The Council of Europe and Roma: 40 years of action

Jean-Pierre Liégeois

in co-operation with the Roma and Travellers Division of the Council of Europe

Council of Europe Publishing

French edition:
Le Conseil de l'Europe et les Roms : 40 ans d'action

ISBN 978-92-871-6944-0

The opinions expressed in this work are the responsibility of the authors and do not necessarily reflect the official policy of the Council of Europe.

All rights reserved. No part of this publication may be translated, reproduced or transmitted, in any form or by any means, electronic (CD-Rom, Internet, etc.) or mechanical, including photocopying, recording or any information storage or retrieval system, without prior permission in writing from the Directorate of Communication (F-67075 Strasbourg Cedex or publishing@coe.int).

Cover design: SPDP, Council of Europe
Layout: Jouve, Paris

Council of Europe Publishing
F-67075 Strasbourg Cedex
http://book.coe.int

ISBN 978-92-871-6945-7
© Council of Europe, September 2012
Printed at the Council of Europe

Tribute to Claudio Marta,

Italian member of the Council of Europe Committee of Experts on Roma and Travellers (MG-S-ROM) from 1996 to 2008 and vice-chair of that committee in 2004

Claudio loved the Roma; indeed, some of them were his childhood friends. He loved them, not as the subject of any academic study but as his brothers and sisters.

His contribution to the work of the Council of Europe over nearly 10 years was to bring to the discussions and projects that human dimension without which everything is reduced to cold administrative action.

A man's greatness is not measured solely by his knowledge – and Claudio possessed immense knowledge – but above all by the courage of his convictions, his contempt for compromise, the sincerity of his ideas and the simplicity of his human relationships.

The Claudio we knew had that greatness of soul, and that is why we shall remember him.

Claudio is not dead: he has merely passed through to the other side of the mirror. We cannot see him, but he sees us and will continue to encourage us and guide us in our work.

Henry Scicluna
Council of Europe Co-ordinator for Activities concerning Roma and Travellers

Contents

Background 7
1. The Council of Europe's terminological glossary 11
2. The number of Roma and Travellers in Europe 19
3. The Roma in Europe: seven centuries of history 23
4. The Parliamentary Assembly: a driving force since 1969 33
5. The Committee of Ministers on Roma since 1975 51
6. The Congress of Local and Regional Authorities of the Council of Europe and Roma since 1981 71
7. The impact of the two fundamental treaties on minority languages and protection of national minorities 83
8. Co-ordination and stronger follow-up to action on Roma 97
9. The Education of Roma Children in Europe project: implementing a Committee of Ministers recommendation 111
10. Consolidating the approach through law 127
11. Beyond prejudice to culture and partnership 153
12. Issues for the future 173

Appendices

The Council of Europe and Roma: references to the principal texts and key dates 195

Testimonials from former and current MG-S-ROM members 199

Background

The Council of Europe is the oldest of the European institutions, having been created in 1949 by the 10 founding states. In 2009, it celebrated its 60th anniversary. The year 2009 also marked an important stage in activities relating to Roma:[1] 40 years earlier, in 1969, the Council of Europe Parliamentary Assembly (then known as the "Consultative Assembly") adopted its first text on Roma.

Among many other activities let us merely note that:

- in 1995, 15 years earlier, an intergovernmental committee was set up to oversee Roma questions;
- in 2005, five years earlier, the European Roma and Travellers Forum (ERTF) was established and the Decade of Roma Inclusion, a major project in which the Council of Europe plays an important part, was launched.

The year 2010 was also an important milestone.

An integrated approach

Today, after some 40 years of discussion and work, the Council of Europe's various bodies are strengthening their commitment in fields which have practical repercussions for monitoring and improving the situation of Roma communities, and for the involvement of their representatives in the framing of policies relating to them. This action derives from the implementation of instruments adopted explicitly on Roma and from that of texts concerning minorities or minority languages, and also the fight against discrimination. These all have a major impact on Roma, and it will be helpful to present an overview.

Institutional memory is lacking: over the years people and programmes change, and projects launched are limited in duration and give way to others. So it is important to propose an overall approach and give historical depth to the work that has been accomplished. It is crucial to give visibility to facts which are often isolated or lost in a mass of events, and to make them more readily understandable so that a forward-looking view may be obtained,

---

1. The term "Roma" as used in this publication refers to Roma, Sinti, Kale, Travellers and related population groups in Europe, and is intended to encompass the wide range of groups concerned, including groups which identify themselves as "Gypsies" and those referred to as "Traveller communities".

over and above a mere stocktaking exercise. Such a view makes it easier to understand the present and define suitable guidelines for future work.

This background will afford a clearer historical grasp of the origin and development of the Council of Europe's activities, a fuller picture of the fields which have been examined, and an updated view of the subjects which deserve further action.

A source of inspiration

More broadly, Roma community issues are able to shed useful light on institutional dynamics, and provide inspiration at a time when the Council of Europe is considering how to reorganise its activities. Roma are at the crossroads of priorities and sensitivities in the 21st century: European citizens for centuries, they represent, with a population of 10 to 12 million, the largest of all its minorities. They live against a background of strong cultural dynamism set in 1 000 years of history, but they also suffer the most discrimination and are the victims of processes of exclusion, usually in situations of poverty. These characteristics and sensitivities all represent priority areas for the Council of Europe – minorities, migrations, discrimination, exclusion, poverty – and relate to its fundamental values in the spheres of culture, education, social cohesion and human rights.

So this study sets out to be, for all partners concerned, an instrument of knowledge and reflection, of reference and analysis, providing immediate access to information which is often misunderstood, generally piecemeal and difficult to find. It will be useful not only to policy makers and those with administrative responsibility, whether at European, national or local level, but also to anyone active in non-governmental organisations (NGOs). However, it is not a mere catalogue of activities, for that would not make the movement which has evolved over the past four decades comprehensible. It is a working tool, with each chapter including references to the texts mentioned and the publications available, often in several languages, on the Council of Europe's website and those produced in member states. It also contains short extracts from texts, giving a sense of their character and a better understanding of the genesis and adoption of the policies leading to and guiding the action advocated. Lastly, the ability to assess the hierarchy and institutional weight of texts adopted allows all partners involved to make better use of them in the context of their own work as bases for action, negotiating tools and a source of suggestions. A knowledge of the major action taken in the fields of education, language and culture, as well as the measures taken against prejudice, makes it possible to draw on the experience acquired and, by engaging in that action, to benefit from its dynamism.

Structure of the study

The first step was to define the subject. The first chapter therefore provides a glossary of the terms employed to designate all or part of the groups concerned. The glossary shows that these groups are varied, but at the same time united in their diversity. It reveals the usage of terminology which constitutes administrative designations or categorisations, and also the way in which terms change over time, in the Council of Europe as elsewhere. This is followed by a table listing estimated Roma populations in the member states, ending with a historical account of their centuries-old presence within Europe.

The chapters which follow describe the engagement of Council of Europe bodies with the Roma. In covering institutional dynamics a chronological account has been employed, starting with the Parliamentary Assembly's adoption of its first text in 1969, and moving on to statements from the Committee of Ministers and then the Congress of Local and Regional Authorities of the Council of Europe. After a discussion of the importance to Roma of conventions on minorities or minority languages, there is an analysis of the establishment of specific structures and activities, and examples are given of the strategic elements in project implementation. There follows a discussion of the more systematic intervention of mechanisms relating to respect for rights. Lastly, after presenting three recent, complementary activities which are significant for Roma, the study suggests ways forward, emphasising the priorities for today and explaining why, after 40 years of the Council of Europe's activities for Roma, they are right at the heart of Europe's future challenges.

1. The Council of Europe's terminological glossary

It is important to stress that the terminology used in this field by the Council of Europe has varied considerably since the early 1970s: the subjects of this study have been designated by terms such as "Gypsies and other Travellers", "nomads", "populations of nomadic origin", "Gypsies", "Roma (Gypsies)", "Roma", "Roma/Gypsies", "Roma/Gypsies and Travellers", and "Roma and Travellers".

From 2006 until autumn 2010, official Council of Europe texts abided by the following terminology, as explained in Committee of Ministers Recommendation Rec(2008)5:

> The term "Roma and Travellers" used in the present text refers to Roma, Sinti, Kale, Travellers and related groups in Europe, and aims to cover the wide diversity of groups concerned, including groups which identify themselves as Gypsies.

A slightly modified definition has been used at the Council of Europe since October 2010:

> The term "Roma" used at the Council of Europe refers to Roma, Sinti, Kale and related groups in Europe, including Travellers and the Eastern groups (Dom and Lom), and covers the wide diversity of the groups concerned, including persons who identify themselves as Gypsies.

An updated glossary is available at www.coe.int/roma/.

The earlier definition of "Roma and Travellers" should be borne in mind when reading this study, even though we usually use only the term "Roma", and even though official texts adopted some time ago, and to which reference may be made, employ such terms as "nomads" or "Gypsies".

In view of the many variants found in the different Council of Europe documents and on its website, it was thought essential to harmonise terminology within the Organisation. In December 2006 the Translation Department, together with staff at the Roma and Travellers Division and the Education of Roma Children in Europe project, drew up a terminological glossary in consultation with the Roma and Travellers community.

Some of the decisions on terminology also derive from the conclusions of a seminar held at the Council of Europe in September 2003 on Cultural Identities of Roma, Gypsies, Travellers and Related Groups in Europe, which brought together representatives of different groups in Europe (Roma, Sinti, Kale, Romanichals, Boyash, Ashkali, Egyptians, Yenish, Travellers, etc.) as well as representatives of various international organisations (Organization for Security and Co-operation in Europe – Office for Democratic Institutions and Human Rights, European Commission, Office of the United Nations High Commissioner for Refugees, among others).

The glossary has been updated for this publication in order to reflect the present consensus in the Council of Europe. It takes account of recent developments with regard to usage and acceptance in everyday language.

Even though the glossary developed by the Council of Europe has been taken up by numerous international organisations, the recommendations below apply primarily to the terminology employed in the Organisation.

Terms designating groups

ROMA

a Rom (n)
Roma (pl)
Roma (adj)
Romani (adj, restricted use)

Some variants of Romani double the "r" in "Rrom"; this spelling is also used for political reasons in certain countries, e.g. Romania (to distinguish Rroma from Romanians).

In English, both "Roma" and "Romani" are used as an adjective, as in "a Roma(ni) woman" or "Roma(ni) communities". But there is a clear preference for "Romani" when referring to the language and culture, as in "Romani language" or "Romani culture".

"Rom" means "man of the Roma ethnic group" or "husband", depending on the variant of Romani or the author. The Roma are – with the Sinti and Kale – one of the three main branches of the Roma (generic term), a people originally from northern India.

Roma are most numerous in the Balkans and central and eastern Europe. Most of them speak the Romani language *(romani čhib)*. They are divided into sub-groups (e.g. Kelderash, Lovari, Gurbeti, Churari, Ursari).

In the Balkans, there are also groups who regard themselves as Roma, but do not speak Romani. These include the Boyash (Beash, Bayash, Banyash, Baieşi or Rudari, depending on the country), whose language derives from Moeso-Romanian, and some Ashkali, who speak Albanian. Other groups, who resemble the Roma in certain respects, such as the Egyptians (so-called because they reputedly came from Egypt, and who also speak Albanian) and some Ashkali, insist on their ethnic difference.

SINTI (MANUSH)

a Sinto (n)
Sinti (pl)
Sinti (adj)

The Sinti are mainly found in German-speaking regions (Germany, Switzerland, Austria), Benelux and certain Scandinavian countries (e.g. Sweden), as well as in northern Italy (Piedmont, Lombardy) and southern France (Provence).

In France, Sinti are called *"Manouches"* (English: Manush). "Manush" comes from a Romani word meaning "human being".

Sinto, the language spoken by the Sinti, (called *"romnepen"* in the language itself) is a Germanised version of the Romani language.

The southern sub-branch of the Sinti living in northern Italy and southern France speaks another variant of the Sinto language, using a partly Italian-based vocabulary.

KALE (SPANISH GYPSIES)

a Kalo (n)
Kale (pl)
Kale (adj)

The Kale (more commonly called "Gypsies") of the Iberian peninsula and southern France have practically lost the use of Romani. They speak Kaló, which is Spanish (in vocabulary and grammar) with some vestiges of Romani. Today there are two variants (Spanish Kaló and Catalan Kaló). In Spanish it is written with a "c" (Caló, Calé), but the spelling with "k" is the recommended international version.

There is also a "Kaalé" group in Finland which is striving to maintain its traditions, and there are Kale in Wales who lost the use of Kaló in the 1950s.

TRAVELLERS

a Traveller (n)
Travellers (pl)
Traveller (adj)

Travellers proper are to be found in Ireland and Great Britain and are quite distinct ethnically from Roma/Sinti/Kale groups. Travellers' ancestors do not originate from northern India, unlike Roma/Sinti/Kale.

In Ireland they are officially considered an indigenous community which is not distinct from the majority in terms of race, colour, descent or ethnic origin. Originally, they were itinerant but 80% are now sedentary. It should not, therefore, be assumed that Travellers live on the road: in Norway, Travellers are sedentary while Roma move around!

Irish Travellers call themselves *"Pavee"* in their own language. This language, known as "the Cant", "Shelta" or "Gammon" by native speakers themselves, has a mainly English and Irish vocabulary (with some borrowings from Romani) and a grammar close to that of English. Many words are formed by reversing syllables. For a long time Travellers were also known as "Tinkers" or "Tinklers", a term that is pejorative in their eyes, just as "Gypsy" can be to Roma – see below.

In French, the term "Travellers" is usually translated as *"Voyageurs"* or *"Gens du voyage"*. Within a French-speaking context, it is, however, best to keep the term *"Voyageurs"* in French to designate these populations, just as in English texts the use of "Travellers" is recommended, the two terms not being wholly equivalent. *"Gens du voyage"* used exclusively in France is an administrative term which also applies to non-Roma groups with a nomadic way of life. It thus covers not only the various branches of Roma (Roms, Sinti/Manush, Kale/Spanish Gypsies) but also other populations with a nomadic lifestyle.

There are no "British Travellers" as such in the United Kingdom, where the only terms used, particularly in England, are "Irish Travellers", or "Travellers of Irish Heritage". Like Roma/Gypsies (see under Gypsies below), they are regarded as a distinct ethnic group and are covered by the Framework Convention for the Protection of National Minorities (unlike Travellers in Ireland).

However, in Northern Ireland and Scotland, the terms "Scottish Travellers" and "Irish Travellers" are used. In Scotland, the Scottish Gypsies/Travellers (some of them accept the term "Gypsies", others do not) have sometimes been called "Nawkins" or "Nachins", which are pejorative terms (see "Tinkers" above).

In Wales there are two groups, the Romanichals (see below), who nowadays speak Anglo-Romani and, in the north, the Kale (who arrived from Spain via France and Cornwall).

ROMANICHALS

In the United Kingdom, mainly in England and south Wales, the Romanichals identify themselves as "Gypsies" (sometimes "Roma/Gypsies" in official texts). They speak Anglo-Romani, a mixture of English and Romani vocabulary with English grammar.

YENISH

a Yenish (n)
Yenish (pl)
Yenish (adj)

Like the Irish Travellers, the Yenish are an indigenous non-Roma people living mainly in Switzerland. Some lead an itinerant lifestyle, but the majority (over 90%) are now sedentary. Local names sometimes applied to them include *"Karner"*, *"Laninger"*, *"Kessler"*, *"Fecker"* and *"Spengler"*. They speak German with some Romani, Latin and Hebrew borrowings.

GYPSIES

a Gypsy (n)
Gypsies (pl)
Gypsy (adj)

The term "Roma/Gypsies" was used by the Council of Europe for many years as these two names covered most areas and situations in Europe. The term "Roma" is fairly widely employed in central and eastern Europe, while "Gypsies" has a pejorative ring for many European Roma and Sinti, who reject it as an alien term, linked with negative, paternalist stereotypes which still pursue them in Europe.

In western Europe (e.g. United Kingdom, Spain, France, Portugal), in Hungary and certain parts of Russia, "Gypsy" or its national equivalent (*Gitano, Tsigane, Cigano, Cigány, Tsyganye,* etc.) is more acceptable and sometimes more appropriate. Thus many NGOs or federations of associations set up in western European states have "Gypsies" or "*Tsiganes*" in their title.

The term "Gypsy" is also generally accepted and used in the artistic sphere (e.g. "Gypsy music"), even in countries which otherwise prefer the use of "Roma".

The fact that some groups accept the use of "Gypsies" or *"Tsiganes"* was used (until July 2006) as an argument by the former chairman of the MG-S-ROM, previously called the Group of Specialists on Roma, Gypsies and Travellers, in favour of keeping these terms in the committee's name.

GADJE/GADGE (NON-ROMA)

a gadgo (n)
gajde/gadge (pl)
gajde/gadge (adj)

This term means "non-Roma" in Romani. It is recommended not to use a capital "G", unlike in "Roma/Sinti/Kale", since they are not a people. In fact, this is the name given by Roma to all those who do not belong to their community (just as *"goy/goyim"* means "non-Jew/non-Jews"). The sound "dj" is rendered by a special letter in the Romani alphabet [3], and for this reason the transcription is different in English (gadje) and French *(gadjé)*.

In Kaló, spoken in the Iberian peninsula, the term used to designate non-Roma is *"payo"* (plural: *"payos"*).

Terms designating the language

ROMANI

Romani/Romani language

Romani, or *"Romani ćhib"* in Romani, is an Indo-European language (Indo-Aryan sub-branch) like Greek and the Romance, Germanic, Slav, Baltic and Celtic languages.

It is a language in its own right – one cannot speak of Romani languages in the plural, and it is understood by a very large proportion of European Roma despite the many variants (it is preferable to speak of "variants" of Romani rather than "dialects"). The variants are explained by the fact that some groups have borrowed to differing degrees from the vocabulary of their surroundings.

In English, "Romani" is to be preferred to "Romany", though the latter still appears frequently in dictionaries.

In western Europe, and particularly in France, the term *"romanes"* (pronounced "romanèss") is quite often used for the Romani language. In fact, it is the adverb: *"parler romanes"* means "to speak in Romani".

Interpretation into Romani has been provided as a matter of course for a decade now at events organised by the Council of Europe on this subject (it is also the third working language of the Committee of Experts on Roma and Travellers, alongside French and English, the official languages). Interpretation into Romani has also become routine in the other international organisations.

Some Romani populations have virtually lost the use of Romani or now speak a language (a kind of "pidgin" or hybrid language) influenced to varying degrees by the official language of the country they live in, as for example in the case of the Kale in Spain, the Sinti in the Germanic countries, the Romungrès in Hungary and the Gypsies in the United Kingdom.

Council of Europe structures or projects

Migration and Roma Department
attached to DG III (Directorate General of Social Cohesion)
www.coe.int/t/dg3/default_EN.asp

Roma and Travellers Division
attached to the Migration and Roma Department
www.coe.int/t/dg3/RomaTravellers/Default_EN.asp

(Council of Europe) Co-ordinator for Activities concerning Roma and Travellers
attached to the Private Office of the Secretary General but located in DG III
www.coe.int/t/dg3/romatravellers/coordinator_EN.asp

Committee of Experts on Roma and Travellers (MG-S-ROM)
This has been the name of this intergovernmental committee since the adoption of its new terms of reference on 12 July 2006. Between 1995 and 2002 it was known as the "Group of Specialists on Roma and Gypsies", and from 2002 to July 2006 as the "Group of Specialists on Roma, Gypsies and Travellers".
www.coe.int/t/dg3/romatravellers/mgsrom_EN.asp

Project: Education of Roma Children in Europe
This is a project developed by the Division for the European Dimension of Education to implement Committee of Ministers Recommendation No. R (2000) 4 on the education of Roma/Gypsy children in Europe, which is why the term "Gypsies" was retained during the first stage of the project (2003-05). The Steering Committee for Education adopted the terminology recommended in the glossary for the next stage of the project, Education of Roma Children in Europe.
www.coe.int/t/dg4/education/roma/default_EN.asp

Project: Route of Roma Culture and Heritage
The project was developed by the Directorate of Culture and Cultural and Natural Heritage, DG IV. The initial work on this subject, in particular the reports by Jean-Pierre Liégeois in 1993 and 1997, used the name "Gypsy Cultural Route". In 2003 at Brno in the Czech Republic, it was decided to change the name. Some texts still use "Roma/Gypsy Cultural Route" to refer to the project.
www.coe.int/t/dg4/cultureheritage/culture/routes/roma_EN.asp

Campaign: *Dosta!* Go Beyond Prejudice, Meet the Roma!
This is an awareness-raising campaign launched by the Roma and Travellers Division of the Directorate General of Social Cohesion, aimed at bringing non-Roma citizens closer to the Roma. Initially launched in five Balkan states in 2006-07 under a joint Council of Europe/European Commission programme, this campaign has been gradually extended to other member states of the Council of Europe. It seeks to eliminate a number of prejudices and stereotypes, and to recognise the contribution made by Roma culture to European cultural heritage.
www.dosta.org

Teaching the Roma genocide ("*Samudaripen*" or "*Pharrajimos*" in Romani)
Remembrance, particularly remembrance of the events which occurred during the Second World War, remains a sensitive and painful issue for Roma. Work covered by the project includes the production of teaching materials on Roma history and culture, the organisation of events and working meetings on the Roma genocide, and the setting-up of a website devoted to Roma remembrance.
www.romagenocide.org

2. The number of Roma and Travellers in Europe

There are 10 to 12 million Roma in Europe (as estimates vary from 6 to 16 million, the "10 to 12 million" range seems most appropriate for all 47 Council of Europe member states taken together). If we consider only the 27 European Union (EU) states, the estimate should be reduced to about 6 million.

As our knowledge stands at present, no precise data are available. Censuses are unreliable because the criteria for membership of this community, the definition of which is usually political, vary from one state to another. In addition, a significant number of people may avoid calling themselves Roma for various reasons, given the centuries of persecution and the fear of being registered and coming to the notice of the authorities. Migration, substantial at certain times, also makes exact counting difficult, especially as families can move within a very short period of time, may then return rapidly to their point of departure either voluntarily or arbitrarily, or may actually settle more permanently in a country.

At present, states are becoming more aware of the size of their Roma populations, and of the need to improve the situation by devising suitable programmes based on exact data. Roma organisations, which have strengthened their political position, are persuading Roma families and individuals that it is important to declare their membership of a minority claiming its rights.

Table 1: Official numbers and estimates of Roma and related populations in Europe

Countries are listed in decreasing order of average estimated number of Roma or related persons.

Country	Total population (World Bank 2010)	Official number (self-declared)	Last census	Minimum estimate	Maximum estimate	Average estimate (used by the Council of Europe)	Average estimate as a percentage of total population
Turkey	72 752 325	4 656	1945	500 000	5 000 000	2 750 000	3.78%
Romania	21 442 012	619 007	2011	1 200 000	2 500 000	1 850 000	8.63%
Russian Federation	141 750 000	205 007	2010	450 000	1 200 000	825 000	0.58%
Bulgaria	7 543 325	325 343	2011	700 000	800 000	750 000	9.94%
Hungary	10 008 703	190 046	2001	500 000	1 000 000	750 000	7.49%
Spain	46 081 574	Data unavailable		500 000	1 000 000	750 000	1.63%
Serbia (excl. Kosovo *)	7 292 574	108 193	2002	400 000	800 000	600 000	8.23%
Slovak Republic	5 433 456	89 920	2001	380 000	600 000	490 000	9.02%
France	64 876 618	Data unavailable		300 000	500 000	400 000	0.62%
Ukraine	45 870 700	47 917	2001	120 000	400 000	260 000	0.57%
United Kingdom	62 218 761	Data unavailable		150 000	300 000	225 000	0.36%
Czech Republic	10 525 090	11 718	2001	150 000	250 000	200 000	1.90%
"The former Yugoslav Republic of Macedonia"	2 060 563	53 879	2002	134 000	260 000	197 000	9.56%
Greece	11 319 048	Data unavailable		50 000	300 000	175 000	1.55%
Italy	60 483 521	Data unavailable		120 000	180 000	150 000	0.25%
Albania	3 204 284	1 261	2001	80 000	150 000	115 000	3.59%
Republic of Moldova	3 562 062	12 271	2004	14 200	200 000	107 100	3.01%
Germany	81 702 329	Data unavailable		70 000	140 000	105 000	0.13%
Bosnia and Herzegovina	3 760 149	8 864	1991	40 000	76 000	58 000	1.54%
Portugal	10 642 841	Data unavailable		34 000	70 000	52 000	0.49%
Sweden	9 379 116	Data unavailable		35 000	65 000	50 000	0.53%
Belarus	9 490 500	9 927	1999	25 000	70 000	47 500	0.50%
Netherlands	16 612 213	Data unavailable		32 000	48 000	40 000	0.24%
Kosovo *	1 815 000	45 745	1991	25 000	50 000	37 500	2.07%

Ireland	4 481 430	22 435	2006	32 000	43 000	37 500	0.84%
Croatia	4 424 161	9 463	2001	30 000	40 000	35 000	0.79%
Austria	8 384 745	6 273	2001	20 000	50 000	35 000	0.42%
Poland	38 187 488	12 731	2002	15 000	50 000	32 500	0.09%
Switzerland	7 825 243	Data unavailable		25 000	35 000	30 000	0.38%
Belgium	10 879 159	Data unavailable		20 000	40 000	30 000	0.28%
Montenegro	631 490	8 305	2011	15 000	25 000	20 000	3.17%
Latvia	2 242 916	8 517	2011	9 000	16 000	12 500	0.56%
Finland	5 363 624	Data unavailable		10 000	12 000	11 000	0.21%
Norway	4 885 240	Data unavailable		4 500	15 700	10 100	0.21%
Slovenia	2 052 821	3 246	2002	7 000	10 000	8 500	0.41%
Lithuania	3 320 656	2 571	2001	2 000	4 000	3 000	0.09%
Denmark	5 544 139	Data unavailable		1 000	4 000	2 500	0.05%
Armenia	3 092 072	50	2004	2 000	2 000	2 000	0.06%
Georgia	4 452 800	1 200	1989	1 500	2 500	2 000	0.04%
Azerbaijan	9 047 932	Data unavailable		2 000	2 000	2 000	0.02%
Cyprus	1 103 647	502	1960	1 000	1 500	1 250	0.11%
Estonia	1 339 646	584	2009	600	1 500	1 050	0.08%
Luxembourg	505 831	Data unavailable		100	500	300	0.06%
Malta	412 961	Data unavailable		0	0	0	0.00%
Iceland	317 398	Data unavailable		0	0	0	0.00%
Andorra	84 864	Data unavailable		0	0	0	0.00%
Liechtenstein	36 032	Data unavailable		0	0	0	0.00%
Monaco	35 407	Data unavailable		0	0	0	0.00%
San Marino	31 534	Data unavailable		0	0	0	0.00%
Total in Europe	828 510 000	1 809 631		6 206 900	16 313 700	11 260 300	1.36%
Council of Europe (47)	817 204 500	1 753 959		6 156 900	16 193 700	11 175 300	1.37%
European Union (27)	502 087 670	1 292 893		4 338 700	7 985 500	6 162 100	1.18%

* All reference to Kosovo, whether to the territory, institutions or population, in this text shall be understood in full compliance with United Nations Security Council Resolution 1244 and without prejudice to the status of Kosovo.

3. The Roma in Europe: seven centuries of history

The Roma are very widely misunderstood, and over the centuries attitudes towards them, or the political decisions taken in respect of them, have been prompted more by prejudice than by a knowledge of historical and cultural realities. Most people asked do not know where the Roma families who are their neighbours come from, and are unaware that some of them, having arrived centuries ago, comprise the state's oldest communities. People are also ignorant of the history of families arriving today from other countries, and unaware of the reasons why they move and of the fact that they may be related culturally and socially to families who have been settled throughout Europe since the Middle Ages.

This misunderstanding, the everyday effects of which are usually negative except where they relate to folklore or stereotyped elements such as music and dance, is the result of prejudices that have built up over centuries. The absence of Roma even today from history books, especially school textbooks, has made it impossible to inculcate knowledge leading to understanding and respect in a context of interpersonal relations, or leading to appropriate institutional action to improve a difficult situation.

Before moving on to present the activities of the Council of Europe, therefore, it is appropriate to look at the Roma from a socio-historical and political dynamic.

A long history

Roma were imagined to have come from Egypt because, in medieval Europe, the whole of Syria, Greece, Cyprus and the neighbouring lands was given the name "Little Egypt", a name also given to the Izmir region by the Turks. So Roma were called "Egyptians": hence the name given to them in some ancient texts, and such current names as *"Gitans"*, *"Gitanos"*, "Gypsies" and many more besides. They were confused with a group of seers and magicians known for several centuries in Greece as *"Atsinganos"* or *"Atsinkanos"* ("untouched/untouchables"). The name of this sect, given to groups of travellers from the east, was to remain attached to them in many countries and languages (*"Tsiganes"* in French, *"Zigeuner"* in German, *"Zigenare"* in Swedish, *"Zingari"* in Italian, *"Ciganos"* in Portuguese, etc.).

Not until the end of the 18th century did linguists discover that the language, Romani, was an Indian language, probably from north-western India, and derived from popular speech close to Sanskrit. Migrations took place from India, probably between the 9th and the 14th centuries. It has also been possible, by examining the vocabulary and grammatical structures of Romani variants in different countries, to guess at the migration routes followed.

The first known texts relating to Roma concern the situation of family slavery in Moldova and Wallachia from 1385 onwards. Group dispersal continued in the 14th century into Wallachia and Bohemia and then, until 1430, throughout western Europe except for the northern countries. In Poland, an early document mentions the presence of Roma in Cracow in 1401. Between 1407 and 1416, various chronicles allude to the presence of Roma in Germany. In 1417, Emperor Sigismund of Germany gave one group a letter of recommendation and protection, asking for them to be well received. As Sigismund was also King of Bohemia, groups from Bohemia are sometimes called "Bohemians", *"Boemianos"*, etc. One group bearing these recommendations, led by "Duke" André, presented themselves at Deventer in the Netherlands in 1420. This was probably the same group which had been welcomed by the city of Brussels in January 1420. In 1423, Sigismund gave "Duke" Ladislav a safe-conduct. Families were arriving in Hungary from Transylvania during the same period.

In August 1419 the French village of Châtillon-en-Dombes (Châtillon-sur-Chalaronne, in Ain) made a gift to a group bearing letters from the Emperor and the Duke of Savoy. Italy was certainly approached from the south and the north simultaneously. However, the first documented appearance was in the north in 1422, initially in Bologna. In Spain, the first text indicates an arrival from the north, by way of a safe-conduct delivered in Saragossa by Alfonso V on 12 January 1425 to "Don Johan de Egipte Menor". The document ordered that he be "suffered to go, stay and pass" for three months, together with his entourage and everyone accompanying him. As regards Portugal, in an early text in 1526 – almost a century later – King D. João III ordered that *"Ciganos"* be expelled. But it is likely that they were present much earlier on Portuguese territory: the first known reference appears in a poem which can be dated to 1510, and Gypsies probably arrived in Portugal during the second half of the 15th century.

The first mention of Roma in the British Isles was in 1505 in Scotland, in 1514 in England and in 1530 in Wales. However, Roma probably arrived earlier, as accounts exist which appear to refer to well-established groups. In 1505, Gypsies arrived in Denmark from Scotland. As for Sweden, information is contained in the Swedish chronicle of Olai Petri showing that in 1512 "those who journey from one country to another and who are called *tater* have come to this country and to Stockholm. They were never seen here before". In 1540, a group was deported from England to Norway. Families arrived in Turku, Finland, in 1584. Perhaps others had arrived previously or later from the east or directly from the south; in Estonia, the first text dates from 1533 and concerns people probably arriving from Sweden. In Russia – at least in the regions which were to form part of its empire, as the frontiers changed – the first group arrived from the south in 1501, though Siberia was apparently not reached until 1721. Family migration also took place to Africa and the Americas, mainly following the deportation measures taken by the Portuguese authorities (to Brazil) and the Spanish authorities in the

17th century, followed by similar actions by the English and French authorities. Angola was doubtless the principal Portuguese colony to receive Gypsies, starting in the 16th century.

This outline gives an idea of the direction and scale of family movements. The archives show that groups which came to western Europe often continued to move from one region to another and from one country to another. However, at all times and in every country some groups have migrated less or ceased to migrate. Many families restrict their nomadic way of life and seek employment in a rural area. Sometimes they become semi-sedentary, which is practical for the development of commercial and craft activities and seasonal rural work. Thus they become locally settled and experience some degree of acculturation.

The first wave of migration, therefore, spread throughout Europe ultimately, coming to a halt in places. This led to reduced movement on the part of some groups. It also happened that travellers of Indian origin came into contact with native travellers, resulting in cultural exchange.

Mobility

In every country the first wave was followed by others. Many examples of such movements over the centuries can be given. For instance, in Bulgaria at the end of the 17th century and the beginning of the 18th, migration took place because of the conflict between Austria and the Ottoman Empire. Similarly in the 19th century, migration took place when slavery was abolished in the Romanian principalities of Moldova and Wallachia. In Italy in the late 19th century, "Hungarian" Roma appeared. After the end of the First World War, other "German" and "Slav" families came from the north and east. During the Second World War, "Gypsies" were driven out of Italy, Slovenia and Croatia. Many families arrived in France in the late 19th century from Hungary and Romania, and that movement continued fairly regularly until the First World War. The same happened in Norway and Germany. Since the 1960s there has been migration from Yugoslavia in successive waves, including in the late 1980s when thousands of Roma left "the former Yugoslav Republic of Macedonia", particularly for Germany, where they applied for political refugee status.

The migratory movements that have had the greatest impact in terms of number of persons and number of receiving states are those which started from Romania in the second half of the 19th century, from Yugoslavia in the 1960s and from Romania and Yugoslavia – and also from other states – in the early 1990s. After a few movements originating in central and eastern Europe at the end of the 1980s (in particular from "the former Yugoslav Republic of Macedonia" and from Romania to Germany), the early 1990s was indeed a period of migration, the first wave being of such size and of such visible consequences that very few citizens of the states of origin or the states to which the Roma went were unaware of them. It was also probably the first time in history that Roma communities got themselves so talked about, this time on a continental and even global scale (with many migrations to America, especially North America).

The reasons for migration have varied. First among them are the persecutions to which Roma have been subject. Over the centuries there have been very many expulsions and banishments, and in modern times refusal of permission to stay and forced return. These are present-day revivals of the policies carried out ever since Roma first appeared. Deportations have taken place at various times in history, whether from Portugal to Africa, from England to Australia, or within states (to Siberia in Russia, to Transnistria in Romania, etc.), resulting in considerable mobility. After centuries of Roma slavery in Romanian principalities, its abolition around 1860 sent families off in every possible direction. Pressures of every kind, especially on families living in precarious housing, made them travel further afield, and countless cases of expulsion, sometimes at state level, have amounted to banishment. At the present time this may take the form of planned expulsion through the implementation of bilateral agreements between two states.

Faced with hostility from those around him, the only possibility open to a Rom is to go and see whether he receives a better welcome elsewhere: the 1990s and 2000s are a cruel illustration of this, with Roma faced with physical aggression, racist pogroms, destruction of housing and unbearable living conditions in many European regions. Periods of unrest within a country cause Roma to leave because, generally speaking, at such times they become scapegoats. For example, about 120 000 of the 150 000 Roma who lived in Kosovo before the events of the late 1990s had to flee the country fearing for their lives.

Economic activities and trade in particular are another reason to move to a different region or indeed another country. There are others reasons too: for families who feel that they belong to the same group, travel – when it is possible – enables them to meet others and forge and maintain social ties. So on the one hand there is structural mobility due to a form of social and economic organisation and a desire to travel, and situational mobility imposed by events brought about by others – exclusion or its opposite, confinement (slavery, imprisonment, various prohibitions). As a general rule, both forms are combined in the resulting move.

It must be underlined that the majority of Roma are not nomadic, and many would prefer not to be but are obliged to be so in order to adapt to changing and often threatening living conditions. The fact that it is not easy to park caravans in a single place for those who are itinerant in certain countries often makes nomadic life a necessary response to a hostile environment. Nomadic Roma are few in number, but all Roma have had to accept mobility as part of their existence in adapting to a still prevailing spirit of rejection. So nomadism is neither a product nor a producer of Roma culture, but a way of adapting to living conditions imposed on them. That said, mobility is fundamental in some cases, especially for engaging in economic activities, and it is important to respect it. Moreover, the present increase in discrimination, of which Roma are the main victims in Europe (as all international reports show), will not help families to settle.

Since the 1990s, migratory movements, and above all the image they convey, have taken centre-stage, leading almost everywhere in Europe to policies which have taken on unforeseeable dimensions and new forms, often backed by scarcely rational argument. Recent concern about immigrants in general, and fear of "invasion by Gypsies from the east" in particular, has given rise to much discussion. Most of the international organisations have carried out studies on the question. This interest on the part of the international community has been aroused mainly by the sudden visibility of Roma migrating from certain Balkan states (Romania, Bulgaria, the former Yugoslavia) in search of temporary residence or political asylum in western Europe. The present situation of Roma communities (worsening social situation, violent assaults, increasing xenophobia, etc.) is perceived mainly from the standpoint of actual or potential migration as a "problem" likely to cause difficulties, one with an "international dimension".

The "danger" of mass migration by Roma has been exaggerated, and the reality of these movements is usually poorly understood for lack of precise figures. So people base their opinions on impressions which are not free from the effect of stereotypes. A similar dynamic arose a century ago, at the start of the 20th century, when states were fearful of all mobility and introduced a system of supervision and registration of individuals, one which is now seen again in new forms assisted by the available technical (primarily IT) resources.

Policies of negation

Over the centuries, relations between Roma and non-Roma have never been smooth. Regarded as intruders as soon as they discovered Europe, where states were seeking to organise and control societies, Roma aroused mistrust, fear and rejection by virtue of their mobility as compared with local populations settled in a given territory. Though rejection was initially local, it very soon became a state matter and overarching policies were developed. A suggested typology of these policies, which evolved over more than half a millennium, includes:

- policies of exclusion: disappearance is achieved in particular through banishment from the territory of a kingdom or state. This has usually taken the form of geographical disappearance, through expulsion from the territory in question, but it may constitute physical disappearance, as suffered by most of the families of European Roma under the Nazi regime;

- policies of confinement: disappearance that is desired in geographical terms, by banishment synonymous with expulsion, comes to be desired in social terms, this being effected by confining and splitting up the group and its families. This can be accompanied by use of the Roma community as a potential labour force, for example by sending them to the galleys, to colonies needing population, or through deportation or slavery;

- policies of assimilation: disappearance is cultural, and Roma are considered merely as outsiders who pose social problems; they are no longer banned but controlled, no longer rejected but assimilated. Their language, dress and cultural traditions are prohibited. Together with the technocratic management of society and the development of humanist ideas, these policies spread throughout Europe during the second half of the 20th century.

These three categories may follow a chronological pattern, but they may also coexist: the desire to assimilate has never precluded the desire to exclude. There has never been so much talk of integration as today, while exclusion has never been so common. There has never been so much said about inclusion, nor so much discrimination in practice.

However, we are now at a crossroads. The current situation can be seen as:

- a period of indecision: noting that the above policies are not producing the hoped-for effects, and that the situation is deteriorating, we are undecided and ask ourselves questions. This can be seen in a positive light, because indecision and doubt open the way to the formulation of new ideas, and to more relaxed practices;
- a period of innovation: since opportunities exist, it is the task and the responsibility of all those concerned – politicians, administrators, members of associations, whether Roma or non-Roma – to ensure that the present time can be seen as a period of innovation.

The present situation

No detailed factual account is needed to show how difficult living conditions are for Roma, so extensive are their issues: all the national and international reports make this clear. Let us take a "press review" as our indicator. It is a particularly interesting one, since it reflects the reality of actual facts and reveals the prejudices behind certain policies.

Whichever country we consider, anyone reading its newspapers or listening to its news bulletins will receive information which is doubly negative with regard to Roma. On one hand, they report the day-to-day hardships suffered by Roma families. On the other, they usually do so in negative ways, such that the persons described are seen as undesirable and as being responsible for their own difficulties, expulsions, deportations, etc.

Anyone in receipt of such information will deduce from it that Roma constitute a "problem", or indeed a host of "problems". Concluding that the disappearance of Roma is a way of solving the problems is a step that is quickly taken, leading to rejection, expulsion and violence in all its forms.

This resurgence of negative reporting, which has become more marked over recent years, brings with it a threefold risk of:

- exacerbation of conflict and mounting violence against Roma – a kind of vicious circle. Violence breeds violence, and the fact that it is shared – because everyone starts joining in – gives it both reason and legitimacy;
- such occurrences beginning to be perceived as commonplace. This is extremely serious. When people begin to lose interest, they may cease to react, resistance may tail off and democracy fails;

- the victims becoming stigmatised and devalued by those around them, leading ultimately to their losing value in their own eyes.

It must be said that the present state of affairs has deep roots, both historical and ideological, which have developed over centuries. They are hard to remove, embedded as they are in the historical policies of which we have outlined a typology, and in the history of attitudes.

Attitudes

The perceptions of Roma, based on prejudice and stereotypes which those around them have, are of major importance: these are the perceptions which largely determine attitudes and behaviour towards them. They convey the most important, and often the only information about Roma to surrounding communities. Roma are not unknown quantities: everyone who is asked expresses an opinion (often a categorical opinion) about them. In fact they are misunderstood, and reality is masked by the imagination.

For centuries, a whole set of images has built up, developed and crystallised into stereotypes. Thus a stock of perceptions, some firmly rooted and others perhaps less so, has come about. These can be drawn on by those who reject Roma as well as those who seek to assimilate them; everyone can always find something to bear out what they say and justify what they do.

Roma are rarely seen for what they are but as they have to be, for reasons of politics and the behaviour exhibited towards them. The spread of perceptions induces a circular cause-and-effect phenomenon: regulations, dictionaries, books of various kinds, press and television feed on public opinion, seizing on scraps which vary with the mood of the day, give them the force of truth, amplify them and send them back to those who already have them and who thus see their opinions validated.

Any attempt to put new policies in place comes up against this set of perceptions. If respectful attitudes and policies are to become possible in practice, if suitable ideas are to emerge from the present period of "indecision", it is vital that the centuries-old images which block all understanding and impede all communication between Roma and their surroundings be shaken off.

Racism, intolerance and xenophobia

A great many studies throughout Europe underline the rise of intolerance, and its manifestations may be with us for a long time. Opinion polls also show that Roma are always the first to be stigmatised. Ignorance leads to incomprehension, in turn leading to rejection and then to potential conflict. Thus one proceeds from a negative attitude to negative behaviour.

The fundamental importance of education for an intercultural approach, and the importance of providing quality information, must be emphasised. Informing people, and informing oneself, are the first steps to recognition and understanding. In relations between societies, information is a major factor in preventing conflict by transforming oppositions of principle into differences that are better understood. In other words, information brings knowledge. Knowledge affords better understanding. From understanding, mutual respect may emerge. This is the basis on which several Council of Europe activities, particularly in the field of education and combating prejudice, have been pursued.

However, one must remain cautious, and perhaps pessimistic, knowing that very often the new knowledge contributed comes up against very strong prejudices and that this new knowledge, instead of upsetting, contextualising, modifying and breaking down prejudice and stereotypes, is actually reinterpreted by them. Conversely – perhaps a cause for optimism – we observe that stereotypes are learned, and that different types of learning are possible, especially among the young.

Four grounds for hope

The present situation is characterised by several negative aspects, but we may also hope that the situation will improve because of:
- the above-mentioned period of indecision, which is a feature of policies and may open the way to innovations;
- the possibility of curbing the effect of stereotypes as part of the intensified intercultural approach now accepted by the majority of states, and by an increase in quality information.

We may add further grounds for optimism, characteristic of the present context and synonymous with the development of a new space for Roma. These are:
- the emergence of a Roma political movement taking its place on the European stage and within states;
- the fact that the international organisations are coming to grips with Roma issues.

Strong political dynamics

As regards the political emergence of the Roma, their organisation through associations or in any other form such as elective representation is a recent phenomenon and a departure – a radical one – from the tradition of centuries. It is hard to expect of Roma communities, within the space of a few decades, a process of organisation which other communities have taken centuries to develop. Moreover, the hitherto unstructured nature of their political movement has made it vulnerable and susceptible to the influence of other policies which have claimed to assist it in order better to exploit it.

In the cultural and political world of the Roma, diversity – a response to the reality of a diversified community – is an asset which must not be downgraded by the requirement of a single, unified partnership. The reality is plural, and political realism requires respect for the plurality of organisational and political tendencies. Moreover, it is paradoxical to demand of the Roma what no democratic state accepts – a single-party organisation.

In recent years there has been a consolidation of the Roma political movement, marked by the emergence and development of NGOs in almost all states and the development of international organisations such as the International Romani Union, set up at the first World Romani Congress in 1971. That congress adopted a flag and an anthem, symbols of identity shared throughout the world by Roma communities, and the opening day of that first congress, 8 April, which Roma wanted to be an international day, has gradually become recognised and celebrated in different countries. A Roma partnership has been established in numerous states, at both local and national level, to monitor Roma issues, and as part of activities supported by the Council of Europe the ERTF, a pan-European partner organisation, was set up in 2005.

As regards the international institutions, apart from the age-old conflict which typifies relations between public or local authorities and Roma, they have both the power to move innovative policies forward and the responsibility for doing so. They are also best equipped for this, because as international institutions they are actually familiar with the transnational aspects of Roma communities.

Let us look at just one indicator of the extent to which the activities of the international institutions have developed: the number of texts they have adopted. In 1994, the collected texts of the international institutions concerning Roma were published; that publication contained 89 documents (up to the end of 1993) explicitly concerning Roma. The 2000 update of the same publication shows that the number of documents almost doubled in just six years. Between 2000 and 2010 the number has again increased significantly.

Furthermore, many reference texts relate not only to Roma but can be used in the context of an action strategy. Particular mention should be made here of the Council of Europe's Framework Convention for the Protection of National Minorities and the European Charter for Regional or Minority Languages.

Apart from the texts, a stocktaking exercise shows that the EU, the Council of Europe and the Organization for Security and Co-operation in Europe (OSCE) have stepped up their work and increased their activities in respect of Roma in recent years. The same is true of the United Nations Sub-Commission on the Promotion and Protection of Human Rights (subsumed within the UN Human Rights Council since 2006) and of the Committee on the Elimination of Racial Discrimination (CERD). It is now clear also that the efforts are beginning to bear fruit in a tangible manner (significant number of projects, numbers of protagonists, distribution of reports, spread of information, growing awareness on the part of administrative authorities, etc.). However, these efforts must be sustained, despite difficult conditions, to maintain the positive results.

Having outlined the global context, let us now examine the activities of the Council of Europe.[4]

---

4. Each paragraph in this chapter is considerably amplified in the Council of Europe study: Liégeois J-P. (2007), *Roma in Europe,* Council of Europe Publishing, Strasbourg (now available in Albanian, Azeri, Croat, English, French, Hungarian, Romanian and Turkish, with other translations in preparation). For up-to-date information, see the Council of Europe website: www.coe.int.

4. The Parliamentary Assembly: a driving force since 1969

On 5 May 1949, 10 governments signed the instrument by which the Council of Europe was founded. The Parliamentary Assembly of the Council of Europe, then called the "Consultative Assembly", held its first session on 10 August 1949. It is the oldest international parliamentary assembly consisting of democratically elected parliamentarians.

All the parliaments of the Council of Europe's member states send representatives to the Parliamentary Assembly. Their numbers are determined in proportion to the population of each state, with between 2 and 18 representatives per state.

Recommendation 563 (1969) on the situation of Gypsies and other travellers in Europe

The first text concerning Roma was adopted by the Parliamentary Assembly on 30 September 1969. It was also the first text adopted by any European institution (the first adopted by the EU, a European Parliament resolution, was adopted in 1984, 15 years later).[5]

Recommendation 563 is a politically powerful text. There are three kinds of text: recommendations, resolutions and opinions. The characteristic of a recommendation is that it contains proposals addressed to the Committee of Ministers, for application by the governments of the member states, while a resolution commits only the Assembly. This text deals broadly with the question of "travellers", their reception and their rights in the member states. The parliamentary delegations representing them at that time were western European and were often concerned by the situation of travellers forming part of the population in their states. The report on the "Situation of Gypsies and other travellers in Europe" presented to the Assembly before the vote by the Committee on Social and Health Questions explains the choice of the terms employed as follows:

> In some countries the word "Gypsy" has been introduced in legislation, for instance, to indicate a person without fixed abode who leads a nomadic life. For

---

5. The titles of the texts discussed, and the extracts quoted, reflect the wording used at the time, for example in this case "Gypsies and other travellers". This will also show how the terminology has evolved. See Chapter 1, "The Council of Europe's terminological glossary".

these reasons and because it is difficult to separate these people into distinct ethnic groups, the two terms – Gypsy and Traveller – are used interchangeably throughout this report. (Wiklund report, Doc. 2629, 18 September 1969. Mr Wiklund had tabled a motion for a resolution two years earlier: Doc. 2290 of 25 September 1967, on the "Situation of the gypsy population of Europe").

It is important to quote the recommendations addressed to the Committee of Ministers by the Parliamentary Assembly, because the approach to the issues in question reveals an in-depth analysis of the situation and has remained relevant to the present day:

> The Assembly ... Recommends that the Committee of Ministers urge member governments:
>
> i. to take all steps necessary to stop discrimination, be it in legislation or in administrative practice, against Gypsies and other travellers;
>
> ii. as a minimum measure, to promote actively the construction by the authorities concerned, for Gypsies and other travellers, of a sufficient number of caravan sites which should be provided with sanitary installations, electricity, telephones, community buildings, and fire precautions, as well as working areas, and should be situated near to schools and villages or towns;
>
> iii. to ensure, wherever possible, that local authorities provide houses for travellers' families, especially in regions where climate conditions make caravans unsuitable for permanent residence;
>
> iv. where attendance at existing schools is not possible, to encourage the provision of special classes near caravan sites or other places where groups of travellers gather regularly to facilitate the integration of children from travellers' families into normal schools and to ensure that the educational programmes for the children from travellers' families link up satisfactorily with those of secondary school or other forms of continued education;
>
> v. to create or improve the possibilities for professional education of adult Gypsies and travellers with a view to improving their employment opportunities;
>
> vi. to support the creation of national bodies consisting of representatives from governments, Gypsy and travellers' communities as well as voluntary organisations working in the interests of Gypsies and other travellers, and to consult these bodies in the preparation of measures designed to improve the position of the Gypsies and other travellers;
>
> vii. to adapt existing national laws with a view to ensuring that Gypsies and other travellers have the same rights as the settled population with regard to social security provisions and medical care.

Various interventions

The 1970s were marked by a text adopted by the Committee of Ministers, a resolution in which it referred to the work of the Assembly (see Chapter 5), and the 1980s by the activities of the Conference (which became the Congress in 1994) of Local and Regional Authorities of Europe (see Chapter 6). This general development went hand in hand with the intensification of the work of the Parliamentary Assembly, which took various forms. Some examples are given below, followed by a presentation of other recommendations adopted by the Assembly.

Assembly Opinion No. 108 (1982) on the texts adopted at the 16th session of the Conference of Local and Regional Authorities of Europe, in specifically referring to its Resolution 125 (1981), states that the Assembly:

> i. approves this text, and in particular the concrete measures proposed to improve the situation of nomads;

> ii. recalls, in this connection, its own Recommendation 563 (1969), on the situation of Gypsies and other travellers in Europe, and Resolution (75) 13 of the Committee of Ministers;

> iii. regrets that the public authorities in the majority of European countries have not been apprised of these important texts, and expresses concern at the fact that, in spite of certain isolated efforts undertaken by a few public authorities, the situation of the nomad populations and especially Gypsies has scarcely improved since Recommendation 563 was adopted in 1969;

> iv. considers that it is for the conference itself to ensure that local and regional authorities are better informed;

> v. invites the governments of the member states, the Committee of Ministers and the Secretary General of the Council of Europe to implement without delay the proposals and recommendations contained in paragraphs 13 to 20 of Resolution 125;

> vi. invites its Legal Affairs Committee to examine the question afresh and submit a new report if appropriate.

This document reveals the encouraging and questioning role played by the Assembly, which is also apparent in the questions raised by Assembly members. It is interesting to list some of those questions and to see what subjects were considered over the years. These questions include:

– Written Question No. 158 by Mr Wiklund on the protection of the human rights of Gypsies (Doc. 3349 of 27 September 1973);

– Written Question No. 187 by Mr McNamara on the situation of nomads in Europe (Doc. 3867 of 20 September 1976);

– Written Question No. 267 by Mr Ramírez Pery on the cultural and social problems of populations of nomadic origin (Doc. 5096 of 28 June 1983);

– Written Question No. 269 by Mr Ramírez Pery on the discriminatory treatment of populations of nomadic origin (Doc. 5141 of 3 October 1983);

– Written Question No. 270 by Mr Ramírez Pery on the demographic characteristics of Gypsy populations (Doc. 5142 of 3 October 1983);

– Written Question No. 274 by Mr Ramírez Pery on the exclusion of Gypsies from among the ethno-linguistic minorities in Italy (Doc. 5182 of 2 February 1984);

– Oral Question No. 3 by Mr Franck on concrete measures to protect Gypsies and improve their opportunities (Doc. 7115 of 29 June 1994);

- Written Question No. 358 by Ms Verspaget on citizenship legislation in the Czech Republic (Doc. 7196 of 24 November 1994);
- Written Question No. 372 by Ms Verspaget on the appointment of a mediator for Roma/Gypsies (Doc. 7802 of 18 April 1997);
- Written Question No. 411 by Mr Cilevičs on the visit to Greece of the Group of Specialists on Roma (Doc. 9528 of 23 July 2002);
- Written Question No. 430 by Mr Tabajdi on the legal situation of Roma in Europe (Doc. 9877 of 10 July 2003);
- Written Question No. 474 by Mr Cilevičs on forced evictions of Roma in Greece (Doc. 10694 of 1 October 2005);
- Written Question No. 502 by Mr Cilevičs on implementation of the European Social Charter by Greece: Forced evictions of Roma (Doc. 11014 of 1 September 2006);
- Written Question No. 549 by Mr Lindblad on the persecution of people of Roma origin (Doc. 11655 of 23 June 2008).

As their wording and content indicate, the questions cover a range of subjects. Put to the Committee of Ministers, they keep attention focused on the question of Roma, Gypsies and Travellers. In order to reply, the Committee of Ministers has to conduct research and in return presents a sometimes substantial overview of the situation concerning the points raised before making proposals. This process makes it possible to initiate and consolidate political and institutional advances at both state and European level.

Another means of action is for a group of parliamentarians to propose the adoption of a new text. In 1981, for example, a motion for a recommendation on the legal situation of travellers in the member states of the Council of Europe was tabled by Mr Scholten and others (Doc. 4696 of 30 March 1981). At that time, however, although growing attention was being paid to the question of Roma and Gypsies, the approach sometimes lacked coherence both in the vocabulary employed and in the subject areas dealt with. One example is a motion for a resolution which in the French version uses the term "Romanichels", a highly pejorative term, to describe Gypsies (Document 1, 229/81 of 14 May 1981, CPL (16) 5). To take another example, the Assembly Committee on Culture and Education carried out a survey of minority languages and dialects in which Romani and its variants were not even mentioned among the 50 covered by the report (Doc. 4745, 12 June 1981).

In 2000, a motion for a recommendation on the improvement of living and social conditions of the Roma/Gypsy population in order to decrease possible Romani migration from the countries of central and eastern Europe was tabled by Mr Tabajdi and others (Doc. 8830 of 22 September 2000):

> The Assembly notes that the problems faced by Roma/Gypsies of central and eastern Europe in their living and social conditions are largely the result of long-standing social, employment and educational policies of the past, which prevented the Roma/Gypsies from real social integration and forced them either to accept assimilation or to live at the periphery of society ... The Assembly is concerned that

the social and economic system in the central and east European countries finds the Roma/Gypsy population unprepared to adapt themselves to the basically new conditions of market economy ... It is particularly worrying that social solidarity has markedly decreased in the new democracies, which has given room to rapidly growing discrimination, even racist intolerance, against the weakest of society.

In 2006, a motion for a resolution on the double discrimination of Romani women and girls was tabled by Ms Zapfl-Helbling and others (Doc. 11074 of 9 October 2006). The authors call upon Council of Europe member states:

to urgently gender mainstream their policies on the Romani, in order to ensure that:

i. Romani women and girls cease to be discriminated against, both within their own community and in society at large;

ii. special attention is paid to the educational, health and housing needs of Romani women and girls;

iii. the practice of forced and underage marriages is no longer tolerated, and that Romani women and girls in such marriages and/or subjected to domestic violence are given the necessary assistance to leave such relationships;

iv. the practice of coercive sterilisations ends and victims receive proper redress.

Another motion for a recommendation on the situation of Roma in Europe and relevant activities of the Council of Europe was tabled by Mr Cilevičs and others in 2007 (Doc. 11206 of 23 March 2007). It notes that "the Roma issue is at the heart of three of the Organisation's priorities: protection of minorities, the fight against racism and intolerance and the fight against social exclusion."

In 2009, a motion for a recommendation on Roma asylum seekers in Council of Europe member states was tabled by Ms Memecan and others (Doc. 12073 of 15 October 2009):

Over the last two decades, Roma and related groups – often described as Europe's forgotten people – have left their countries in Eastern and Central Europe to seek asylum in other parts of Europe and the world. Due to the Yugoslav wars in the 1990s, many tens of thousands of Roma left their countries. As a result of the conflict in Kosovo about 120 000 Roma had to leave Kosovo. Recently, a wave of violence against Roma entailing eight deaths and many injured has swept the Czech Republic, Hungary and Slovakia. Many hundreds of Roma from the Czech Republic have been granted asylum in Canada as a result. Those who have sought asylum in European Union member states have, however, been denied protection. The EU Qualification Directive provides that EU member states shall be regarded as "safe countries of origin" with regard to claims of persecution. The Assembly should propose action aimed at dealing with the issue of Roma asylum seekers. All action must be prepared and undertaken in consultation and co-operation with the Roma themselves.

Recommendation 1203 (1993) on Gypsies in Europe

Nearly a quarter of a century after Recommendation 563 (1969) was adopted, and following repeated references by its members, the Parliamentary

Assembly deemed it necessary to take stock of the situation of Roma and to present a new text, especially because the changes which had come about in Europe since 1989, and the accession of new member states to the Council of Europe, had put the Roma question in a new perspective. Moreover, the other European institutions, the EU and the OSCE, had also become active in this field. A detailed report was drawn up by a member of the Assembly, accompanied by a draft recommendation on Gypsies in Europe (Doc. 6733 of 11 January 1993), presented by Ms Verspaget for the Committee on Culture, Science and Education:

Summary

Intolerance of Gypsies and other travellers has long existed. It has mainly been associated with their generally unfavourable social and economic condition and has worsened with the recent changes in central and eastern Europe.

Much attention has been paid to Gypsy problems by international bodies and in particular the Council of Europe. But little improvement in their situation has resulted in practice.

The report proposes to replace the socio-economic image of Gypsies by a cultural definition. Gypsies have after all been part of the European cultural tradition for over five centuries. Their culture and language should be respected and promoted as more than simple folklore.

Gypsies should be recognised as a non-territorial minority. While they should respect the laws of the countries in which they live, they should also be allowed to enjoy equal rights with other citizens of those countries.

Special measures are necessary in the fields of education, information and everyday life. As a general principle it is stressed that Gypsies should be consulted over measures that directly affect them.

The explanatory memorandum reveals how the terminology evolved:

For the purposes of this report the term "Gypsy" is used for all people and groups of people who are by dominant society called "Gypsies", "travellers", "Zigeuner", "Gitanos", "Tsiganes", "Gitanos", or other similar terms. The term is also used here for other people who experience similar treatment as "Gypsies" because of their real or alleged itinerant existence or the supposed itinerant existence of their ancestors, and because of their lifestyle, including people and groups of people who call themselves Roma, Sinti, Kale or suchlike.

Recommendation 1203 was adopted by the Assembly on 2 February 1993. It proposed a new approach, along the lines developed during the 1980s, to activities carried out at European level – mainly a cultural and legal approach, as is clearly stated in the opening paragraphs:

2. A special place among the minorities is reserved for Gypsies. Living scattered all over Europe, not having a country to call their own, they are a true European minority, but one that does not fit into the definitions of national or linguistic minorities.

3. As a non-territorial minority, Gypsies greatly contribute to the cultural diversity of Europe. In different parts of Europe they contribute in different ways, be it by language and music or by their trades and crafts.

4. With central and east European countries now member states, the number of Gypsies living in the area of the Council of Europe has increased drastically.

5. Intolerance of Gypsies by others has existed throughout the ages. Outbursts of racial or social hatred, however, occur more and more regularly, and the strained relations between communities have contributed to the deplorable situation in which the majority of Gypsies lives today.

6. Respect for the rights of Gypsies, individual, fundamental and human rights and their rights as a minority is essential to improve their situation.

7. Guarantees for equal rights, equal chances, equal treatment, and measures to improve their situation will make a revival of Gypsy language and culture possible, thus enriching European cultural diversity.

8. The guarantee of the enjoyment of the rights and freedoms set forth in Article 14 of the European Convention on Human Rights is important for Gypsies as it enables them to maintain their individual rights.

The recommendations brought to the attention of the Committee of Ministers relate to culture, education, information, equality of rights, consultation of the populations concerned and the appointment of a mediator for Gypsies.

Recommendation 1557 (2002) on the legal situation of Roma in Europe

Some 10 years after the adoption of Recommendation 1203 (1993), the Committee on Legal Affairs and Human Rights presented a report drawn up by Mr Tabajdi (Doc. 9397 of 19 April 2002):

Summary

The report offers a new approach towards the subject of Roma, based on the significant changes that have taken place in Europe and in the framework of the Council of Europe since the last recommendation.

Today the Roma are still subjected to discrimination, marginalisation and segregation. Discrimination is widespread in every field of public and personal life, including access to public places, education, employment, health services and housing. The Romani community is still not regarded as an ethnic or national minority group in every member state, and thus it does not enjoy the rights pertaining to this status in all the countries concerned. The effective participation of the Romani minority in public life is a vital element in all democratic societies, but the participation must always take a voluntary form. There is a need to strengthen, clarify and harmonise the work of multilateral organisations.

The Council of Europe can and must play an important role in improving the legal status, the level of equality and the living conditions of the Roma. The report supports the proposal of establishing a European Roma Consultative Forum. A charter on the fundamental rights of Roma should be initiated. The report advocates the need for the institution of a European Roma Ombudsman. A European Roma study and training centre is also envisaged.

The approach is intentionally legal, and it is significant that the text was tabled on behalf of the Assembly's Committee on Legal Affairs and Human Rights. It refers to Recommendation 1203 (1993) and stresses that "although international organisations, national governments, local authorities and non-governmental organisations have made great efforts, the aims set by this recommendation have been achieved to a restricted extent." Discrimination was actually greater in every sphere, and the difficult economic situation was making the plight of Roma even worse.

Major migratory movements had given rise to a new element, according to Recommendation 1557:

> The nature and direction of the migration of the Roma has changed recently, as its illegal aspect has grown markedly, and even former transit countries have become final destinations. Ethnic conflicts and civil wars of the last 10 years in certain parts of Europe intensified the phenomena of the migration of the Roma. This migration is still not higher than the average migration trend from central and eastern Europe, but it attracts greater public attention because of its specific nature, as it is usually not an individual, solitary enterprise, but a family affair for the smaller or larger Romany families.

On a matter as important as the migration of Roma (still a topical issue), it is interesting to mention Doc. 9417 of 22 April 2002 (rapporteur Mr Cilevičs), presented by the Parliamentary Assembly's Committee on Migration, Refugees and Population (then the Committee on Migration, Refugees and Demography), which was asked for its opinion:

> 2. Several questions, lying in the field of interest of the Committee on Migration, Refugees and Demography need, in your rapporteur's opinion, closer examination. They constitute different aspects of Roma migration: increasing number of Roma asylum seekers from central and eastern Europe, discrimination of Roma migrants and asylum seekers, specific case of Roma displacement due to the conflict in Kosovo, and itinerant style of life of numerous Roma communities (so-called nomadism).
>
> ...
>
> *Migratory movements of Roma population*
>
> 17. Roma migration has deep historical roots, and it is a natural tradition of numerous Roma communities. Movement and migration is intrinsic for Roma, and the respect for diversity and different cultures cannot abstract from this fact.
>
> 18. A number of factors determines Roma's high mobility and their movement across borders. These are economic factors, in particular search for employment, political and social insecurity caused by systematic discrimination and social marginalisation, and the existence of family networks.
>
> 19. The right to move into any country is not a human right. Any state has the right to impose restrictions and establish procedures regulating the movements in and out of its borders. However, these rules should be applied in a non-discriminatory way and Roma migrants should be treated like all other migrants.
>
> 20. Finally, your rapporteur would like to express his concern that the problem of Roma migration, is discussed, as a rule, in terms of migration control and prevention, and not in the context of full and fair implementation of the 1951 Geneva Convention and the principle of non-discrimination.

21. In your rapporteur's opinion, migration should not be treated as a negative phenomenon but rather as an inevitable tendency of modern society necessary for economic development, and cultural enrichment of Europe. The right to move is after all a fundamental human right.

Recommendation 1557 was adopted on 25 April 2002. It contains several paragraphs on the difficult economic and social situation of Roma and the discrimination they face in every field. A series of recommendations is addressed to the member states (only the headings are listed here, but detailed guidelines are suggested for each specific point):

15. The Council of Europe can and must play an important role in improving the legal status, the level of equality and the living conditions of Roma. The Assembly calls upon the member states to complete the six general conditions, which are necessary for the improvement of the situation of Roma in Europe:

a. to resolve the legal status of Roma

...

b. to elaborate and implement specific programmes to improve the integration of Roma as individuals and Romany communities as minority groups into society and ensure their participation in decision-making processes at local, regional, national and European levels

...

c. to guarantee equal treatment for the Romany minority as an ethnic or national minority group in the field of education, employment, housing, health and public services

...

d. to develop and implement positive action and preferential treatment for the socially deprived strata, including Roma as a socially disadvantaged community, in the field of education, employment and housing

...

e. to take specific measures and create special institutions for the protection of the Romany language, culture, traditions and identity

...

f. to combat racism, xenophobia and intolerance and to ensure non-discriminatory treatment of Roma at local, regional, national and international levels.

Recommendation 1633 (2003) on the forced returns of Roma from the former Federal Republic of Yugoslavia, including Kosovo, to Serbia and Montenegro from Council of Europe member states

As the preceding texts show, the Parliamentary Assembly can adopt texts of a general nature, although each of the recommendations quoted has one dominant theme which has a logical link to the Assembly committee which proposed it for adoption after preparing a report on the subject. Thus we have:

- Recommendation 563 (1969), by the Committee on Social and Health Questions;
- Recommendation 1203 (1993), by the Committee on Culture, Science and Education;
- Recommendation 1557 (2002), by the Committee on Legal Affairs and Human Rights.

However, when the situation demands it the Assembly can also adopt texts on topical questions, in the sense that they are linked to major events or a geographical area. This was the case with Recommendation 1633. In 2003, the Assembly's Committee on Migration, Refugees and Population presented a report on the forced returns of Roma from the former Federal Republic of Yugoslavia, including Kosovo, to Serbia and Montenegro from Council of Europe member states (Doc. 9990 of 31 October 2003, rapporteur Mr Einarsson):

Summary

Forced returns of Roma have been carried out on the basis of bilateral readmission agreements concluded between Serbia and Montenegro on the one hand and different European countries on the other. They started shortly after the democratic changes following the presidential elections in Yugoslavia in September 2000. So far, approximately 1 000 Roma have been forcibly returned, mainly from Germany. According to estimates, a further 50 000 to 100 000 Roma staying in different Council of Europe member states fall into the category foreseen for readmission.

Although this question cannot be considered in abstraction from the general issue of forced returns of rejected asylum seekers and migrants without legal status originating from the Balkans, Roma population constitute a particularly vulnerable and exposed group requiring effective policy measures in many areas.

The recommendation was adopted on 25 November 2003. In it, the Assembly emphasises that:

6. The main concerns relating to forced returns of Roma can be divided into three areas. The first group of issues calls into question the legitimacy of certain decisions on expulsion taken by the host countries. The second group relates to the conditions in which forced returns take place, and the third to the situation in which forcibly returned Roma find themselves upon their return to Serbia and Montenegro.

7. It is particularly worrying that readmission agreements do not clearly define the conditions for the reception of returned persons and do not put any responsibility on the receiving state with regard to the reintegration of returnees.

8. The Assembly is also concerned by so-called "voluntary returns" which in some cases are so strongly encouraged that they may amount to disguised forced returns.

The Assembly went on to adopt a list of recommendations to the Committee of Ministers asking it to invite the member states concerned to take organisational, humanitarian, legal and financial measures such as required to respect the rights of families and individuals.

Recommendation 1708 (2005) on the current situation in Kosovo

Other Assembly texts are directly, if not exclusively, relevant to Roma. Over recent years, several texts have been adopted on the situation in central or eastern European states or the Balkans. One example is Resolution 1123 (1997) on the honouring of obligations and commitments by Romania as a member state, in which "the Assembly therefore earnestly requests that the Romanian authorities ... promote a campaign against racism, xenophobia and intolerance and take all appropriate measures for the social integration of the Rom population." Another example is Recommendation 1338 (1997) on the obligations and commitments of the Czech Republic as a member state, which lays emphasis on the question of "minorities: notably, measures to reduce discrimination against the Roma/Gypsy community".

Mention may also be made of Recommendation 1708 (2005). The Assembly's Political Affairs Committee presented a report on the situation in Kosovo (Doc. 10572 of 3 June 2005, rapporteur Ms Tritz). On the basis of that report, on 21 June 2005 the Assembly adopted Recommendation 1708 on the situation in Kosovo, but with special reference to the Roma question.

Other texts relate to the situation of the Roma, in particular those which the Assembly has adopted on migrations or the right of asylum, for example Recommendation 1440 (2000) on restrictions on asylum in the member states of the Council of Europe and the European Union, Resolution 1695 (2009) on improving the quality and consistency of asylum decisions in the Council of Europe member states, and Recommendation 1889 (2009) which bears the same title.

On the question of migrations and asylum seekers, a motion for a recommendation on Roma asylum seekers in Council of Europe member states was tabled in 2009 by Ms Memecan and others (Doc. 12073 of 15 October 2009).

> 1. Over the last two decades, Roma and related groups – often described as Europe's forgotten people – have left their countries in Eastern and Central Europe to seek asylum in other parts of Europe and the world. Due to the Yugoslav wars in the 1990s, many tens of thousands of Roma left their countries. As a result of the conflict in Kosovo about 120 000 Roma had to leave Kosovo. Recently, a wave of violence against Roma entailing eight deaths and many injured has swept the Czech Republic, Hungary and Slovakia. Many hundreds of Roma from the Czech Republic have been granted asylum in Canada as a result. Those who have sought asylum in European Union member states have, however, been denied protection. The EU Qualification Directive provides that EU member states shall be regarded as "safe countries of origin" with regard to claims of persecution. The Assembly should propose action aimed at dealing with the issue of Roma asylum seekers. All action must be prepared and undertaken in consultation and co-operation with the Roma themselves.
>
> ...

the Parliamentary Assembly of the Council of Europe should:

i. urge Council of Europe member states to ensure that they honour their obligations under the European Convention on Human Rights, in particular its Article 3, and the 1951 Geneva Convention Relating to the Status of Refugees and its 1967 Protocol with regard to Roma asylum seekers.

The proposal goes on to raise several issues relating to the combating of racism and the need to lay down clear rules for asylum seekers so that their rights are respected. The text concludes by urging "Council of Europe member states to enhance understanding and communication between Roma and non-Roma, ensure that the media are not used for the dissemination of hate speech and step up work to address the poverty, exclusion and discrimination of Roma."

The subject was raised again in the ambitious Doc. 12393 on Roma asylum seekers in Europe, presented by Mr Pupovac on 7 October 2010:

Summary

Over the last few years, acts of violence giving rise to death, injury and a climate of fear have forced many Roma to leave their countries, in order to apply for asylum in other countries, some of which are member states of the European Union. European Union legislation provides that it is safe to return asylum seekers to European Union member states; they are considered "safe countries of origin". A citizen of one European Union member state may thus not be granted refugee protection in another European Union member state, save in exceptional cases. Since the requirements for long-term residence in another European Union member are often so stringent that many Roma asylum seekers are unable to fulfil them, they find themselves in a state of limbo and in an irregular situation.

A further issue of importance is that around 100 000 Roma who fled violence in Kosovo are now facing return, after having spent up to 10 years in western European or neighbouring countries. If they are returned they face great social difficulties, discrimination and threats to their personal security. They have little chance of successfully reintegrating. Many of the children of these potential Roma returnees are born in or have lived all their lives in the host countries. Between 70% and 75% of Roma returnees have left Kosovo again following their return.

In order to deal with these different issues, the rapporteur underlines the importance of providing asylum seekers with an individual, specific, fair asylum assessment and the opportunity to rebut the presumption of safety that exists in cases of flight within the European Union. The rapporteur also insists on the prompt re-evaluation of the return policy aimed at Roma from Kosovo and urges member states to consider suspending returns and examining the option of providing for local integration in the host countries. However, if returns are enforced, they should be accompanied by genuine assistance.

The report's author analyses the current situation, which warrants the taking of an urgent decision to deal with these issues politically:

It is indeed frightening that systematic racist violence may occur in a member state of the Council of Europe and that its citizens feel forced to seek protection in other countries. Signatories to the European Convention on Human

Rights (ECHR) owe an obligation to protect everyone within their jurisdiction. Furthermore, it is highly unsatisfactory that the rules of the European Union are such that the people concerned are faced with three equally negative options: to seek asylum outside the European Union (which can be prohibitively expensive and requires travel documents), to live as irregular migrants in the country of asylum once they are refused (without access to housing, health care or education) or to stay in their home country and face persecution. The rapporteur considers that the European Union should reassess its rules in order to avoid this state of affairs. He also considers that member states of the Council of Europe should do their utmost to prevent racism and violent acts from occurring and, if they still do, to abide by the rule of law and bring the perpetrators to justice. Impunity for crimes and human rights violations, which often forces people to flee, must be eradicated once and for all.

...

The concerns addressed in this report stem from the incidents of violence and racism towards Roma today which have forced them to leave their homes in order to apply for asylum in other countries ... In fact, in many places in Europe today, as regards their social situation and exposure to discrimination, Roma face a situation of de facto apartheid. This is unacceptable. ... An important point is the leadership of authorities and politicians in the countries concerned. Extremists may feel that they have a license for their attacks when the message they receive from their government in other spheres is that the Roma are a problem. The rapporteur is consequently of the opinion that politicians must strongly and publicly condemn all forms of racism and stigmatisation of Roma.

...

For many years, the Assembly has been drawing attention to the situation of Roma without much progress being made. To the general and deplorable situation of the Roma in Europe has now been added that of Roma refugees and asylum seekers. In fact, the situation of Roma in Europe, instead of improving, has deteriorated to the point that Roma have again been forced to leave their countries to escape persistent discrimination and racist violence. Instead of finding protection they have been caught in limbo and often forced into living as irregular migrants.

Recommendation 1924 (2010) and Resolution 1740 (2010) on the situation of Roma in Europe and relevant activities of the Council of Europe

In 2010, the Assembly's Committee on Legal Affairs and Human Rights adopted a report on the situation of Roma in Europe and relevant activities of the Council of Europe (Doc. 12174 of 26 February 2010, rapporteur Mr Berényi):

Summary

The Roma, estimated at between 10 and 12 million people, constitute the largest minority in Europe and are present in virtually all Council of Europe member states.

> This minority has been suffering profound discrimination for centuries and, even today, is still frequently rejected by the rest of the population because of deep-seated prejudices. Moreover, in these times of economic crisis, this highly vulnerable minority presents an easy target and is used as a scapegoat.
>
> It has to be recognised that the efforts undertaken to improve the situation of Roma have produced very limited results so far. The situation faced by Roma in terms of access to education, employment, health services and housing or in terms of social integration is still very often deplorable, not to say scandalous.
>
> It is high time that a careful assessment was made of the reasons for the failure of efforts already undertaken or the success of certain projects, in particular by the judicious gathering of ethnic statistics. Determined, effective, co-ordinated and sustainable measures must be taken without delay.
>
> Roma are also extremely under-represented in political bodies. Positive measures should be taken to remedy this situation and enhance the participation and representation of Roma in public and political life, including within the Parliamentary Assembly.

Here again, as with Recommendation 1557 (2002), it was the Assembly's Committee on Legal Affairs and Human Rights which prepared a new text. The rapporteur, Mr Berényi, had already paved the way for the debate with an introductory memorandum presented on 3 September 2008 (AS/Jur (2008) 29 rev), itself a follow-up to a draft report presented on 22 November 2007. This is in-depth, long-term work. In his 2008 memorandum the rapporteur presented a detailed account and a number of conclusions:

> While the Council of Europe's Commissioner for Human Rights concluded in 2007 in one of his "viewpoints" that it is time to take a serious interest in the fundamental rights of the Roma, the rapporteur would point out that the Council of Europe has done this for a long time and developed a set of fairly important instruments and legal provisions. ... It is important to point out that the basis of the Organisation's work is respect for human rights, and the Council of Europe should ensure that all activities relating to the protection of the Roma send out a strong and coherent message on human dignity.

To that memorandum must be added the result of additional discussions organised by the rapporteur, in particular a hearing on "The situation of Roma in Romania", held in May 2009 in Târgu Mureş, Romania.

The rapporteur's preparatory work has had all the more impact as it forms the basis for both an Assembly recommendation and a resolution. In his explanatory memorandum, the rapporteur deliberately takes a judicial stance and "sounds the alarm":

> 7. I have wondered how best to describe the seriousness of the situation in my report. I have decided to let the facts speak for themselves and to outline recent outrageous events and circumstances of which Roma people have been victims in a wide range of Council of Europe member states. These events – in which a number of basic human rights of Roma people are infringed – tell the story better than a long analysis.

8. It must be borne in mind that the following are only a handful of shocking examples, reflecting an increasingly widespread trend in Europe towards anti-Gypsyism of the worst kind.

9. Looking at these examples, it appears clearly that the process of Roma integration has not reached its objectives during the last 20 years. Integration has not reached a level which would prevent the Roma population from becoming an easy target for extremist and populist politicians.

He goes on to present a long list of outrages against Roma in every sphere. He then analyses the measures taken (or not taken) by governments and concludes that:

101. The excessively passive stance of the authorities and the tacit consent of part of the population when faced with this intolerable situation are reminiscent of the darkest hours in Europe's history. The Council of Europe was born out of a categorical desire to prevent those dark hours from repeating themselves. Ever since, the European Court of Human Rights has regularly condemned states in which Roma have suffered from abuse or discrimination.

102. Member states must shoulder their responsibilities and do everything they can to extinguish this dangerous flare-up of anti-Gypsyism as promptly as possible.

103. So far, a lot has been undertaken at different levels to improve the situation of Roma. However, these actions remain merely on paper since, at this stage, the results of positive measures are still unclear, because there are no indicators of their efficacy. Too much theory without practical evaluation tends to make one lose touch with reality.

...

107. The current situation of Roma in Europe gives rise to great concern, not least because of the enormous gulf between the situation of the Roma and that of most other minorities. It is always hard to break out of poverty, and harder still when one suffers discrimination.

108. The member states, the Council of Europe and the Roma themselves still have a long way to go before the situation of the Roma is improved sustainably.

The question was also referred to the Committee on Migration, Refugees and Population, which adopted a positive opinion on the draft resolution presented by Ms Memecan (Doc. 12207 of 13 April 2010). That opinion refers to an earlier motion for a recommendation entitled "Roma asylum seekers in Council of Europe member states" (Doc. 12073 of 15 October 2009, also presented by Ms Memecan). In the 2010 opinion, focusing on the issues of migration within its terms of reference, the committee offers a detailed analysis of migration situations and the lack of protection for the rights of Roma. It stresses the fact that:

1. Roma have a history of migration. They have often had to migrate to survive in a hostile world. Being confronted with persecution, discrimination and lack of understanding, since arriving in Europe centuries ago, Roma have been forced to regularly change domicile, looking for a place where they can settle without being immediately pushed away. This necessity is unfortunately still there today.

In some cases there is even a need for Roma to move within or from Europe in order to seek asylum from persecution.

...

3. The Committee welcomes the strong and unequivocal report of the Committee on Legal Affairs and Human Rights and the constructive proposals that are put forward. The Committee subscribes to the conclusions of the Committee on Legal Affairs and Human Rights, including that monitoring of implementation at local level and a holistic and concerted approach is necessary to improve the situation of Roma, and that enhanced access to housing and education for Roma is of crucial importance.

...

13. In all the problematic fields to which the Committee on Legal Affairs and Human Rights draws attention, Roma that are at the same time migrants face additional difficulties due to their possible lack of citizenship and language skills and the general marginalisation that migrants often face. This issue remains, whether the Roma concerned are regular or irregular migrants, refugees or asylum seekers. In all the social dimensions – housing, health care, employment and education – member states should be urged to specifically consider the needs of Roma migrants.

14. One of the important objectives of the Council of Europe is to promote diversity in society. This aim should be kept in mind when trying to integrate Roma and Roma migrants. Roma migrants should be allowed to exercise and develop their culture, language and lifestyle. This implies a need for knowledge, flexibility and goodwill on the part of the responsible authorities.

The committee then proposed some amendments to the draft resolution. Not all were adopted, but it is important to mention them because they afford a consolidated overview of current trends in taking account of, and showing respect for, Roma communities, in a context marked by discrimination. The proposed amendments to the draft resolution suggested the addition of the following:

"base all action intended to improve the situation of Roma, at every stage of the process, on prior and genuine consultation with the Roma themselves"

...

"consider taking positive action in order to combat discrimination and to improve the opportunities of Roma, in particular in the fields of education and employment, and would expect the Roma to accept that they fulfil all obligations to have an education"

...

"enhance communication, understanding and respect between Roma and non-Roma in society with a view to eradicate racism, xenophobia, discrimination and exclusion"

...

"tackle hate speech vis-à-vis Roma, whether occurring in the media, politics or in civil society"

...

"take firm measures to prosecute all perpetrators of crimes and human rights violations against Roma"

...

"promote the exercise and development of Roma culture, language and lifestyle using for instance the Roma Cultural Route developed by the Council of Europe"

...

"take special measures to afford protection to Roma asylum seekers who have fled racist violence, to ensure that EU citizens have the possibility to rebut the presumption of safety that applies in respect of EU member states, and not to return Roma to Kosovo until the UNHCR has confirmed that the situation there has sufficiently improved in terms of security and access to social rights"

...

"The Assembly encourages member states to apologise for past injustice and sufferings to the Roma community, if they have not already done so".

The Committee on Equal Opportunities for Women and Men was also asked for its opinion. In its report (Doc. 12236 of 28 April 2010, presented by Ms Kovács):

> The Committee congratulates the Committee on Legal Affairs and Human Rights on its comprehensive report, and supports the draft resolution and draft recommendation tabled. However, it wishes to propose some amendments to better integrate the gender dimension, since Roma women and girls risk double, if not triple discrimination: as Roma by the wider community, and as women and girls by both the wider and their own community.

Before proposing some amendments, the document emphasises the many forms of discrimination of which Roma women are victims, the violence they suffer and health issues, in particular the question of sterilisation to which they may be subject:

> Regarding coercive sterilisation, Roma women are particularly vulnerable to abuse by medical practitioners at the time of pregnancy and childbirth. Practices of extreme abuse include death after childbirth, serious damage of the women's health, as well as forceful termination of the women's reproductive capacity through coercive sterilisation. Roma women are at risk of being subjected to sterilisation without their full and informed consent, without an explanation about the intervention, its nature, possible risks, or what the consequence of being sterilised would be. Instances of coercive sterilisation of Roma women have occurred in a number of Council of Europe member states.

Following the report and the committees' proposals and opinions, on 22 June 2010 the Assembly adopted Resolution 1740 (2010) and Recommendation 1924 (2010).

Following the three major recommendations 563 (1969), 1203 (1993) and 1557 (2002), this latest text proposes a global, comprehensive approach again in 2010. It reactivates the documents adopted earlier and stresses that their implementation leaves something to be desired, and it focuses not only on rights but also on the need for Roma to play a part in decisions affecting them. Thus in 2010 this text can be seen as a stocktaking report on action taken, with a critical approach both in the text of the resolution and in the rapporteur's explanatory memorandum, and as opening up possibilities for the immediate future and emphasising the paths to be followed. This approach within a broad political framework is in keeping with a general movement which, as we shall see in the next chapter, is one pursued by the Committee of Ministers.

Furthermore, in Resolution 1740, the Assembly expresses anxiety over the fact that states tend to offload their responsibilities onto "Europe":

> The Assembly notes a new trend within member states to consider that the Roma issue falls under the responsibility of international and European organisations. Whilst convinced of the importance of the role of international organisations – and especially of the Council of Europe – in this field, the Assembly reiterates that the main responsibility lies with the member states. There should be no shirking of responsibility: education, employment, social inclusion, health services and housing are almost entirely national responsibilities.

Consequently, later in the adopted text the Assembly urges member states, offering a detailed list of actions to be taken, to tackle Roma issues in depth, both globally from the standpoint of a cultural minority, from the standpoint of combating discrimination and adopting action plans and consolidated strategies, and in a targeted fashion in the field of education, housing, employment, health and political representation. In Recommendation 1924 the Assembly points to the leading role of the Council of Europe and encourages the organisation to step up its action:

> 1. The Parliamentary Assembly ... considers the issue to be crucial enough for the Council of Europe to increase its involvement in this field by reinforcing the visibility of its existing activities and so avoiding its *acquis* being diluted or misinterpreted.
>
> 2. The Council of Europe, which has been a pioneer in promoting the protection of Roma, should renew its impetus in its long-standing commitment to ensure greater protection and social integration of Roma.[6]

---

6. The full versions of the texts mentioned in this chapter are available on the Council of Europe Parliamentary Assembly website http://assembly.coe.int/ under the heading "Documents/Adopted texts".

5. The Committee of Ministers on Roma since 1975

The Committee of Ministers consists of the ministers of foreign affairs of all the member states or their representatives in Strasbourg. The decision-making organ of the Council of Europe, it is an emanation of the governments of the member states. In addition to the decisions it takes, as set out in the texts it adopts, it ensures that the commitments entered into are complied with by the member states.

The texts adopted by the Committee of Ministers are of different kinds. The Committee may issue declarations. It replies to recommendations and questions from the Parliamentary Assembly and to recommendations of the Congress of Local and Regional Authorities of the Council of Europe. In the administrative sphere, where the operation of the institutions is concerned, decisions are taken in the form of resolutions. As for the most important texts – conventions or agreements in fields where a strong common policy must be defined – the Committee of Ministers proposes them for signature and ratification by the states, and the states which have ratified them are committed to their implementation.

The Committee of Ministers may also adopt recommendations to the member states seeking to define a common policy in a particular field. It is not mandatory for the states to implement these recommendations, but the Committee of Ministers may ask states to inform it of the action they have taken on them.

With regard to Roma, the Committee of Ministers has produced many texts on a wide range of questions, for example the opening of a special "Programme on Roma/Gypsies in Europe" account, the setting-up of working groups such as the one tasked with examining the question of a forum for Roma and Travellers (the GT-ROMS group), replies to questions from members of the Parliamentary Assembly and replies to Assembly recommendations. This latter point is well illustrated, among other examples, by the reply given by the Committee of Ministers to Assembly Recommendation 1557 (2002) on the legal situation of Roma in Europe (CM/AS(2003)Rec1557 final of 13 June 2003):

> 1. The Committee of Ministers has examined with interest Recommendation 1557 (2002) of the Parliamentary Assembly on the legal situation of Roma in Europe. It has requested and received opinions on the recommendation from the Specialist Group on Roma, Gypsies and Travellers (MG-S-ROM) and the Steering Committee for Education (CD-ED).

2. The Committee of Ministers notes that the Assembly considers that although great efforts have been made since the adoption of its Recommendation 1203 (1993) on Gypsies in Europe, nearly 10 years ago, the aims set by that recommendation have been achieved to a restricted extent. In the 1993 recommendation, the Assembly stressed the need for special protection for Gypsies and condemned the various forms of discrimination suffered by them. In Recommendation 1557 (2002), the Assembly stresses that Roma are still "subjected to discrimination, marginalisation and segregation" and that "most Roma are currently faced with a rather severe economic situation in most of the member countries of the Council of Europe".

3. The Committee of Ministers shares the view of the Assembly that the Council of Europe can and must play an important role in improving the general situation of the Roma and their living conditions. It agrees that there is a need to improve, speed up and harmonise all the efforts towards a better integration of Roma into society in order to improve their present situation.

The Committee of Ministers goes on to reply point by point to the various paragraphs of the Assembly recommendation and concludes by saying that:

> The Committee of Ministers would like to underline the complexity and relevance of the issues raised by the Parliamentary Assembly. It will continue its examination of these issues in one of its forthcoming meetings, also in the light of a number of major events taking place in this field in the near future.

Similarly, the Committee of Ministers replied to Parliamentary Assembly Recommendation 1203 (1993) in January 1994 and October 1995.

Resolution (75) 13 containing recommendations on the social situation of nomads in Europe

In chronological sequence, the first text concerning Roma adopted by the Committee of Ministers is Resolution (75) 13 of 22 May 1975. Although classed as a resolution, the document is the equivalent of a recommendation in today's terminology. As the text makes clear:

> For the purposes of this resolution, the expression "nomads" means persons who for historical reasons are accustomed to following an itinerant way of life, as well as persons of nomadic origin who experience difficulties in integrating into society for sociological, economic or similar reasons.

Remember that in 1969 the Parliamentary Assembly was using the expression "Gypsies and other travellers".

The text presents an overall picture, mentioning housing difficulties, economic difficulties, unfavourable prejudice and discriminatory attitudes, the low level of school attendance, inadequate social protection, and "bearing in mind the concern expressed in Recommendation 563 of the Consultative Assembly on the situation of gypsies and other travellers in Europe", the Committee of Ministers:

> I. Recommends the governments of the member states to take all measures they consider necessary to give effect to the principles set out in the appendix to the present resolution, of which it forms an integral part;

II. Invites the governments of member states to inform the Secretary General of the Council of Europe in due course of the action taken on the recommendations contained in this resolution.

The appendix lays down principles on general policy, encampments and housing, education, vocational guidance and training, health and social welfare, and social security.

Recommendation No. R (83) 1 on stateless nomads and nomads of undetermined nationality

Eight years later, in 1983, the Committee of Ministers prefaced recommended principles thus:

> Recalling its Resolution (75) 13 containing recommendations on the social situation of nomads in Europe and taking into account action taken by governments of the member states to implement these recommendations;
>
> Noting that many nomads experience difficulties with regard to their legal status, particularly in matters of travel and stay, because they lack a sufficient link of nationality or residence with a given state;
>
> Considering that it is desirable to contribute at European level to a harmonised solution of these problems particularly for humanitarian reasons in a way consistent with the legislation of each member state, while at the same time respecting the nomads' way of life;
>
> ...
>
> Having regard to the wish expressed by the Conference of European Ministers of Justice, which met at Athens in May 1982, that the problems raised by nomads should be examined in greater depth within the framework of the existing structures of the Council of Europe.

The Committee of Ministers went on to state principles in respect of non-discrimination, the link with a state, residence and movement of nomads, family reunification, measures of a general character and extended protection. Although family migrations were later to increase because of conflicts in several states and a strong sense of rejection, this Committee of Ministers recommendation adopted nearly 30 years ago retains its topicality, and is referred to in texts proposed today.

Recommendation No. R (2000) 4 on the education of Roma/Gypsy children in Europe

The year 2000 marked a turning point in the texts concerning Roma adopted by the Committee of Ministers. Parliamentary Assembly Recommendation 1203 (1993), presented by its Committee on Culture, Science and Education, had already influenced thinking on the subject, and introduced a strong cultural component over and above the nomadic way of life which was very much in evidence in the early texts. The Assembly recommendation was itself greatly influenced by a process initiated in 1981 by the Congress of

Local and Regional Authorities, which gave rise to a series of activities in the field of education. Other factors emerged to play their part in this change of approach by the Committee of Ministers. We shall return to them in later chapters.

As well as the new perspective introduced in the 2000 texts, the fact that, from Recommendation No. R (2000) 4 onwards, the Committee of Ministers began to organise its activity systematically and to adopt a series of complementary texts covering specific areas constituted a second change. The series started with the priority subject of education, and Recommendation No. R (2000) 4 on this question was adopted on 3 February 2000.

The first tangible activities concerning Roma in the field of education were carried out in 1983. Over the years, that experience was developed and consolidated. But it remains an urgent matter, and sustained political attention is still needed if this field is to be the subject of priority action. For example, the group of governmental experts responsible for Roma questions in the Council of Europe (see below) has been working on this question and in 1997 submitted a memorandum for the attention of the Committee of Ministers entitled "Roma children education policy paper: strategic elements of education policy for Roma children in Europe" (MG-S-ROM (97) 11 of 16 October 1997). After a short historical account analysing policies and the obstacles to school education for Roma children, the group laid the foundations for further developments, basing itself on the similarly directed Council of Europe texts. Finally, it proposes the strategic outlines of an education policy and concludes as follows:

> the Specialist Group stresses that there is an urgent need for a thorough evaluation of past and ongoing policies and actions in the member states, regarding the education of Roma/Gypsy children, especially in the new member states.
>
> ...
>
> 20. Taking these principles and general framework as a basis for future educational strategies and policies toward Roma children, and recognising the crucial importance of education as a means of overcoming disadvantage, marginalisation and deprivation and upgrading the status of the Roma minority in society, the Specialist Group proposes to the Committee of Ministers that the Council for Cultural Co-operation (CDCC) should be invited, in co-operation with the Specialist Group, to draw up a recommendation or resolution devoted specifically to the education of Roma children in Europe.

This proposal went through the usual administrative process. The Council for Cultural Co-operation proposed a text which was examined at several meetings of the Ministers' Deputies. At those meetings, several states suggested amendments (France, Portugal, Hungary, Finland) before the text was finalised and led to the adoption of Recommendation No. R (2000) 4 on the education of Roma/Gypsy children in Europe. The text refers to earlier work:

> Bearing in mind the work carried out by the Council for Cultural Co-operation (CDCC) to respond to Resolution 125 (1981), and in particular, the publication of the report *Gypsies and Travellers* (1985), updated in 1994 (*Roma, Gypsies, Travellers*, Council of Europe Publishing);

Having welcomed the memorandum prepared by the Specialist Group on Roma/Gypsies entitled "Roma children education policy paper: strategic elements of education policy for Roma children in Europe" (MG-S-ROM (97) 11).

The innovative character of the text, already mentioned, also lies in its critical approach to the policies pursued hitherto, which not only did not improve the situation but were in significant measure responsible for it:

Recognising that there is an urgent need to build new foundations for future educational strategies toward the Roma/Gypsy people in Europe, particularly in view of the high rates of illiteracy or semi-literacy among them, their high drop-out rate, the low percentage of students completing primary education and the persistence of features such as low school attendance;

Noting that the problems faced by Roma/Gypsies in the field of schooling are largely the result of long-standing educational policies of the past, which led either to assimilation or to segregation of Roma/Gypsy children at school on the grounds that they were "socially and culturally handicapped";

Considering that the disadvantaged position of Roma/Gypsies in European societies cannot be overcome unless equality of opportunity in the field of education is guaranteed for Roma/Gypsy children;

Considering that the education of Roma/Gypsy children should be a priority in national policies in favour of Roma/Gypsies;

Bearing in mind that policies aimed at addressing the problems faced by Roma/Gypsies in the field of education should be comprehensive, based on an acknowledgement that the issue of schooling for Roma/Gypsy children is linked with a wide range of other factors and pre-conditions, namely the economic, social and cultural aspects, and the fight against racism and discrimination.

The Committee of Ministers recommended that:

in implementing their education policies the governments of the member states:

– be guided by the principles set out in the appendix to this recommendation;

– bring this recommendation to the attention of the relevant public bodies in their respective countries through the appropriate national channels.

The text also emphasises the need for a comprehensive approach, and the link between education and families' living conditions in "the economic, social and cultural aspects, and the fight against racism and discrimination". The appendix details "Guiding principles of an education policy for Roma/Gypsy children in Europe". There are sections on structures, curriculum and teaching material, recruitment and training of teachers, information research and assessment, consultation and co-ordination. Reference is made – a novel approach – to flexibility, co-ordination, involvement of parents and the community through mediators and support structures, and the taking of culture into account is clearly called for:

8. Educational policies in favour of Roma/Gypsy children should be implemented in the framework of broader intercultural policies, taking into account the particular features of the Romani culture and the disadvantaged position of many Roma/Gypsies in the member states.

9. The curriculum, on the whole, and the teaching material should therefore be designed so as to take into account the cultural identity of Roma/Gypsy children. Romani history and culture should be introduced in the teaching material in order to reflect the cultural identity of Roma/Gypsy children. The participation of representatives of the Roma/Gypsy community should be encouraged in the development of teaching material on the history, culture or language of the Roma/Gypsies.

10. However, the member states should ensure that this does not lead to the establishment of separate curricula, which might lead to the setting-up of separate classes.

11. The member states should also encourage the development of teaching material based on good practices in order to assist teachers in their daily work with Roma/Gypsy pupils.

12. In the countries where the Romani language is spoken, opportunities to learn in the mother tongue should be offered at school to Roma/Gypsy children.

These recommendations were put into effect in the Council of Europe by way of a project that is presented below as an example of the implementation of Committee of Ministers recommendations.

The innovative character of this recommendation adopted in 2000 has been mentioned, highlighting its approach based on recognition of Romani culture, history and language; the fact that it was the first recommendation in a series of texts each of which had one main theme, in this case school education, and its critical approach. There is a fourth aspect of its originality, an important one when seen in a historical and institutional perspective, namely its link with a text adopted in 1989 by the EU: the recommendation, and the memorandum that went before, make explicit reference to action taken in the EU framework and to the resolution adopted by the EU's ministers of education in 1989:

> The Committee of Ministers ... considering that, as there is a text concerning the education of Roma/Gypsy children for member states of the European Union (Resolution of the Council and of the Ministers of Education meeting with the Council on School Provision for Gypsy and Traveller Children, of 22 May 1989; 89/C 153/02), it is urgently necessary to have a text covering all of the member states of the Council of Europe.

Furthermore, Recommendation No. R (2000) 4 of the Council of Europe is structured in the same way and along the same lines as the EU resolution. This institutional similarity in the preparation and adoption of a text, thus making it possible for the two texts to be interlinked, and their reciprocal validation, give added force to both. The text adopted in 1989 covers the member states of the EU, and the 2002 text covers the member states of the Council of Europe. So the countries of the EU saw the 1989 text confirmed and extended to the whole of Europe.

The political and practical implications are important, and constitute the underlying issue for Roma. Thus it is possible for the two institutions, in implementing these texts, to acquire the necessary means with regard to reflection, research, information, evaluation and financing, and so encourage their member states to pursue the requisite action along the lines recommended, and confirm their wish to organise their work in following up and co-ordinating the activities in question.

Recommendation Rec(2001)17 on improving the economic and employment situation of Roma/Gypsies and Travellers in Europe

One year after adopting its recommendation on education, the Committee of Ministers tackled the question of the economic and employment situation. The institutional dynamic was similar. The Committee of Ministers based itself on earlier thinking:

> Bearing in mind the publication of the book *Gypsies and Travellers* (1985), updated in 1994, *Roma, Gypsies, Travellers*, Council of Europe Publishing;
>
> Welcoming the document prepared by the Specialist Group on Roma/Gypsies entitled "Economic and employment problems faced by Roma/Gypsies in Europe" (MG-S-ROM(99)5rev2).

The ground realities are also acknowledged before recommendations are made:

> Recognising that large groups of Roma/Gypsies and Travellers in Europe suffer from the effects of long-term unemployment and poverty, which could present a threat to the social cohesion of member states;
>
> Noting that the persistent problems of poverty and unemployment are the result of discrimination against and social exclusion of Roma/Gypsies and Travellers, and are closely interlinked to problems in areas such as accommodation, education, vocational training and health;
>
> Recognising that the labour market will not open up many job opportunities for Roma/Gypsies and Travellers in the near future without proactive measures;
>
> Considering that the economic problems of Roma/Gypsies and Travellers cannot be overcome unless member states consider equal opportunities as a policy priority for access to the labour market and income-generating activities;
>
> Bearing in mind that policies aimed at addressing the problems facing Roma/Gypsies and Travellers in the areas of employment and economic activity should be comprehensive, based on an acknowledgement that employment is linked to other factors, namely educational and training aspects, accommodation and the fight against racism and discrimination;
>
> ...
>
> Recommends that in implementing their policies aimed at improving the economic and employment situation of Roma/Gypsies and Travellers, the governments of the member states should:
>
> – be guided by the principles set out in the appendix to this recommendation;
>
> – bring this recommendation to the attention of the relevant public and private bodies in their respective countries through the appropriate channels.

As with Recommendation No. R (2000) 4, the need for a comprehensive approach is stressed. The appendix, entitled "Guiding principles for employment and economic policies concerning Roma/Gypsies and Travellers in Europe", sets out the recommendations under several headings: general principles; employment policies and access to the labour market; income-generating activities; financial instruments; training and education; and information, research and assessment. The need to involve communities and organisations is highlighted under the general principles:

> 1. Roma/Gypsy communities and organisations should participate fully in the processes of designing, implementing and monitoring programmes and policies aimed at improving their economic and employment situation.
>
> 2. Governments should fully support empowerment and capacity building among Roma/Gypsy communities to improve their economic and labour market situation.
>
> ...
>
> 11. Authorities should recognise and legitimise economic activities initiated by Roma/Gypsies and Roma/Gypsies' economic contribution to income-generating.

The need for flexibility, synergy and co-ordination of action is also underlined, together with more determined action to combat discrimination. Proposals are made in respect of efforts to develop projects and sectors for income-generating activities, and strategies for financial backing. Economic development must be accompanied by policies on training leading to skills, and innovation is important:

> The member states should encourage innovative small-scale projects and research, in order to find local responses to local needs using available local potential, in co-operation with the appropriate bodies and individuals.

It is noted that "the present recommendation covers Roma/Gypsies and Travellers, to be referred to as Roma/Gypsies in the text."

A report on the implementation of Recommendation Rec(2001)17 drawn up by the Committee of Experts on Roma and Travellers (MG-S-ROM) was released in 2011. It highlights certain good practices such as employment fairs, Roma mediators in employment agencies, suitable training, validation of experience acquired (in the absence of paper qualifications), aids to setting up in business, tax reductions for employers recruiting Roma, etc.

Recommendation Rec(2004)14 on the movement and encampment of Travellers in Europe

In May 2004 the European Committee on Migration (CDMG) debated and adopted the draft Committee of Ministers recommendation to member states on the movement and encampment of Travellers in Europe. Travellers from France and Switzerland took part in the preparatory work. In November 2004 the Rapporteur Group on Social and Health Questions (GR-SOC) examined the draft and recommended its adoption. The text was adopted by the Committee of Ministers on 1 December 2004, which:

> Considering that those among the Roma/Gypsy and Traveller communities who wish to continue to lead a traditional nomadic or semi-nomadic lifestyle should have the opportunity, in law and in practice, to do so, by virtue of the freedom of movement and settlement guaranteed to all citizens of member states and the right to preserve and develop specific cultural identities;
>
> Considering, also, that in order to allow Travellers to exercise their right to move and set up camp, a co-ordinated, coherent system of legal safeguards for their freedom of movement is necessary;
>
> Recognising that policies for dealing with movement and encampment problems should be part of a coherent policy for improving the living conditions of Roma/Gypsies and Travellers;
>
> ...
>
> Recommends that, when devising, implementing and monitoring policies concerning the movement and encampment of Travellers, the governments of member states:
> – take as their basis the principles appended to this recommendation;
> – bring this recommendation to the attention of the national, regional and local public authorities concerned through the appropriate channels.

The scope of the text is defined at the beginning of the appendix:

> The present text covers those Travellers, Roma, Sinti, Yenish and other related groups in member states who have traditionally a nomadic or semi-nomadic lifestyle and who are citizens of those states or legally residing in these countries. For the sake of convenience the term "Travellers" will be used in this recommendation.

Definitions of the terms "encampment area", "encampment", "mobile home", etc., are also given. The appendix then lists general principles for guaranteeing the rights of "individual Travellers, particularly in respect of the following: ownership rights and social benefits equal to persons who are sedentary/settled, fair and proportionate rent and land occupation charges" and security of residence. Measures relating to equality of rights are especially advocated (these are some of the points in a long list which are cited since they may serve today as a source of inspiration for suitable action). Member states should:

> 10. encourage the use of an official Internet site hosting a range of public services in order to facilitate exchanges between Travellers and administrations: revenue declarations, civil status declaration, requests for social benefits, etc. Member states should furthermore support Travellers' organisations so that they can advise and assist their members, and thus facilitate exchanges between Travellers and administration;
>
> ...
>
> 12. give Travellers' mobile homes or, where relevant, the place of residence to which the Traveller is linked, the same substantial rights as those attached to a fixed abode, particularly in legal and social matters;
>
> 13. encourage the signing of quality contracts or charters between local authorities and Travellers, on the basis of the mutual interests of the parties involved;
>
> ...

14. in the case of circulating on the national territory, refrain from requiring of national Travellers documents other than ordinary-law identity papers and/or documents authorising an itinerant economic activity (hawker's professional card) in countries in which such papers are required;

...

25. encourage a number of options with regard to encampment sites, and, in particular, that members of a group who are no longer mobile, because of their age or state of health, can stay all the year round on encampment areas where their families could join them when they want to make a stop;

26. set up a body to monitor and assess the establishment and operation of encampment sites and short-stay areas; such a body should be able to ensure that needs are regularly assessed and provide information as to the sites' locations and facilities. The authorities should ensure that Travellers are fully involved in the work of such a body;

...

establish a legal framework that conforms with international human rights standards, to ensure effective protection against unlawful forced and collective evictions and to control strictly the circumstances in which legal evictions may be carried out. In the case of lawful evictions, Roma must be provided with appropriate alternative accommodation if needed, except in cases of force majeure. Legislation should also strictly define the procedures for legal eviction, and such legislation should comply with international human rights standards and principles, including those articulated in General Comment No. 7 on forced evictions of the United Nations Committee on Economic, Social and Cultural Rights. Such measures shall include consultation with the community or individual concerned, reasonable notice, provision of information, a guarantee that the eviction will be carried out in a reasonable manner, effective legal remedies and free or low-cost legal assistance for destitute victims. The alternative housing should not result in further segregation;

...

34. define as part of a Traveller's caravan, and therefore of his or her place of residence, an area bound by a perimeter of a few metres around the caravan.

Recommendation Rec(2005)4 on improving the housing conditions of Roma and Travellers in Europe

Following questions of education, the economy and employment, then movement and encampment of nomadic families, attention focused on housing for Roma. In May 2004 the CDMG examined and approved the draft Committee of Ministers recommendation to member states on improving the housing conditions of Roma and Travellers in Europe. The GR-SOC examined the draft at three meetings in 2004 and one in 2005. At the last of these meetings, it was agreed to submit the text as amended to the Committee of Ministers for adoption. The text was adopted on 23 February 2005. It reveals once again a comprehensive, cultural approach, the different fields being seen as interlinked, and the scale and consequences of discrimination mentioned once more:

The Committee of Ministers ...

Recognising that Roma/Gypsies and Travellers have been contributing to European culture and values, just as other European people, and recognising that despite this asset, Roma/Gypsies and Travellers have been experiencing widespread discrimination in all areas of life;

Recognising that there is an urgent need to develop new strategies to improve the living conditions of the Roma/Gypsy and Traveller communities all over Europe in order to ensure that they have equality of opportunities in areas such as civic and political participation, as well as developmental sectors, such as housing, education, employment and health;

Bearing in mind that policies aimed at addressing the problems faced by Roma/Gypsies and Travellers in the field of housing should be comprehensive, based on an acknowledgement that the issue of housing for Roma/Gypsies and Travellers has an impact on a wide range of other elements, namely the economic, educational, social and cultural aspects of their lives, and the fight against racism and discrimination;

Bearing in mind the under-used potential of Roma/Gypsy and Traveller communities and their capacity to contribute to the improvement of their own situation, especially in the field of housing;

Bearing in mind that some member states do not have, or do not implement, a clearly defined national housing-related legislation, addressing various practices such as housing discrimination, discriminatory harassment in housing, discriminatory boycotts, ghettoisation, racial and residential segregation, and other forms of discrimination against nomadic and semi-nomadic Roma/Gypsies and Travellers, as well as unequal housing conditions and access to housing, such as social housing, public housing, do-it-yourself housing and co-operative housing;

...

Recommends that, in designing, implementing and monitoring their housing policies, the governments of member states:

– be guided by the principles set out in the Appendix to this recommendation;

– bring this recommendation to the attention of the relevant public bodies in their respective countries through the appropriate national channels.

A very detailed appendix follows. While the main text mostly employs the terms "Roma/Gypsies and Travellers", the appendix uses only the term "Roma" and defines it as follows: "The term 'Roma' used in the present text refers to Roma/Gypsies and Traveller communities and must be interpreted as covering the wide diversity of groups concerned." The notion of "housing" and "adequate housing" are defined as follows:

"Housing" in this recommendation includes different modes of accommodation, such as houses, caravans, mobile homes or halting sites.

The definition provided for by the United Nations Habitat Agenda for "adequate housing", paragraph 60, should be borne in mind in the context of the present text: "Adequate shelter means more than a roof over one's head. It also means adequate privacy; adequate space; physical accessibility; adequate security; security of tenure; structural stability and durability; adequate lighting, heating and ventilation; adequate basic infrastructure, such as water-supply, sanitation and waste-management facilities; suitable environmental quality and health-related factors; and adequate and accessible location with regard to work and basic facilities: all of which should be available at an affordable cost".

The appendix goes on to present several sets of recommendations, under the headings of:

- General principles: integrated housing policies; principle of non-discrimination; freedom of choice of lifestyle; adequacy and affordability of housing; prevention of exclusion and the creation of ghettos; participation, partnership, co-ordination; and the role of regional and local authorities;
- Legal framework: legal framework for housing rights; legal framework for related rights; implementation of the legal framework; the need for legal aid; transparency, good governance and access to information; support to NGOs; monitoring of housing policy implementation; and control mechanisms;
- Preventing and combating discrimination: adopting anti-discrimination legislation; monitoring and review of existing housing legislation; protection of the rights of Roma women; preventing segregation in environmentally hazardous areas; and providing effective sanctions;
- Protection and improvement of existing housing: security of land, housing and property tenure; legalisation of Roma settlements and encampments; access to property; legal protection from unlawful evictions and the procedure for legal evictions; and provision of adequate services;
- Framework for housing policies: policies to promote access to housing; comprehensive and integrated housing policies; participation in the preparation of housing policies; the need for adequate housing models; housing policy adapted to specific situations; providing equipped transit/halting sites; access to health and sanitary services; role of regional and local authorities; international relief; awareness-raising; employment initiatives and construction; and statistical data-base and housing policy indicators;
- Financing of housing: sustainability of financial resources; financing housing projects from various sources; integrated funding; international support for Roma housing; access to funding possibilities to acquire housing; funding infrastructure and services; and specific budgetary provisions;
- Housing standards: adequate housing as a basis for all housing standards; standards for housing location and surroundings; legal standards for public and social services; the need for non-discriminatory security standards; minimum construction standards; and standards for adaptability and enhancement of housing.

Recommendation Rec(2006)10 on better access to health care for Roma and Travellers in Europe

After examination and approval by the CDMG, the Committee of Ministers adopted this recommendation on 12 July 2006, which begins by:

Noting that many Roma and Travellers are living in marginal situations in member states and experience widespread discrimination in all areas of life;

Aware that as a result of poor living conditions, *inter alia,* many Roma and Traveller communities have a poorer health status than that experienced by the general population.

It recommends that the governments of member states follow the principles and implement the provisions set out in the appendix. The text is based on the earlier documents adopted by the Council of Europe, other recommendations on Roma, charters and conventions. It is important to note that this recommendation, like its predecessors but probably to an even more marked degree, refers to the texts of other institutions (United Nations, EU, OSCE), which points to the possibility of international co-operation and the convergence of analyses and political proposals.

As with the preceding recommendations, the appendix begins with a definition:

The term "Roma and Travellers" used in the present text refers to Roma, Sinti, Kalé, Travellers, and related groups in Europe, and aims to cover the wide diversity of groups concerned. In the context of the United Kingdom "Roma and Travellers" also refers to self-proclaimed "Gypsies".

It then sets out the general principles for action in the fields of health, the legal framework for preventing and combating discrimination in health care, the framework for health policies (effective access, planning, prevention, participation of Roma and Travellers, and staff training). The section on prevention emphasises housing conditions in particular:

Recognising that decent housing and a satisfactory sanitation infrastructure is a sine qua non for improvement of the health status of Roma and Traveller communities, governments of member states should ensure:

i. that Roma and Traveller settlements and encampment sites are located in decent places in a healthy environment, with own toilet and water facilities, electricity, paved roads, rubbish containers, sewage, etc., under the same conditions as the general population of the region concerned;

ii. that members of mobile populations without access to legal caravan sites have access to health care and other public services;

iii. that local health bodies should work with local housing and other agencies to address these wider issues. When doing so they should ensure that Roma and Traveller communities are engaged effectively in these processes.

Participation also attracts detailed recommendations:

i. Wherever appropriate local health services should ensure that they have in place specific services such as gender equality advisers and health mediators to meet the health needs of these communities. Members of Roma and Traveller communities, where applicable, should be involved in developing those services and, where possible, health professionals should be recruited from their communities.

ii. Where applicable training should be undertaken to improve Roma and Travellers' skills in policy making and health public administration.

iii. Adequate resources should be provided for capacity-building training to enable representatives of the Roma and Traveller communities to engage effectively in the consultation process when drawing up strategies and policies affecting their health.

iv. The actual focus of training programmes for Roma and Travellers in the field of health should be expanded from health mediators – whose role is to mediate between Romani patients and health professionals, provide basic health education and assist Roma communities in obtaining necessary insurance and documents – to include more ambitious targets.

v. Roma and Travellers, if they so wish, should be encouraged to take up professions such as those of nurses and doctors at all levels of the health system.

The recommendation, which was drawn up in close collaboration with Roma women, does not explicitly mention questions of forced sterilisation, but it does mention "respect of the principle of informed consent". The text of the explanatory memorandum drawn up by the MG-S-ROM in 2009, Document MG-S-ROM(2009)10, states that:

Governments should ensure that physicians and other health-care workers properly counsel Romani and Traveller women on all available family planning methods, including voluntary sterilisation, and that the canon of free and informed consent be rigorously followed, especially in the case of sterilisation. No incentives should be given or coercion applied to promote or discourage any particular decision regarding sterilisation.

Recommendation CM/Rec(2008)5 on policies for Roma and/or Travellers in Europe

More than 30 years after the Committee of Ministers adopted its first text on Roma in 1975, this particularly detailed recommendation appears as the keystone of the political edifice constructed over the years.

The communities concerned are defined as follows:

The term "Roma and/or Travellers" used in the present text refers to Roma, Sinti, Kale, Travellers, and related groups in Europe, and aims to cover the wide diversity of groups concerned, including groups which identify themselves as Gypsies.

The text takes as its standpoint rights and access to rights, discrimination and exclusion. The Committee of Ministers states in the preamble:

Recognising that Roma and Travellers have faced, for more than five centuries, widespread and enduring discrimination, rejection and marginalisation all over Europe and in all areas of life; and were targeted victims of the Holocaust; and that forced displacement, discrimination and exclusion from participation in social life have resulted in poverty and disadvantage for many Roma and Traveller communities and individuals across Europe;

Recognising the existence of anti-Gypsyism as a specific form of racism and intolerance, leading to hostile acts ranging from exclusion to violence against Roma and/or Traveller communities;

Recognising the role of the media and education in the persistence of anti-Roma prejudices and their potential to help overcome them;

Aware that discrimination and social exclusion can be overcome most effectively by comprehensive, coherent and proactive policies targeting both the Roma and the majority, which ensure integration and participation of Roma and Travellers in the societies in which they live and respect for their identity;

> Considering that all human rights are indivisible, interdependent and interrelated and that economic and social rights are human rights, and should be supported by concrete community and governmental efforts to ensure they are equally accessible to the most deprived and disadvantaged groups and communities.

It is important to underline that this is the first time the term "anti-Gypsyism" is used in a Committee of Ministers text. Reference is then made to fundamental instruments on the protection of rights, in particular those of the United Nations, the EU, the OSCE and the Council of Europe, before it is recommended that governments of the member states:

> – adopt, in accordance with the principles and provisions set out in the appendix to this recommendation, a coherent, comprehensive and adequately resourced national and regional strategy with short- and long-term action plans, targets and indicators for implementing policies that address legal and/or social discrimination against Roma and/or Travellers and enforce the principle of equality;
>
> – monitor and publish regular evaluation reports on the state of the implementation and impact of strategies and policies to improve the situation of Roma and/or Travellers;
>
> – bring this recommendation to the attention of and ensure the support of the relevant national and local or regional, self-governing public bodies, Roma and/or Traveller communities and the broader population in their respective countries through the appropriate channels, including the media.

Definitions of the terms employed follow, such as "policy", "strategy", "programme", "project", "objective", "result", "impact/outcomes", "participation", "evaluation", "positive action", etc. The overall aim is stated:

> A national and/or regional strategy should aim at ensuring equality and integration of Roma and/or Travellers in social, economic and political life, promoting community empowerment and capacity building, increasing awareness and understanding of Roma and/or Traveller culture and lifestyle among the rest of society, and ensuring respect for Roma and/or Traveller identity and effective protection from direct and indirect discrimination and segregation and from racism.

The general principles for action are then set out:

> i. allow a rights-based, comprehensive, dynamic and integrated approach;
>
> ii. recognise the diversity of Roma and/or Traveller communities and their different needs warranting diverse and flexible responses;
>
> iii. support Roma and/or Travellers' participation as an essential component of all stages of design, implementation, monitoring and evaluation of strategies concerning them, and promote community capacity building;
>
> iv. ensure gender and age balance of Roma and/or Traveller representation;
>
> v. ensure effective monitoring of the implementation of the strategy with clear benchmarks and criteria for success;
>
> vi. integrate ongoing evaluation of strategies and make it a subject for ongoing review and improvement;
>
> vii. ensure that targeting and mainstreaming approaches are used.

The headings that follow cover each of the general principles: they concern the legislative framework, with recommendations for improving the efficacy of anti-discrimination laws; the development of a strategy (establishing needs, developing a coherent and co-ordinated strategy, participating in policy/strategy development, risk management, continuous monitoring and evaluation, funding); adopting the strategy; implementation of the strategy (implementation mechanism, positive action, mediators or assistants, guidance and training, the role of civil society, mainstreaming); and finally, the monitoring and evaluation of the implementation of the strategy.

The combination of these series of recommendations, as advocated in a high-level text such as that of the Committee of Ministers, offers an innovative instrument which proposes the application of a comprehensive structural approach, placed in a long-term perspective and based on substantive action. For example, here is what the section on "Guidance and training" says:

> i. Any new legislation on combating discrimination should be accompanied by guidance for the law-enforcement authorities to assist them in effective implementation of the law. Law-enforcement personnel should be provided with training on their duty to refrain from racially-motivated acts themselves and actively prevent and expeditiously prosecute such acts in order to ensure the long-term safety and security of Roma and/or Traveller communities. They should have regular contact with Roma and/or Traveller communities and their leaders to foster co-operation and understanding.
>
> Public officials (such as teachers, police officers, health-care practitioners, social welfare workers) should be made aware of direct and indirect racism and anti-gypsyism in the course of their general training.
>
> ii. Member states should ensure that municipal and other local authorities undergo a process of institutional development to ensure they relate to Roma and/or Traveller communities on a fair and equal basis. Staff training, clear leadership, effective management and supervision, practical guidance, monitoring of performance, and effective complaints procedures are useful tools for securing institutional change.

Or the section on mainstreaming:

> i. The needs of Roma and/or Traveller communities should be incorporated in broader national strategies. Access to and participation in society at large are essential goals, but targeted measures for Roma and/or Travellers should also be pursued where necessary. Mainstreaming should ensure linkage with the rest of activities in the same area, facilitate acceptance of the issue at all levels, and permit access to all necessary administrative mechanisms to ensure Roma and/or Travellers have a say in decisions affecting them. Targeted policies should ensure that specific concerns are not diluted and that the Roma and/or Traveller populations do not become invisible in generic policies.
>
> Mainstreaming should include the gender perspective, which takes into account the specific needs of men and women.
>
> ii. Implementation should go beyond project-based improvements to systemic changes.

Or again, that on evaluation:

> i. Evaluations should take place within a multi-annual programme or strategy, at a set frequency (for example, twice every five years), and after the completion of programmes and strategies to identify long-term impacts and outcomes for the range of intended beneficiaries.
>
> ii. Evaluations should:
>
> – be conducted by independent bodies with competence in development issues, monitoring and evaluation and having a wide representation of interested parties;
>
> – be evidence-based and draw on the results of monitoring and involve not only donors and the implementing bodies but also the perspective of other actors, in particular the relevance to the intended beneficiaries and the real impact on their lives;
>
> – review the performance, cost effectiveness and efficiency of the implementing bodies to ensure accountability and be transparent in their findings to promote confidence;
>
> – become tools for learning and for use in strengthening future programmes and strategies for Roma and/or Travellers in similar areas at national, regional and/or local level.

Recommendation CM/Rec(2009)4 on the education of Roma and Travellers in Europe

Nearly a decade after the Committee of Ministers adopted Recommendation No. R (2000) 4 on the education of Roma/Gypsy children in Europe, it seemed appropriate to review the question of schooling for Roma children and young people, to draw conclusions from the existing situation and to make fresh proposals. A new draft recommendation was prepared and examined, and adopted by the Steering Committee for Education.

The purpose of Recommendation CM/Rec(2009)4, adopted on 17 June 2009, was to update and reinforce Recommendation No. R (2000) 4 in the light of the situation existing in the first decade of the 21st century. The Committee of Ministers:

> Taking into consideration the weight of centuries-old discrimination and rejection of Roma and Travellers and the persistence of widespread inequalities and difficulties in the field of education that affect Roma and Traveller children across Europe;
>
> Noting that the problems faced by Roma and Travellers in the field of schooling are also the result of long-standing educational policies of the past, which can lead either to assimilation or to segregation of Roma and Traveller children at school on the grounds that they were "socially and culturally handicapped";
>
> Condemning the existence of situations of de facto segregation in schooling, as recalled by recent judgments of the European Court of Human Rights concerning the education of Roma children;

Considering that the disadvantaged position of Roma and Travellers in European societies cannot be overcome unless access to quality education is guaranteed for Roma and Traveller children;

Taking into consideration the new challenges raised by the recent intra-European migration phenomenon, that engages numerous Roma children in temporary or permanent residence in other member states, with negative consequences for access to education and recognition of acquired competencies;

...

1. Recommends that the governments of member states, with due regard for their constitutional structures, national or local situations and educational systems:

a. draw on the principles set out in the appendix to this recommendation in their current or future educational reforms;

b. elaborate, disseminate and implement education policies focusing on ensuring non-discriminatory access to quality education for Roma and Traveller children, based on the orientations set out in the appendix to this recommendation;

c. bring this recommendation to the attention of the relevant public bodies in their respective countries through the appropriate national and linguistic channels;

d. ensure, through local and regional authorities, that Roma and Traveller children are effectively accepted in school;

e. monitor and evaluate the implementation of the provisions of this recommendation into their policies, and inform the Steering Committee for Education of the measures undertaken and progress achieved.

2. Calls on the Secretary General of the Council of Europe to bring this recommendation to the attention of the States Parties to the 1954 European Cultural Convention (ETS No. 18) that are not members of the Council of Europe.

The appendix which follows contains a section on the principles of policies to be pursued, among them the following basic principles:

1. Educational policies aiming at ensuring non-discriminatory access to quality education for Roma and Traveller children should be devised at national level. These policies should be formulated with a view to guaranteeing access to quality education with dignity and respect, based on the principles of human rights and on the rights of the child. Existing educational policies need to be reviewed to identify actual and potential hindrances preventing Roma and Traveller children from enjoying full rights in the field of education.

2. In consultation with the national/international Roma and Travellers stakeholders, educational policies should include references to Roma and Travellers as part of wider recognition of cultural and/or linguistic diversity and should, where appropriate, provide opportunities for Roma and Traveller children to benefit from instruction in/of their mother tongue, based on the principles set out in the Framework Convention for the Protection of National Minorities and in the European Charter for Regional or Minority Languages.

Then come recommendations on structures and provision for access to education. The emphasis is laid on flexibility, the development of pre-school education, the transition between pre-school and primary education, then between primary and secondary, and on suitable vocational training, with validation of knowledge acquired through experience. There are measures to improve the conditions of school education:

> 14. Schools should make strong efforts to engage Roma and Traveller parents in school-related activities in order to enhance mutual understanding. When involving parents, the school must respect their values and culture and acknowledge their contribution to the education of their children.

> 15. School mediators and/or assistants recruited from Roma and Traveller communities should be employed to facilitate the relations between teachers and Roma or Traveller families, as well as between schools and the Roma or Traveller community. They should be provided with adequate training and support and be accepted as far as possible as full members of the school's professional team.

Curricula, teaching materials and teacher training are then covered, together with European exchanges and the sharing of experience and best practice.

Other ministerial action

While recommendations focusing on a specific subject are the most direct form of intervention by ministers and the governments they represent, other forms are also possible, such as conferences at which ministers discuss the situation of Roma. Examples are the general conclusions of the European Conference against Racism (EUROCONF (2000)7 final) and the political declaration adopted by the ministers of Council of Europe member states in October 2000 at the closing session of the conference (EUROCONF (2000)1 final). The general conclusions state that:

> The European Conference underlines the necessity for participating States to pay particular attention to and adopt immediate and concrete measures to eradicate the widespread discrimination and persecution targeting Roma, Gypsies, Sinti and Travellers, including through the establishment of structures and processes, in partnership between the public authorities and representatives of the Roma, Gypsies, Sinti and Travellers.

Governments, in the political declaration adopted at the end of the conference, committed themselves "to develop effective policies and implementation mechanisms and exchange good practices for the full achievement of equality for Roma/Gypsies and Travellers."

The question of Roma may be addressed at certain regular meetings of ministers responsible for a given field. An example is the Standing Conference of European Ministers of Education, held on average every two years. Priority subjects considered essential to deal with in education systems are discussed. The education of Roma children is sometimes explicitly mentioned, for example:

– in October 2000 in Cracow, the Standing Conference of European Ministers of Education took as its theme "Education policies for democratic citizenship and social cohesion: challenges and strategies for Europe". In their final declaration the ministers called on the Council of Europe to turn its attention to the Roma/Gypsy question, and in their resolution on the

2001-03 programme of activities, to conduct work "on educational policies for and the educational needs of Roma/Gypsies in all their dimensions, drawing on relevant experience in member states";

– at the Conference of European Ministers of Education held in Athens in November 2003, the theme chosen was "Intercultural education: managing diversity, strengthening democracy". In the final text, the "Declaration by the European Ministers of Education on intercultural education in the new European context", the ministers "note with satisfaction the progress and results of the projects and activities currently being carried out by the Council of Europe, particularly: ... the implementation, in the framework of Recommendation R(2000)4 of the Committee of Ministers, of the project on 'Education for Roma/Gypsy children', a project that highlights the principles of intercultural education";

– activities in connection with schooling for Roma/Gypsy children since the first Council of Europe seminar in 1983, 20 years before the conference, had indeed "clearly highlighted the principles of intercultural education". A glance at the documents produced on the occasion of the conference of ministers confirms that the activities pursued over several years accorded with the priorities set by the ministers;

– in May 2007 in Istanbul, at the 22nd session of the Standing Conference of European Ministers of Education, on the theme of "Building a more humane and inclusive Europe: role of education policies", the ministers, in their resolution on the 2008-10 programme of activities, recommended "in the field of intercultural and diversity education ... continuing and reinforcing work on the education of Roma children".

Finally, the question of Roma may be raised at summits of Council of Europe heads of state and government, and even placed centre-stage in view of the difficulty of their situation. At the Warsaw Summit in May 2005, the heads of state and government said:

> We ... have outlined the following action plan laying down the principal tasks of the Council of Europe in the coming years
>
> ...
>
> We confirm our commitment to combat all kinds of exclusion and insecurity of the Roma communities in Europe and to promote their full and effective equality.

This constitutes a clear commitment at the highest level in the member states.[7]

---

7. The full versions of the texts mentioned in this chapter are available on the Council of Europe Committee of Ministers website www.coe.int/T/CM/home_en.asp under the heading "Adopted texts".

6. The Congress of Local and Regional Authorities of the Council of Europe and Roma since 1981

Some years after the Council of Europe was founded in 1949, it was thought necessary to take account of the importance of local and regional democracy in the implementation of the Organisation's aims. In 1957 the Conference of Local Authorities was established. It then became the Standing Conference of Local and Regional Authorities of Europe (CLRAE), which brings together the elected representatives of local and regional authorities. The European Charter of Local Self-Government adopted subsequently is a landmark international treaty. It was opened for signature to the member states in 1985 and entered into force on 1 September 1988.

In 1994 the Standing Conference of Local and Regional Authorities of Europe became the Congress of Local and Regional Authorities of Europe, with the same acronym (CLRAE), as a consultative organ of the Council of Europe. In October 2003, the body was renamed by a decision of its Bureau to "Congress of Local and Regional Authorities of the Council of Europe", and is now known simply as "the Congress".

The Congress exists to represent local and regional authorities, and consists of two chambers: the Chamber of Local Authorities and the Chamber of Regions. In Resolution CM/Res(2007)6 containing the Congress Charter, adopted on 2 May 2007, the Committee of Ministers laid down the composition and rules of operation of this assembly.

The Congress adopts different kinds of texts. It may submit draft treaties or conventions which then pass to the Committee of Ministers. It adopts recommendations to the Committee of Ministers for the attention of national governments. It also adopts resolutions addressed directly to the local and regional authorities which it represents. The Congress issues opinions when consulted by the Parliamentary Assembly or the Committee of Ministers on questions relating to the powers of local and regional authorities. Finally, at the end of international meetings the Congress may issue a final declaration containing a series of proposals addressed to local and regional authorities, or to governments or European organisations.

Resolution 125 (1981) on the role and responsibility of local and regional authorities in regard to the cultural and social problems of populations of nomadic origin

In 1979, the Cultural Committee of the Standing Conference of Local and Regional Authorities of Europe organised a hearing on the situation of municipalities faced with the cultural and social problems of populations of nomadic origin (CPL/Cult (14) 10 to 24 and CPL/Cult (15) 14 and 15). Following a report by Mr Lieuwen presented in October 1981, the Standing Conference adopted Resolution 125 (1981). It is important to observe that, as with the other early texts adopted, it contains recommendations which remain relevant, or which anticipated later achievements, or which provided inspiration for the action and programmes of certain states.

The document mentions the Parliamentary Assembly's 1969 recommendation and the 1975 resolution of the Committee of Ministers, and then states in the preamble:

> 5. Regretting that in most of the member countries no full information about these most valuable texts had been made available to the local and regional authorities concerned;
>
> 6. Noting with concern that despite the efforts undertaken in certain countries and, in particular, by certain local and regional authorities, the general situation of travelling people and especially gypsies has not been notably improved since the adoption of the Assembly's recommendation;
>
> ...
>
> 10. Convinced that notable progress will be achieved only if public opinion can be persuaded that minority groups – very often of a different ethnic origin and with a different way of life – must be recognised as having the right to live among us on an equal footing and that they are entitled to the same rights and obligations as other citizens; this also implies that they should be fully rehabilitated where they have been subjected to persecution in the past;
>
> ...
>
> 12. Conscious of the particular responsibility of local and regional authorities with regard to travelling people, these authorities being the framework within which the necessary facilities have to be created, and being, together with their population and the nomads themselves, the first to suffer from the present lack of adequate policies.

Among the actions the recommended to the Committee of Ministers are:

> iii. to draw up a legal instrument providing that travelling people living in any member country shall have the possibility of obtaining identity papers enabling them to travel at least in all member countries
>
> ...
>
> v. to consider the possibility of adding an article to the Convention for the Protection of Human Rights and Fundamental Freedoms in order to ensure more effective protection for the rights of minorities
>
> ...

vi. to study the feasibility of setting up, within the framework of the Council of Europe, an information centre about travelling people, as a European contribution to overcoming prejudices and discrimination and compensating for the injustices suffered in the past; this objective should of course be pursued in close contact with the nomads; it should provide information not only for nomads themselves, but also for the municipalities and regions concerned.

It calls on the governments of member states to ratify the conventions on stateless persons, "to recognise Romanies and other specific nomadic groups such as Samis as ethnic minorities and, consequently, to grant them the same status and advantages as other minorities may enjoy; in particular concerning respect and support for their own culture and language" and to make provision at national level for helping local authorities to receive nomadic people.

Local and regional authorities are called upon to take all necessary reception measures for nomads, with reference to the texts adopted. They are invited "to create ... associations between the municipalities concerned" in order to provide the necessary equipment "at the most efficient level", and:

iii. to seek the participation and the support of the nomads themselves for any such measures and to let them take an active part in the administration of any facilities provided;

iv. to help to overcome prejudices in providing full information about the origins, ways of life, living conditions and aspirations of the nomads to other citizens, or, still better, to give their full support whenever travelling people themselves propose to organise this type of information.

Lastly, among the Council of Europe bodies invited to assist, the Standing Conference asks the Council for Cultural Co-operation:

i. to make provision in its work programme for a thorough study of the education and vocational training problems of nomads

...

ii. to prepare, as part of its work on intercultural education, information on dossiers for teachers on the history, culture and family life of people of nomadic origin in member states

...

iii. to study the possibility of setting up ... a specific training programme for teachers with a view to enabling them to teach the Romany language.

A hearing and a colloquy

Ten years after Recommendation 125 (1981) was adopted, and following the post-1989 political changes, in July 1991 the Standing Conference organised a major hearing in Strasbourg entitled "The Gypsy people and Europe: the continuation of the tradition in a changing Europe". It was organised at the instigation of two committees, the Committee on Culture, Education and the Media and the Committee on Social Affairs and Health. It was attended by Roma from 12 states, and the conclusions stress that member states should help Roma organisations set up a large representative European association to serve as an interface for public authorities and the European institutions. Further, representative organisations of Roma communities at European level should be granted consultative status with the Council of Europe. The conclusions also note that:

> There have been Gypsy communities in all the countries of Europe for so long that their history now merges with Europe's history. Although the Gypsy people have paid a heavy tribute in blood, that history is not made up entirely of betrayals. It is also a history of peoples, a history of rights and of political communities founded on the rule of law.

> The twin aspects of human rights, both individual (the right to life, to food, the means of subsistence, and shelter) and collective (rights to a family, education, freedom of expression and communication, freedom of movement and association, political rights), are the foundation on which free and democratic political communities are built. Such communities are the best defence against all forms of violence, racism, intolerance and economic, social and political exclusion

> ...

> However, a genuine solution as regards legal and political status will be achieved only when they are granted European citizenship. It has been observed that the constitution of a political and legal Europe within the framework of the 12 member countries of the European Communities entails creating an area which is by definition multinational and, consequently, as the European process advances, there is bound to be growing dissociation between nationality and European citizenship.

One year later, in October 1992, the Committee on Culture, Education and the Media organised a colloquy at Liptovský Mikuláš in Slovakia attended by about 100 participants: representatives of Roma involved in local action and representatives of the Council of Europe, in particular members of the Standing Conference of Local and Regional Authorities of Europe. Four themes were chosen for discussion and consolidated proposals were put forward for each theme: the reception of Gypsies in the locality; education, vocational training and employment; social action and health; development and promotion of the Gypsy cultural heritage.[8] One of these proposals was highlighted in the closing address by Ms Farrington, chair of the Committee on Culture, Education and the Media:

> The conclusions of this conference suggest a great number of possibilities to improve the situation that will be transmitted for action to concerned persons and organisations. I would like to stress in particular the proposal concerning the organisation of a Network of Local Authorities and of leaders of Gypsy and Travellers communities. Such a network would allow a sharing of experiences and an overall exchange of practical information on strategies to be developed to fulfil the needs of those that often are the most disadvantaged Europeans.

> This project will be implemented with great care in order to make it as efficient as possible thanks to the close co-operation with all the partners concerned at the

---

8. The full collection of papers and studies has been published in book form as Congress of Local and Regional Authorities of Europe (1994), *Gypsies in the locality*, Studies and Texts No. 38, Council of Europe Publishing, Strasbourg.

Council of Europe. I have heard, with great interest, the different speakers that have underlined the Gypsy and Traveller communities' desire that they themselves wish to be actively involved in the organisation of the Network.

I will take back the following message to the Council of Europe: this project should be launched as soon as possible; however, it should be organised with due attention to make it as successful as possible.

Resolution 249 (1993) on Gypsies in Europe: the role and responsibility of local and regional authorities

On the basis of a report and draft resolution presented by the Committee on Culture, Education and the Media by Mr Gémesi and Mr O'Brien, the Standing Conference adopted Resolution 249 in March 1993. In it, the Standing Conference mentions the results of the hearing and the colloquy and the texts adopted previously by the Council of Europe bodies. It observes that: "In this report, the word Gypsy is used to designate the diversified group of those who generally identify themselves as Gypsies and Travellers, for example Rom, Travellers, Yenish, Kale, Sinti, Voyageurs, etc. The Gypsies and Travellers community present in the different European states is made up of nomadic as well as sedentary families." Then, "fully aware of the special responsibility of local and regional authorities towards Rom/Gypsies, particularly with regard to accommodating Gypsies in the municipality, their education, training, health, development and the promotion of their culture", it goes on to invite local and regional authorities:

I. to take necessary measures as part of an overall strategy to facilitate the integration of Rom/Gypsies into the local community, in the area of housing, caravan sites, education, health and support for the expression and development of their identity and culture;

II. to encourage Rom/Gypsies themselves to collaborate and participate in projects to foster such integration;

III. to counter the prejudices suffered by Rom/Gypsies in order to facilitate and promote communication between Gypsy and non-Gypsy communities through comprehensive information;

IV. to help develop networks of municipalities with a view to achieving these aims.

The Committee on Culture, Education and the Media and the Committee on Social Affairs and Health were particularly tasked with launching a network of municipalities most concerned by the reception of Gypsy communities, with a view to facilitating "exchanging experiences and circulating information ... running small-scale projects based on community development ... and analysing data to develop tools for decision-making and appraisal". As in the 1981 resolution, the Committee of Ministers was asked to instruct the Council for Cultural Co-operation "to step up the work pursued over the last 10 years with publications for the purposes of education and information in the field of schooling and training for Gypsy children and young people" and to participate in the development of the network of municipalities proposed at the 1992 colloquy. The Roma were again asked "to set up a European association to represent Gypsy communities which will serve as a political interface for governments and European bodies".

Recommendation 11 (1995), towards a tolerant Europe: the contribution of Roma (Gypsies)

Two years later, following the setting-up of the Network of Cities and the organisation of another hearing on the contribution of Gypsies to the building of a tolerant Europe, both in 1994, the newly reorganised Congress of Local and Regional Authorities of Europe (CLRAE) reverted to the question of Roma in two adopted texts. The first was Recommendation 11, towards a tolerant Europe: the contribution of Roma (Gypsies), adopted on 31 May 1995 on the basis of a report by Mr Slavkovsky, a member of the Congress and organiser of the 1992 colloquy.

The CLRAE recommends that the Committee of Ministers, among other things, take steps to appoint a European mediator or, failing that, "set up a small ad hoc group of experts who could serve as a contact with the Committee of Ministers on Roma (Gypsy) matters", as well as a small unit responsible for Roma (Gypsy) matters within the Council of Europe Secretariat and, with reference to the 1981 resolution, "consider the feasibility of drawing up an international legal instrument on the movement of persons" in order to improve the conditions of movement for Roma in the member states. National legislation should also be examined in depth and if necessary revised in order to enable Roma (Gypsies) "to enjoy their fundamental rights as citizens and take full part in the political, social, cultural and economic life of the member states in which they reside". The CLRAE recommends setting up an information centre on Roma as an instrument in the fight against racism, xenophobia and intolerance, and stepping up the work of the European Commission against Racism and Intolerance (ECRI). The Committee of Ministers is also called upon "to study the possibility of promoting European training programmes for Roma (Gypsy) mediators, thereby providing them with a status enabling them to play their role to the full in local and regional authorities" and "to lend its full support to the urgent efforts of the Council for Cultural Co-operation aimed at instituting a 'Roma (Gypsy) Cultural Route' and to its activities in the field of education, training and information".

Resolution 16 (1995), towards a tolerant Europe: the contribution of Roma (Gypsies)

On the same day (31 May 1995) as the recommendation cited above, addressed to the Committee of Ministers, the CLRAE adopted Resolution 16, which was addressed to local authorities.

The CLRAE, deploring "the pogroms, violence, racial hatred and discrimination" suffered by many Roma, expresses its concern "at an often complacent attitude on the part of local authorities or the police towards these barbaric acts". It "encourages the local and regional authorities to play their part to the full and shoulder their responsibilities towards Rroma (Gypsy) communities" by ensuring respect for their rights, particularly in cultural and educational matters; supporting meetings to foster intensive sharing of experience and know-how and to set up a forum where new ideas can be presented, especially for experimenting at local level; and by "expanding the Network of Cities, in particular by setting up a network of cities in each member state".

The question of setting up the Network of Cities is dealt with in an appendix:

> The Network of Cities is a testing ground for good practice and sound examples in relations between local and regional authorities and Rroma (Gypsy) communities to be developed through dialogue and pooling experience. It is a particularly suitable means of helping prevent conflicts and finding solutions to urgent problems.

After a detailed presentation of the operating principles, the substantive activities are proposed:

> The work of the Network will focus on the following three approaches:
>
> – the social approach, incorporating housing, health and employment;
>
> – the cultural approach, aimed at enhancing Rroma (Gypsy) culture, language and history, and developing education;
>
> – and the "human rights, citizenship and democracy" approach, which can be applied to all minorities and which should be aimed at "inter-community integration". Representatives of Rroma (Gypsies) should be closely involved in devising policies which the city intends to promulgate throughout the Network. The work may also be carried out in collaboration with experts.

The Network of Cities

The Network of Cities was set up on the basis of the 1992 colloquy and Resolution 249 (1993). Its aims are to facilitate exchanges of experience and the circulation of information in fields within the responsibility of local authorities, and to foster twinnings and the implementation of joint projects. In 1994 a hearing brought together the member towns of the network and representatives of Roma organisations. The Working Group on provision for Roma in municipalities was set up in late 1994, with the task of co-ordinating network activities, suggesting new projects and broadening the network. The latter's importance is emphasised in Resolution 16 (1995) and its structure clarified. Resolution 16 also calls for the holding of three hearings on related subjects.

In reply, the Working Group which heads the network organised a hearing at the end of 1995 in Košice (Slovakia) on "Rroma in municipalities: what provision for education and culture, social problems, training and employment? Some innovative experiences and models". The consolidated document AUD/KOS (2) 18 analyses the chronological sequence of action taken by the CLRAE, and places it in the context of overall action taken by the Council of Europe. The importance of a comprehensive approach is then underlined, together with the need to set action strategies in place. Lastly, emphasis is laid on the many advantages afforded by the development of the CLRAE's Network of Cities:

- this is a long-term activity, providing an opportunity for a collective approach which, with a little organisation, offers potential for important work;

- it takes the form of action research: a major European meeting on the theme of action research in relation to school provision for Rroma (Gypsy) children, bringing together 65 participants from 10 states for 8 days of debate on the subject and resulting in a book, which remains an important reference document,[9] revealed that the action-research approach presents a great number of advantages and is applicable to the work being done as part of projects in the city's network;

- Rroma (Gypsy)-related projects are, almost by definition, European; whereas other fields find it very difficult to establish a transnational profile, often compelled to set up ad hoc projects more or less artificially in order to receive international subventions, to speak of a European network in relation to Rroma (Gypsies) is merely a tautology. This point is linked to our earlier observation on the logic of obtaining support for transnational work;

- the Network of Cities, operating in an osmotic manner, provides an opportunity for conducting exchanges, eradicating stereotypes and avoiding blind alleys. Several papers and the ensuing discussions highlighted errors committed in the past, for example in the provision of accommodation or campsites: had it been possible to know what others were doing, and share their experience, considerable amounts of time, energy and money could have been saved, and the chances of carrying out suitable activities increased;

- working through a cities network makes it possible to take a practical, concerted approach, providing reciprocal support and avoiding misreadings of the local situation by persons unfamiliar with it, while conversely making it more difficult merely to pretend to be doing something or to claim that all is well in the best of all possible localities while the facts demonstrate the opposite. Above all, this approach provides what is most needed: not criticism or good advice, but moral, technical and financial support for doing what needs to be done. At the hearing, the debate on this issue was both lively and clear, demonstrating that the sort of intensified mutual exchange made possible by the CLRAE Network of Cities is not only useful, but imperative;

- the practical modus operandi demanded by membership of an active network will make it possible to respond more easily and more concretely to the pressing demands of NGOs for the development of a direct, close partnership between local authorities and Rroma (Gypsy) communities. At the hearing, several cities stressed the importance of encouraging active citizenship among Rroma (Gypsies) in connection with the pursuit of specific projects characterised by increased consultation; cities in a number of states indicated the development of "consultative committees" on which Rroma (Gypsies) are full partners, and the appearance in many areas of Rroma (Gypsies) acting as local and/or regional mediators;

---

9. ACERT (1993), *The Education of Gypsy and Traveller Children: Action-Research and Co-ordination*, report of a meeting held from 5 to 12 July 1989, University of Hertfordshire Press, Hatfield. Also published in French and Spanish.

- networking brings to light the cultural, artistic, documentary, historical, archival and other assets to be found in so many different places, enabling them to be pooled and shared;
- still other advantages were mentioned, confirming the synthesis proposals of the Liptovský Mikuláš[10] colloquy on the launching of the Network of Cities, notably the production of high-quality comparative analyses to be used in developing instruments for decision-making and evaluation, community development, the importance of "pole of excellence" playing a leading role and "pulling up" other projects and the relative independence of projects within a network of international co-operation that provides a degree of protection from various hazards.

At the same hearing, in addition to the European network, the National Network of Czech Cities and the charter adopted when that network was founded were presented. The wish was expressed that further national networks be established. Some have since been set up, for example the Dutch Platform of Roma Municipalities, in Greece the Pan-Hellenic Intermunicipal Roma Network to support Greek Roma, and in France the French Cities Working Group on Roma.

Following the 1995 hearing, mainly on questions of education, culture and employment, a hearing was organised in 1996 in Ploiesti (Romania) on the "Legal and institutional framework of national minorities: the situation of Roma/Gypsies in municipalities". The third hearing was organised by the Working Group in Pardubice (Czech Republic) on "Provisions for Roma in municipalities: housing/sites, health, social affairs". The Working Group's terms of reference expired in 1997, and the Network of Cities took the form of an association: the European Network of Cities on Provision for Roma (Gypsies) in Municipalities. The first partner cities were Budapest, Berlin, Cordoba, Strasbourg, Pardubice, Ankara and Thebes. The network remains open to cities wishing to join. It is planned that there should be a city in every state to head the network and serve as an interface with the Council of Europe. Cities must prepare a multi-annual programme, and as members of the network they will receive information from the Council of Europe to help them develop their activities. The importance of the network was restated at a meeting of the Congress in Rome in October 2003.

Resolution 44 (1997), towards a tolerant Europe: the contribution of Roma

This new resolution was adopted on 7 March 1997, on the basis of a report by Mr Slavovsky. In the preamble, the CLRAE expresses concern:

1. Deploring the crimes, serious violence, racial hatred and discrimination suffered by many Roma throughout Europe, which have caused many Roma deaths, even in recent years;

---

10. See footnote No. 8 above referring to the Congress publication *Gypsies in the locality*.

2. Concerned at a too passive, or even in some cases accommodating, attitude on the part of local authorities or the police towards this inhumanity, xenophobia, racism and intolerance;

3. Regretting the great precarity and the uncertainty of the nationality of many Roma as a result of armed conflict or the dissolution of some states.

It restates parts of documents adopted earlier, clarifying and strengthening their meaning and aims. It encourages the Network of Cities, welcomes "the creation of a Specialist Group on Roma (MG-S-ROM)" as previously requested, decides also "to use the spelling 'Roma', with a single 'r', in future so as to comply with usual practice within the Council of Europe" and decides "in order to provide for better reading and understanding, to comprise under the expression 'Roma' the whole variety of groups such as Roma, Gypsies, Sinti, Manush, Gitanos...".

Recommendation 147 (2004) on migration flows and social cohesion in South-East Europe: the role of local and regional authorities

A detailed report entitled "Migration flows and social cohesion in South-East Europe: the role of local and regional authorities" (CG (11) 9 Part II) was presented by Mr Nazir in April 2004. It was not concerned with Roma alone, but Roma are particularly affected by the situation in Europe:

> The violent dissolution of the former Federal Socialist Republic of Yugoslavia led to the biggest massive flow of population in Europe since the Second World War. Forced displacement on a large scale occurred both within and between the single states of the region (Croatia, Bosnia and Herzegovina, Serbia and Montenegro, "the former Yugoslav Republic of Macedonia") as well as towards other countries outside the region. More than three million people were forced to leave their homes at least for a certain period of time.
>
> ...
>
> The dynamics of these massive population flows has been different; however, this took place over an entire decade between 1991 and 2001, and was especially strong in four different periods:
>
> The first and largest population flow occurred between 1991 and 1995, during the war in Croatia and Bosnia and Herzegovina. Over that period, in Bosnia and Herzegovina alone more than two million citizens (out of a total number of 4.3 million of its pre-war population) left their places of origin. The second phase coincided with the war in Kosovo in 1999, when in a relatively short period almost one million people were forced to leave their homes.
>
> The third and fourth waves of arrivals coincided with the hostilities in "the former Yugoslav Republic of Macedonia" and in Southern Serbia when 250 000 and 20 000 persons respectively left their homes, thus becoming refugees or Internally Displaced Persons (IDPs).
>
> ...

> Among the displaced population, the Roma population seems to be more affected than any other group due to the weak position they occupy in society. The living conditions of the Roma refugees and IDPs are generally extremely poor. They mainly live in illegal settlements or unrecognised collective centres, without access to electricity, drinking water or sewage systems. Some municipalities are reluctant to accept them and provide little or no assistance, consequently they depend on NGOs and international relief. Specific programmes to provide support for this group should be devised and implemented, including those fostering their access to training and employment opportunities ... When analysing the position of the Roma population the reason for their particular vulnerability and social exclusion probably derives on the one hand from the absence of any reliable census data regarding this population and on the other, from the lack of information on the rights and services available to them.

Consequently, Recommendation 147 (2004) recommends that the member states "pay particular attention to the situation of the Roma minority".

The Congress has also adopted many texts not specifically aimed at Roma but which directly concern them. One example is Resolution 192 (1988) on regional or minority languages in Europe, which led to the European Charter for Regional or Minority Languages. A more recent example is Recommendation 286 (2010) on minority languages – an asset for regional development. Other texts relating to minorities such as Resolution 232 (1992) on autonomy, minorities, nationalism and European union, or again the development of intercultural policies as in the Frankfurt Declaration (May 1991), "Towards a new municipal policy for multicultural integration in Europe", or the Charleroi Declaration (February 1992), "European municipalities and democracy: the exclusion of poverty through citizenship".

Still others concern discrimination and racism, for example Recommendation 246 (2008) on a social approach to the fight against racism at local and regional level, in which Roma are mentioned:

> The Congress of Local and Regional Authorities of the Council of Europe has shown a particular interest in Roma and migrants, two of the groups targeted by racism, and is considering ways and means of combating racism at local and regional level. This commitment coincides with the Council of Europe's new anti-discrimination campaign.

7. The impact of the two fundamental treaties on minority languages and protection of national minorities

The European Charter for Regional or Minority Languages

In the preceding chapter, we saw that the Congress proposed a charter on regional or minority languages as long ago as 1988. The project was adopted as a convention by the Committee of Ministers on 25 June 1992 and it was opened to the states for signature on 5 November 1992. The convention came into force on 1 March 1998. As is noted in a document presenting the European Charter for Regional or Minority Languages:[11]

> The Charter is the only internationally binding instrument focused on minority language protection. It benefits its signatory states by offering a common and internationally recognised framework for their language policies. It also offers a rich experience of how languages can be enhanced in practice.

The charter has been signed and ratified by a growing number of states (as of 2012 it has been ratified by 25 states, and signed but not ratified by eight states). It is a treaty whose aims and scope are explained in the summary:

> This treaty aims to protect and promote the historical regional or minority languages of Europe. It was adopted, on the one hand, in order to maintain and to develop Europe's cultural traditions and heritage, and on the other, to respect an inalienable and commonly recognised right to use a regional or minority language in private and public life.
>
> First, it enunciates objectives and principles that Parties undertake to apply to all the regional or minority languages spoken within their territory: respect for the geographical area of each language; the need for promotion; the facilitation and/or encouragement of the use of regional or minority languages in speech and writing, in public and private life (by appropriate measures of teaching and study, by transnational exchanges for languages used in identical or similar form in other States).
>
> Further, the Charter sets out a number of specific measures to promote the use of regional or minority languages in public life. These measures cover the following fields: education, justice, administrative authorities and public services, media, cultural activities and facilities, economic and social activities and transfrontier

---

11. Secretariat of the European Charter for Regional or Minority Languages, *Giving regional and minority languages a say!*, Council of Europe Publishing, Strasbourg.

exchanges. Each Party undertakes to apply a minimum of 35 paragraphs or sub-paragraphs chosen from among these measures, including a number of compulsory measures chosen from a "hard core". Moreover, each Party has to specify in its instrument of ratification, acceptance or approval, each regional or minority language, or official language which is less widely used in the whole or part of its territory, to which the paragraphs chosen shall apply.

Enforcement of the Charter is under control of a committee of experts which periodically examines reports presented by the Parties.

So the charter offers a variable-geometry choice – 98 measures from which, for each language, the state chooses a minimum of 35 measures in at least six fields. In fact, states exceed the required minimum in most cases. This formula enables each state to choose, from among the measures advocated, those which best suit its own political and linguistic situation. According to the explanatory memorandum to the charter:

> On the one hand, the charter establishes a common core of principles, set out in Part II, which apply to all regional or minority languages. On the other hand, Part III of the charter contains a series of specific provisions concerning the place of regional or minority languages in the various sectors of the life of the community: the individual states are free, within certain limits, to determine which of these provisions will apply to each of the languages spoken within their frontiers. In addition, a considerable number of provisions comprise several options of varying degrees of stringency, one of which must be applied "according to the situation of each language".

The explanatory memorandum explains the reasons for, and the scope of, these provisions:

> The demographic situation of such regional or minority languages varies greatly, from a few thousand speakers to several million, and so does the law and practice of the individual states with respect to them. However, what many have in common is a greater or lesser degree of precariousness. Moreover, whatever may have been the case in the past, nowadays the threats facing these regional or minority languages are often due at least as much to the inevitably standardising influence of modern civilisation and especially of the mass media as to an unfriendly environment or a government policy of assimilation.
>
> ...
>
> the charter's overriding purpose is cultural. It is designed to protect and promote regional or minority languages as a threatened aspect of Europe's cultural heritage. For this reason it not only contains a non-discrimination clause concerning the use of these languages but also provides for measures offering active support for them: the aim is to ensure, as far as reasonably possible, the use of regional or minority languages in education and the media and to permit their use in judicial and administrative settings, economic and social life and cultural activities.

Where prospects for the Roma language, Romani or its variants, are concerned, certain provisions of the text mention the possibility of its inclusion in the implementation of the charter, while Romani and some of its variants appear in the list of languages supplied by states at the time of ratification. This is made clear in the explanatory memorandum:

> 19. The authors of the charter were confronted by the problem of the major differences which exist in the situations of regional or minority languages in Europe. Some languages cover a relatively large territorial area, are spoken by a substantial population and enjoy a certain capability of development and cultural stability; others are spoken only by a very small proportion of the population, in a restricted territory, or in a very marked minority context and already with greatly impaired potential for survival and development.
>
> 20. Nevertheless, it was decided not to attempt to define different categories of languages according to their objective situation. Such an approach would not do justice to the diversity of language situations in Europe. In practice, each regional or minority language constitutes a special case and it is pointless to try and force them into distinct groups. The solution adopted was to preserve the single notion of regional or minority language, while enabling states to adapt their undertakings to the situation of each regional or minority language.
>
> ...
>
> 21. The charter puts forward appropriate solutions for the different situations of individual regional or minority languages but does not prejudge what is the specific situation in concrete cases.
>
> ...
>
> 36. "Non-territorial languages" are excluded from the category of regional or minority languages because they lack a territorial base. In other respects, however, they correspond to the definition contained in Article 1, paragraph a, being languages traditionally used on the territory of the state by citizens of the state. Examples of non-territorial languages are Yiddish and Romany.
>
> 37. In the absence of a territorial base, only a limited part of the charter can be applied to these languages. In particular, most of the provisions of Part III aim to protect or promote regional or minority languages in relation to the territory in which they are used. Part II can more easily be applied to non-territorial languages, but only *mutatis mutandis* and on the terms set out in Article 7, paragraph 5.
>
> ...
>
> 78. Some of the provisions contained in paragraphs 1 to 4 can be applied without difficulty also to non-territorial languages; this is the case regarding the recognition of these languages, the measures to develop a spirit of respect, understanding and tolerance towards them, the prohibition of discrimination and the action to afford them positive support, the possibility for the groups speaking those languages to develop links with each other within the state and abroad, and the promotion of language research and study. On the other hand, it will not be possible to apply to non-territorial languages the provisions concerning administrative divisions and the facilities provided for non-speakers of these languages to acquire some knowledge of them, since such measures are capable of being taken only in a specified territory. Lastly, the objectives of making provision for the teaching and study of these non-territorial languages and the promotion of their use in public life can probably, for practical reasons, be implemented only with certain adjustments.

Article 7 paragraph 5 of the charter, concerning the objectives and principles, reads as follows:

> The Parties undertake to apply, *mutatis mutandis*, the principles listed in paragraphs 1 to 4 above to non-territorial languages. However, as far as these languages are concerned, the nature and scope of the measures to be taken to give effect to this Charter shall be determined in a flexible manner, bearing in mind the needs and wishes, and respecting the traditions and characteristics, of the groups which use the languages concerned.

In the list of declarations made with respect to the charter, the states specify which languages are concerned by the charter. Here are a few examples that mention Romani or its variants:[12]

- Austria: "Austria declares that minority languages within the meaning of the Charter in the Republic of Austria shall be the Burgenlandcroatian, the Slovenian, the Hungarian, the Czech, the Slovakian languages and the Romany language of the Austrian Roma minority."

- Finland: "Finland declares, referring to Article 7, paragraph 5, that it undertakes to apply, *mutatis mutandis*, the principles listed in paragraphs 1 to 4 of the said Article to the Romanes language and to the other non-territorial languages in Finland."

- Germany: "The Romany language of the German Sinti and Roma in the territory of the Federal Republic of Germany and Low German language in the territory of the *Länder* Brandenburg, North-Rhine/Westphalia and Saxony-Anhalt shall be protected pursuant to Part II of the Charter."

- Hungary: "The Government of the Republic of Hungary, based on the authorisation of the Parliament and according to Article 2, paragraph 2, of the Charter, undertakes to apply the following provisions in respect of the Romani language:"

- Montenegro: "In accordance with Article 2, paragraph 2, of the Charter, Montenegro has accepted that the following provisions be applied in the Republic of Montenegro, for the Albanian and Romany languages:"

- Netherlands: "The Kingdom of the Netherlands further declares that the principles enumerated in Part II of the Charter will be applied to the Lower-Saxon languages used in the Netherlands, and, in accordance with Article 7, paragraph 5, to Yiddish and the Romanes languages."

- Poland: "The Republic of Poland declares, in accordance with Article 3, paragraph 1, of the European Charter for Regional or Minority Languages that, within the meaning of the Charter, minorities languages in the Republic of Poland are: Belorussian, Czech, Hebrew, Yiddish, Karaim, Kashub, Lithuanian, Lemko, German, Armenian, Romani, Russian, Slovak, Tatar and Ukrainian."

---

12. Full information, and in particular the list of paragraphs applicable to Romani in the case of the states mentioning it, is available on the Council of Europe website, www.coe.int.

Other states, notably Norway, the Czech Republic, Romania, Serbia, Slovakia and Sweden, mention Romani. By contrast, it may be noted that Croatia has entered a reservation under Article 7, paragraph 5, excluding Romani from the scope of the charter. The committee of experts responsible for implementation of the charter has asked the Croatian authorities to withdraw this reservation and to apply the charter to Romani.

In order to monitor the application of the charter, a report is presented every three years by each state in which it has come into force, and according to the explanatory memorandum, "in order to ensure the efficiency of this system for monitoring the implementation of the charter, the latter provides for the setting-up of a committee of experts to examine the reports submitted by the various parties. It will also be possible for the committee of experts to be approached by bodies or associations wishing to supply further information or describe specific situations relating to the application of the Charter".

The reports submitted by the states at regular intervals address the question of Romani and clearly show how the charter has been applied with respect to this language. Reference should be made to them for details (see the Council of Europe website, www.coe.int). Furthermore, various colloquies, meetings and hearings have added to the thinking on implementation. For example, the question of Romani was raised at the international conference organised in Noordwijkerhout (Netherlands) in 2001 on "From theory to practice – the European Charter for Regional or Minority Languages".[13] The question was tackled in depth at a hearing of the ERTF organised in 2005 by the committee of experts for the charter (MIN-LANG (2005) 19). The working paper drawn up by the charter secretariat states that Article 7, paragraph 5, concerning non-territorial languages, "offers a gateway for protection" and that the committee of experts "has increasingly recognised the worth of this provision". So Article 7, paragraph 5, "far from being a lesser form of protection, has actually become an extremely important and worthy basis for protection of the Roma languages".

The document goes on to examine the relationship between language policy and social and economic situation, the question of education in terms both of language protection and of the "severe lack" of trained teachers, training and teaching materials. It recommends in particular substantial investment in teacher training. It then addresses the question of the development of common standards because "the lack of a standard written form is a considerable obstacle to the implementation of many of the undertakings under the Charter". Finally, the question of awareness-raising within the majority population is discussed; action to combat discrimination should be developed for this reason. Thus it is clear that the committee of experts proposes comprehensive reflection and action, language issues being a constant source of friction in the overall context of the existence of Roma communities. The hearing report (MIN-LANG (2005) 19) is supplemented by a "Policy paper on the Romani language" drawn up by the ERTF.

---

13. Council of Europe (2002), *From theory to practice – the European Charter for Regional or Minority Languages*, Regional or minority languages No. 3, Council of Europe Publishing, Strasbourg.

Every three years, when a state sends its report, the Committee of Experts examines it, puts questions to the state on points needing clarification and organises on-the-spot visits to complete the picture. Following a possible consultation with organisations (especially associations), the Committee of Experts draws up its own report, together with proposals to the state concerned, and submits it to the Committee of Ministers. The latter may decide to publish it and may address recommendations to states calling on them to take the necessary steps to bring their policy, legislation and practice into line with their requirements under the charter. The cycle thus results in three documents: a state report, an assessment report by the Committee of Experts, and a recommendation addressed by the Committee of Ministers to the state concerned. Depending on the dates on which states ratified the treaty, some of them have already supplied three and in some cases four reports, enabling the changes – and in particular the extent to which Romani has been catered for – to be measured. They constitute a substantial corpus of documents that allow for analysis over a lengthy period. The monitoring mechanism also enables the content of the reports to be made public.

Most Committee of Ministers recommendations mention the Romani language and call on the state to take or strengthen provisions in one field or another. Thus the implementation of the charter, affording a political framework within which languages, and especially Romani, are taken into account, respected and developed, offers a tool for evaluation, guidance and encouragement. It is also an alarm mechanism, because the Committee of Experts pinpoints, in the case of Romani, not only omissions and instances of negligence but also errors in the measures taken with regard to the language, which is sometimes treated in a discriminatory or imbalanced way relative to other languages.

In this process, NGOs are seen as a vital partner, especially in providing information for those with national responsibilities and members of the Committee of Experts. A practical guide to the charter has been published on NGOs and minority languages;[14] its aim is to encourage synergies between NGOs and the Committee of Experts to promote regional and minority languages in Europe.

Thanks to the monitoring process and to consultation among the players involved, the charter remains a living instrument that is achieving its goal of protecting and promoting regional and minority languages in Europe, including the Romani language.

The Framework Convention for the Protection of National Minorities

The question of minorities has received the attention of Council of Europe bodies over some 50 years. In Recommendation 285 (1961) on the rights of national minorities, the Parliamentary Assembly proposes adding the following article to the European Convention on Human Rights:

---

14. Ruiz Vieytez F.J. (2004), *Working together – NGOs and regional or minority languages*, Council of Europe Publishing, Strasbourg.

> Persons belonging to a national minority shall not be denied the right, in community with the other members of their group, and as far as compatible with public order, to enjoy their own culture, to use their own language, to establish their own schools and receive teaching in the language of their choice or to profess and practise their own religion.

Other ideas subsequently emerged, reports were written and the work intensified from the early 1990s onwards in the course of the major political changes which began in Europe in 1989. The Parliamentary Assembly, particularly in Recommendation 1134 (1990) on the rights of minorities, offered a list of principles for the protection of minorities which largely anticipated the wording of the convention adopted later. The same is true of Recommendation 1177 (1992) on the rights of minorities, adopted in February 1992. In 1992 the Committee of Ministers adopted Recommendation No. R (92) 10 on the implementation of rights of persons belonging to national minorities, in which it stated that "the rights of persons belonging to national minorities are not fully respected" and that "states do not always fulfil their obligations and commitments under international instruments, resulting in national minorities being treated badly". The Committee of Ministers then asked the Steering Committee for Human Rights to look into possible ways of protecting minorities. Finally, the 1st Summit of Heads of State and Government of the Council of Europe, in Vienna in October 1993, was organised around the question of minorities. Among the documents adopted, "Appendix II" is concerned with national minorities. The heads of state and government emphasise that:

> Having regard to its fundamental vocation, the Council of Europe is particularly well placed to contribute to the settlement of problems of national minorities.
>
> ...
>
> In consequence, we decide to instruct the Committee of Ministers:
>
> – to draw up confidence-building measures aimed at increasing tolerance and understanding among peoples;
>
> – to respond to requests for assistance for the negotiation and implementation of treaties on questions concerning national minorities as well as agreements on transfrontier co-operation;
>
> – to draft with minimum delay a framework convention specifying the principles which contracting States commit themselves to respect, in order to assure the protection of national minorities. This instrument would also be open for signature by non-member States;
>
> – to begin work on drafting a protocol complementing the European Convention on Human Rights in the cultural field by provisions guaranteeing individual rights, in particular for persons belonging to national minorities.

The paragraph on confidence-building measures was rapidly acted on by establishing a programme bearing the same title to support activities designed to improve relations between minorities and majority populations. In this context, and over several years, dozens of ongoing projects and short-term activities relating to Roma were launched. The text cited above clearly calls for the drafting of a framework convention, and in November 1993 the Committee of Ministers established the ad hoc Committee for the Protection of National

Minorities (CAHMIN), which became operational in January 1994. CAHMIN submitted proposals in April 1994, and in October of that year submitted the draft convention to the Committee of Ministers, which adopted it in November 1994. The treaty was opened for signature to the member states in 1995 and entered into force in February 1998. The summary explains that:

> The Convention is the first legally binding multilateral instrument concerned with the protection of national minorities in general. Its aim is to protect the existence of national minorities within the respective territories of the Parties. The Convention seeks to promote the full and effective equality of national minorities by creating appropriate conditions enabling them to preserve and develop their culture and to retain their identity.
>
> The Convention sets out principles relating to persons belonging to national minorities in the sphere of public life, such as freedom of peaceful assembly, freedom of association, freedom of expression, freedom of thought, conscience and religion, and access to the media, as well as in the sphere of freedoms relating to language, education, transfrontier co-operation, etc.

By 2012 the treaty had been ratified by 39 states, and signed but not ratified by another four states. The signatory states to the Framework Convention:

> Being resolved to protect within their respective territories the existence of national minorities;
>
> Considering that the upheavals of European history have shown that the protection of national minorities is essential to stability, democratic security and peace in this continent;
>
> Considering that a pluralist and genuinely democratic society should not only respect the ethnic, cultural, linguistic and religious identity of each person belonging to a national minority, but also create appropriate conditions enabling them to express, preserve and develop this identity;
>
> ...
>
> Have agreed as follows:
>
> Section 1
>
> Article 1
>
> The protection of national minorities and of the rights and freedoms of persons belonging to those minorities forms an integral part of the international protection of human rights, and as such falls within the scope of international co-operation.
>
> Article 2
>
> The provisions of this framework Convention shall be applied in good faith, in a spirit of understanding and tolerance and in conformity with the principles of good neighbourliness, friendly relations and co-operation between States.
>
> Article 3
>
> 1. Every person belonging to a national minority shall have the right freely to choose to be treated or not to be treated as such and no disadvantage shall result from this choice or from the exercise of the rights which are connected to that choice.
>
> 2. Persons belonging to national minorities may exercise the rights and enjoy the freedoms flowing from the principles enshrined in the present framework Convention individually as well as in community with others.

There follows a statement of the principles to be applied with regard to rights and access to equality. It is important to note that Article 4 of the text advocates measures to promote "full and effective equality" without this being considered discriminatory:

> 2. The Parties undertake to adopt, where necessary, adequate measures in order to promote, in all areas of economic, social, political and cultural life, full and effective equality between persons belonging to a national minority and those belonging to the majority. In this respect, they shall take due account of the specific conditions of the persons belonging to national minorities.
>
> 3. The measures adopted in accordance with paragraph 2 shall not be considered to be an act of discrimination.

Article 5 gives a comprehensive definition of the spirit in which the protection of minorities is to be implemented:

> 1. The Parties undertake to promote the conditions necessary for persons belonging to national minorities to maintain and develop their culture, and to preserve the essential elements of their identity, namely their religion, language, traditions and cultural heritage.
>
> 2. Without prejudice to measures taken in pursuance of their general integration policy, the Parties shall refrain from policies or practices aimed at assimilation of persons belonging to national minorities against their will and shall protect these persons from any action aimed at such assimilation.

The articles which follow are concerned with a spirit of tolerance, intercultural dialogue, measures to be taken to ensure respect for the fundamental freedoms of members of minorities, freedom of religion, freedom of expression (in particular through access to the media), use of the language, knowledge of the culture, education and organisation of teaching, participation in cultural, social and economic life and in public affairs, maintenance and development of culture and preservation of identity, protection from arbitrary measures involving displacement of population (expulsion, expropriation) which alter the proportions of the population in areas inhabited by persons belonging to national minorities, and transfrontier co-operation. The Committee of Ministers is in charge of monitoring the implementation of the Framework Convention, with assistance from an Advisory Committee. Periodic reports are submitted by each state on implementation.

In the declaration made by states when signing or ratifying the Framework Convention, they sometimes specify the minorities concerned, and Roma are occasionally mentioned. For example:

- Germany: "National Minorities in the Federal Republic of Germany are the Danes of German citizenship and the members of the Sorbian people with German citizenship. The Framework Convention will also be applied to members of the ethnic groups traditionally resident in Germany, the Frisians of German citizenship and the Sinti and Roma of German citizenship."

- Slovenia: "In accordance with the Constitution and internal legislation of the Republic of Slovenia, the provisions of the Framework Convention shall apply also to the members of the Roma community, who live in the Republic of Slovenia."

– Sweden: "The national minorities in Sweden are Sami, Swedish Finns, Tornedalers, Roma and Jews."

– "The former Yugoslav Republic of Macedonia": "The term 'national minorities' used in the Framework Convention and the provisions of the same Convention shall be applied to the citizens of the Republic of Macedonia who live within its borders and who are part of the Albanian people, Turkish people, Vlach people, Serbian people, Roma people and Bosniac people."

The reports submitted on the implementation of the Framework Convention may also refer to Roma. Some 30 of the 39 states which have ratified the convention have mentioned them.

In 2001 the Parliamentary Assembly reverted to the question of minorities in Recommendation 1492 on the rights of national minorities, which regrets the slow pace of implementation of the text, and then in 2003 in Recommendation 1623 (2003) on the rights of national minorities:

> 2. The Assembly welcomes the success of the Framework Convention for the Protection of National Minorities, a privileged instrument in the field of protection of national minorities, which celebrated the fifth anniversary of its entry into force this year. The entry into force of the Framework Convention marked a new stage in the development of the minority protection system within the Council of Europe. Instead of elaborating basic standards for minority protection, the Organisation is concentrating on monitoring mechanisms and improving the efficiency of institutions and procedures aimed at ensuring the compliance with these basic principles by all Council of Europe member states.
>
> ...
>
> 5. The Assembly reiterates the positions it undertook in Recommendation 1492 (2001) with regard to the Framework Convention, that is the demand for a swift signature and ratification by member states without reservations or declarations.[15] Persistent refusal to sign or ratify this instrument, and to implement its standards, should be the subject of particular attention in the monitoring procedures conducted by the Committee of Ministers, the Parliamentary Assembly and the Congress of Local and Regional Authorities of Europe (CLRAE), as appropriate.

The Assembly also calls on "the States Parties to pay particular attention to the possibility for the most vulnerable Roma minorities to fully benefit from the protection envisaged in the Framework Convention". Lastly, it submits a series of recommendations to the Committee of Ministers asking it to take steps to improve monitoring of the implementation of the Framework Convention.

The machinery for monitoring the implementation of the Framework Convention has generated a large volume of documents. The five-year cycle

---

15. Four out of 47 member states of the Council of Europe had not signed the framework convention as of 1 April 2012: Andorra, France, Monaco and Turkey.

of document production operates as follows. The state submits a report on the basis of which the Advisory Committee prepares an opinion, which is sent to the state and the Committee of Ministers; the state may then comment on the opinion received, and the Committee of Ministers adopts a resolution on the implementation of the Framework Convention in the state in question. Meetings may be held in the states, bringing the governmental and non-governmental persons concerned together for discussions. Representatives of Roma organisations or NGOs dealing with Roma questions thus have an opportunity to express their views and priorities.

Depending on the date of ratification, some states are in their third monitoring cycle. As with the European Charter for Regional or Minority Languages discussed above, the implementation of the Framework Convention offers a tool for evaluation, guidance and encouragement. In its opinions, the Advisory Committee very often addresses the situation of the Roma minority and the question of failure to apply the Framework Convention because of anti-Roma discrimination. The principal articles concerned are Article 3, cited above, and Article 6:

> Article 6
>
> 1. The Parties shall encourage a spirit of tolerance and intercultural dialogue and take effective measures to promote mutual respect and understanding and co-operation among all persons living on their territory, irrespective of those persons' ethnic, cultural, linguistic or religious identity, in particular in the fields of education, culture and the media.
>
> 2. The Parties undertake to take appropriate measures to protect persons who may be subject to threats or acts of discrimination, hostility or violence as a result of their ethnic, cultural, linguistic or religious identity.

The Advisory Committee emphasises the persistence of prejudice and stereotypes and intolerance of Roma, violence against them, including violence on the part of the security forces; calls on the authorities to shoulder their responsibilities; and, when incidents occur, to conduct investigations impartially and ensure that the appropriate penalties are applied.

With regard to Article 3, issues of recognition and citizenship have arisen in several states, especially in the Balkans. There are also difficulties over censuses and data collection, in particular because of the Roma minority's fears. The committee further finds that all too often the Roma minority is simply not taken into account in the application of the Framework Convention, or else is merely seen as an "ethno-linguistic" minority with lesser rights recognised, and consequently treated differently from other minorities. It also happens that Roma are assimilated to another minority and regarded as such, or that only some of the Roma, considered "indigenous", are recognised as forming a minority.

With regard to Article 6, the committee highlights the blatant violence committed against Roma, and urges the authorities to make every effort to combat that violence, whose origins lie in negative prejudice towards them. Roma are the victims of hostile attitudes and behaviour on the part of populations as well as the media and representatives of the public authorities.

Some individuals campaigning for election make use of this in their election speeches, and Roma are sometimes subject to acts of group violence.

Special attention must also be paid to discrimination in the fields of education, political representation, employment and housing, and the media and the image of Roma which the media convey. It also appears that Roma have more difficulty than other minorities in obtaining financial support and help in developing their culture, language and traditions. Relations with the police and access to justice are problematic. In some states, the committee emphasises, Roma who are refugees or asylum seekers are not treated in the same way as other people.

Each of these points can be tangibly illustrated by the Advisory Committee's opinions. Some states having reached their second or third monitoring cycle, more than 80 opinions are now available and provide a very complete picture. These opinions are public and are available on the Council of Europe website. We have not quoted particular states or particular opinions in the preceding paragraphs, for lack of space and also because differential treatment of Roma by states is among the most commonly shared patterns of behaviour across Europe. It is also important to read the comments made by states in reply to the Advisory Committee's opinions, as well as the Committee of Ministers resolutions addressed to each member state concerned (nearly 70 resolutions to date).

The Advisory Committee has also produced thematic commentaries. In its commentary of 2 March 2006 on education (ACFC/25DOC52006)002), the Roma minority appears in each section. A few sentences will serve as examples:

> The equal access of Roma children to good quality education and their integration in the societies is a persistent problem in many States Parties to the Framework Convention. Segregated education, often of lower standard than that offered to other students, is one of the most extreme examples of the precarious position of Roma parents and pupils. The Advisory Committee has repeatedly criticised practices of segregation of Roma students and welcomed efforts to end such practices. Other problems encountered are the bullying of Roma children by other children or, even by teachers, inappropriate and culturally biased tests used in the educational systems, the lack of recognition of the Romani language in schools, low income and lack of school meals for Roma. The Advisory Committee has observed differences in the treatment of girls and boys. The Advisory Committee has welcomed efforts to tackle such problems, for instance through offering of school meals, introduction of public transportation, training of Roma school assistants and teachers. ... The importance of teaching of and through the medium of the Romani language is increasingly discussed in State Reports and in the Opinions of the Advisory Committee as a necessary element of the efforts to ensure access to education for the Roma. ... The particularly disadvantaged position of the Roma and Travellers needs to be taken into account in all countries that have ratified the Framework Convention.

During the conference organised in 2008 to celebrate the 10th anniversary of the entry into force of the Framework Convention, entitled "Enhancing the impact of the Framework Convention: past experience, present achievements and future challenges", the Council of Europe Commissioner for Human Rights observed: "I have noted with interest that one of the themes that is under consideration for a new thematic commentary is the implementation of minority rights for Roma". At that same conference, in a paper entitled "Justice, relevance and participation: transnational activism in the field of minority protection in Europe. A perspective from Central and Southeast Europe", Anna-Mária Bíró stressed that:

> As of 5 September 2008, 39 state reports were submitted under the first cycle and 34 state reports under the second cycle. Sixty shadow reports from 27 state parties were submitted under a total of 73 state reports under both cycles. Out of the 60 shadow reports 18 address the situation of a single ethnic group, nearly half of which focus on the Roma.

Asbjørn Eide, in his report on the work of the Advisory Committee on thematic commentaries, noted that:

> It is mentioned, among others, that the particularly disadvantaged position of the Roma and Travellers needs to be taken into special account ... An ever recurring issue is the implementation of the minority rights for Roma and Travellers. Both Commentaries have mentioned it, but again it might be useful to have a full and separate treatment of all aspects of that issue. In this connection, consultations with the EU's Fundamental Rights Agency and with the High Commissioner on National Minorities would be important. Much work on this has also been done by the UN Committee on the Elimination of All Forms of Racial Discrimination, the OSCE/ODIHR, the Department at the Council of Europe specifically dealing with Roma and Travellers' issues, and the CoE Commissioner on Human Rights.

Of all the minorities in Europe to which the Framework Convention applies, Roma clearly require quite special attention by reason of their situation.

8. Co-ordination and stronger follow-up to action on Roma

The 1990s were years of intense Council of Europe activity on Roma. New texts of direct relevance to them were adopted, as well as more general texts with a strong impact on them, such as the treaties covered in the preceding chapter. This trend emerged against a background of growing discrimination and increasing difficulties for Roma, at a time when Europe was being transformed by the upheavals of the 1990s following the fall of the Berlin Wall.

In order to forestall possibly counter-productive effects linked to this intensification of activity (repetition or duplication from one sector to another, lack of follow-up, dispersion, failure to capitalise on knowledge from experience, etc.), measures were needed both within the internal organisation of the Council of Europe Secretariat (the executive body) and in relations with the member states on questions affecting Roma.

Co-ordinator for Roma/Gypsy activities

In 1994, the Secretary General of the Council of Europe appointed a Co-ordinator for Roma/Gypsy activities, with the task of:

— co-ordinating Roma activities in the various Council of Europe departments; in particular, he/she organises meetings between departments on topical questions affecting Roma, so that each sector's priorities can be discussed;

— developing relations with various Roma organisations, in order to respond to their requests and to advise the Secretary General in this connection;

— co-operating with the other international organisations concerned, in particular the OSCE and the EU. In 1995 the Co-ordinator was appointed Council of Europe correspondent for the OSCE's Roma and Sinti contact point.

The function was quickly appreciated by the various Council of Europe bodies. The CDMG, having been instructed by the Committee of Ministers "to conduct an in-depth study on the various aspects of the situation and conditions of life of Gypsies in the new European context", noted in its 1995 report on "The situation of Gypsies (Roma and Sinti) in Europe" that:

the Secretary General has appointed within the Secretariat a Co-ordinator of activities on Roma/Gypsies. In view of the increased importance attached by the Council of Europe to Gypsy questions, this function is acquiring growing significance and the CDMG points out that it needs to be adequately resourced.

The Committee of Ministers, replying to the Parliamentary Assembly in the form of a decision in October 1995 on the subject of Recommendation 1203 (1993) (CM/Del/Dec/Act(95)544/6.3), stressed the importance of the function and its aims:

> The Committee of Ministers also wishes to inform the Assembly that fruitful co-operation has been established between the Council of Europe, the Office for Democratic Institutions and Human Rights (ODIHR) of the Organization for Security and Co-operation in Europe and the Commission of the European Communities on questions of common interest relating to Roma/Gypsies.
>
> The Co-ordinator of activities on Roma/Gypsies designated by the Secretary General of the Council of Europe is responsible for these contacts, for promoting dialogue on policies and problems relating to Roma/Gypsies, and for developing working relations with Roma/Gypsy organisations, with a view to developing the appropriate synergies while avoiding duplication of activities. These functions should make it possible to attain, at least to some extent, the objectives advocated by the Assembly in paragraph xxii of the recommendation. However, the Committee of Ministers has not seen fit to act on the proposal concerning the appointment of a mediator for Roma/Gypsies.

The role of Council of Europe Co-ordinator for Roma activities was consolidated over the following years. As a Committee of Ministers meeting paper states:[16]

> 51. The Co-ordinator organised until recently twice-yearly interdepartmental meetings to address topical issues relating to Roma and Travellers and discuss the priorities of all sectors concerned. Since last year, and with a view to focus on Roma rights from the human rights perspective, these regular internal co-ordination meetings have been taken over by the Commissioner for Human Rights, in close co-operation with the Co-ordinator.
>
> 52. The Co-ordinator ensures external co-ordination by organising the regular meetings of the Informal Contact Group (ICG) of international organisations/institutions involved in Romani affairs, which includes the Council of Europe, the Office for Democratic Institutions and Human Rights (OSCE/ODIHR), the European Commission, the EU Fundamental Rights Agency, the European Parliament, the UNDP, the UNHCR and the World Bank. This Informal Contact Group meets under each EU Council presidency to exchange information and co-ordinate activities.

The Parliamentary Assembly, in Recommendation 1924 (2010), after urging the Committee of Ministers to "keep the issue of the situation of Roma in Europe high on its agenda", invited it to:

> allocate a structural post and an office for the Council of Europe Co-ordinator for activities concerning Roma and Travellers, to enable her/him to play her/his role as an adviser to the Secretary General, as well as to efficiently co-ordinate the Organisation's activities.

---

16. CM/Inf(2009)23, 22 April 2009, Thematic exchange of views: "Facing the future: Council of Europe action in the field of Roma and Travellers", 1056th meeting, 6 and 7 May 2009.

The role of the Co-ordinator in the Informal Contact Group

The Informal Contact Group (ICG) was set up in 1999 under the Finnish presidency of the EU, following the Tampere summit on the situation of Roma and other excluded groups in Europe. Its purpose is to provide an informal working framework for the exchange of information and co-ordination of activities between the different international players involved in Roma issues, in particular the Council of Europe, the Office for Democratic Institutions and Human Rights (OSCE/ODIHR), and the institutions of the EU (the European Commission, European Union Agency for Fundamental Rights and European Parliament).

These meetings were subsequently broadened to include other international organisations such as the United Nations Development Programme (UNDP), the United Nations High Commissioner for Refugees (UNHCR) and the World Bank. Following its inception and by reason of its special links to the Council of Europe, the ERTF was invited to meetings, as was the European Roma Information Office (ERIO), which is closely linked to the European Commission in Brussels. The group was later joined by the European Roma Rights Centre (ERRC), which is active in defending the rights of Roma, and the Open Society Institute (OSI) which was at the origin of the Decade of Roma Inclusion 2005-2015.

At its meeting in May 2000, it was observed that the particular strength of the Council of Europe, as compared with other organisations, lay in the definition of long-term policies.

The group normally meets every six months under the chairmanship of the state chairing the Council of the European Union. However, its meetings do not always follow this pattern. For example, in 2004, when the group had not met during three presidencies, that is, for more than 18 months, the Co-ordinator for Roma/Gypsy activities took steps to relaunch the consultation process. That process, over and above the exchanges of views which keep the different institutions informed of what is being done, makes it possible to set common priorities and sometimes to engage in common action.

The meetings of the ICG have proved useful in keeping the Roma question on the international political agenda, especially since 2008 where the "conclusions" of the presidencies of the EU are concerned.

However, since the meeting of the ICG on 10 February 2010 under Spain's chairmanship, and in order to take into account the creation of the European Roma Platform, it has been suggested that the ICG revert to a smaller membership from among the intergovernmental organisations.

A Council of Europe division for Roma

In 1998, when the Directorate of Social and Economic Affairs became the Directorate General of Social Cohesion (DG III), the original Population and Migration Division was split into two divisions: (i) Population and (ii) Migration and Roma/Travellers.

In 2001 the Migration and Roma/Travellers Division became the Migration and Roma Department, with two divisions, one responsible for migration and the other for Roma and Travellers. Thus Roma questions can be considered for administrative purposes within the Council of Europe in a comprehensive, cross-sectoral manner. They acquire greater visibility and greater coherence, especially as the above-mentioned Co-ordinator works closely with the Roma and Travellers Division, and the secretariat of the intergovernmental committee which monitors Roma questions (MG-S-ROM) is part of the same division. Indeed, it was when the issue arose of placing the activities of the MG-S-ROM within the intergovernmental framework that the Committee of Ministers decided that the CDMG was best placed to deal with Roma questions because its lengthy experience in the matter of migration and inter-community relations would enable it to improve the situation of Roma.

In order to improve the circulation of information and understanding of activities, an information bulletin was launched in July 1995 to serve as a source of regular information on current activities and new developments relating to Roma in the various Council of Europe bodies. Some 10 years later, that *Bulletin of activities on Roma/Gypsies* was replaced by a new website.[17] The website has become a mine of information on the activities carried out – conferences, reports, project developments, work of committees of experts, etc.

An intergovernmental committee for Roma

The CDMG, tasked by the Committee of Ministers with carrying out a study on the situation of Roma, had the following to say in its final report (adopted on 5 May 1995 (CM(95)78)):

> Current discussions within the Council of Europe have demonstrated that the Committee of Ministers lacks a specialised body to advise it on issues concerning Gypsies. This is essentially a multidisciplinary question having economic, social, educational, cultural, legal and human rights aspects and no existing intergovernmental committee of the Council of Europe is fully competent to look at the issues as a whole. To remedy this situation, a number of possibilities are open to the Committee of Ministers: ... to set up under the CDMG a Group of Specialists on Gypsy questions which would also look at Gypsy issues as a whole and make recommendations for work by various Council of Europe bodies according to their competence (the CDMG notes that although it is competent for matters to do with migration and community relations it is certainly not in a position to deal with all aspects of Gypsy questions). The reports and recommendations would be passed on to the Committee of Ministers by the CDMG with any necessary comments. This would also provide a source of specialist advice, but with the advantage of fitting into the usual system of intergovernmental committee structures; its proposals would reach the Committee of Ministers after having been examined by a Steering Committee on which all member states are represented. Once again, it would, however, imply some additional charge to the budget.

---

17. www.coe.int/t/dg3/romatravellers/default_EN.asp.

That initial CDMG proposal was followed up by the Committee of Ministers in the decision it took in October 1995 (CM/Del/Dec/Act(95)544/6.3) in reply to Parliamentary Assembly Recommendation 1203 (1993):

> The CDMG pointed out that the Council of Europe does not at present have a specialised body to monitor the development of the situation of Roma/Gypsies and suggest adequate remedies for any deficiencies found. The Committee of Ministers has therefore decided to set up a group of specialists with instructions to submit to it a detailed plan of action, which will then be approved by the Committee of Ministers and implemented in liaison with the CDMG. Furthermore, the CDMG itself envisages organising in 1996, in the framework of its programme of activities, an exchange of information and experience on the consultative mechanisms set up in certain member states to facilitate dialogue between Roma/Gypsies and travellers and the authorities.

This was how the Group of Specialists on Roma and Gypsies (the MG-S-ROM, to use its Council of Europe title) came into being.

The name of the group later changed in keeping with the terminology used within the Council of Europe. In 2002 the Group of Specialists on Roma/Gypsies became the Group of Specialists on Roma, Gypsies and Travellers, and more recently, in 2006, the Committee of Experts on Roma and Travellers.

This committee is the first Council of Europe body set up on a lasting basis to oversee the situation of Roma in Europe in a coherent, systematic way. It is also the only intergovernmental committee specifically dealing with Roma issues, and has no equivalent in Europe.

Its membership was laid down by the CDMG in 1996: it is a group made up of specialists in Roma questions chosen from among candidates put forward by the member states concerned. The Council of Europe bears the costs of the experts from seven states (Bulgaria, Spain, Finland, Italy, Netherlands, Poland, Romania), those of the experts from other states being borne by their own countries. Representatives of Roma organisations and other organisations, plus the Parliamentary Assembly, the Congress, the OSCE and the EU are also invited as observers. The number of committee members whose costs were to be met subsequently increased, and other Council of Europe bodies which had become active in Roma issues were invited as well as (depending on meeting agendas) competent independent experts and representatives of Roma organisations. The ERTF obtained observer status. The committee normally meets twice a year, in principle once in Strasbourg and once in a member state which must organise a public hearing and a field visit on that occasion. Working sessions use the Romani language in addition to the two official Council of Europe languages, English and French. The first meeting was held in March 1996 with governmental experts from 12 states. The second took place in October 1996, also with 12 states. In 2010, 31 states were represented.[18]

---

18. Albania, Austria, Bosnia and Herzegovina, Bulgaria, Croatia, Czech Republic, Estonia, Finland, France, Germany, Greece, Hungary, Ireland, Italy, Latvia, Moldova, Netherlands, Norway, Poland, Portugal, Romania, Russian Federation, Serbia, Slovak Republic, Slovenia, Spain, Sweden, the "former Yugoslav Republic of Macedonia", Turkey, Ukraine and the United Kingdom.

The committee's terms of reference have also evolved over the years: the terms of reference are limited in time, and are renewed by the Committee of Ministers, which adapts them to the situation and the aims set for the committee. By way of illustration, after the committee had been functioning for a dozen years (1996-2008) and the terms of reference had been renewed several times, the Committee of Ministers redefined the terms of reference in July 2008 (MG-S-ROM (2008) 2), so it would:

> i. study, analyse and evaluate the implementation of policies (national programmes and/or action plans) and practices of member states concerning Roma and Travellers and act as a forum for the exchange of information, views and experience on policies, good practice and issues relating to Roma and Travellers at domestic level and in the context of relevant international instruments, including those of the Council of Europe, without pursuing activities relating to monitoring the situation in individual member states.
>
> ii. draw up guidelines for the development and/or implementation of policies which promote the rights of the Roma and Traveller populations taking into account the findings of the monitoring mechanisms of the relevant legal instruments of the Council of Europe.
>
> iii. keep under review the situation of Roma and Travellers in member states in compliance with relevant legal instruments of the Council of Europe.

The governments of the member states are empowered to appoint a representative with expertise in Roma questions. In order for the committee to work effectively, its members' profile is clearly defined by the Committee of Ministers in accordance with five points:

- They shall have specialised knowledge of the various issues relating to Roma and/or Travellers (legal status, discrimination, health, education, employment, housing and political participation);
- They shall have direct experience of the Roma and/or Traveller populations and of their culture and way of life;
- They shall have a deep knowledge of the policies on Roma and/or Travellers in their country and have a good knowledge of policies in other member states;
- They shall be in close contact in their country with the Roma and Traveller populations, the decision-making bodies and the NGOs working in this area;
- They shall be able to liaise with the authorities of their countries about any decisions, documents or recommendations adopted by the Committee.

Accordingly the Council of Europe covers the costs of the committee's members for 21 states, but that number may increase: the other states bear the costs of sending their delegates. Participation in meetings, without voting rights, has been extended to representatives of the relevant Council of Europe bodies such as the Committee on Education, the committee monitoring the Framework Convention and the European Charter of Regional or Minority Languages, etc., the Parliamentary Assembly, the Congress, the Commissioner for Human Rights, etc., and also the Council of the European Union, the European Commission, the European Union Agency for Fundamental Rights (FRA), and organisations such as the OSCE, UNDP,

UNHCR and the World Bank. The presence of observers is also authorised, in particular organisations such as the ERTF, ERRC and ERIO. A maximum of five representatives of Roma and Travellers, including an ERTF representative, and/or independent experts able to make a useful contribution to the committee's work may also be invited, without voting rights and depending on the work in hand.

The mixed composition of the MG-S-ROM (Roma and non-Roma), the participation of representatives from a variety of institutions and NGOs, the continuity of its work and the accumulation of its experience, and its close co-operation with the Co-ordinator and the Roma and Travellers Division, all make it a hub which serves to foster exchanges, co-operation, evaluation and the piloting of European action. It is a body especially well fitted to draw up European standards. Accordingly, it has instigated or played a crucial part in drafting Committee of Ministers recommendations. It is also involved in the discussions which precede new projects, action plans or the establishment of new bodies, on which it gives its opinion. It was likewise closely involved in the various stages of establishing the ERTF, the question of setting up a European solidarity fund for Roma, and the question of the return of Roma to Kosovo. It is also asked to prepare opinions for the Committee of Ministers in reply to Parliamentary Assembly recommendations.

The work of the committee – missions, studies, recommendations, etc. – may have an impact beyond the Council of Europe. For example, the results of its work provided inspiration for the "Guiding principles for improving the situation of Roma", a reference document for states at the pre-accession stage adopted by the Council of the European Union at the Tampere summit (Finland) in December 1999.

As of late 2010, 30 MG-S-ROM meetings have been held in the 15 years since 1996, the reports of which are available on the Council of Europe website. They bear witness to the range and importance of the exchanges and decisions on the agendas of meetings such as those on education, employment, health, housing, policies on Roma, migrations and freedom of movement, the return of displaced Roma in South-East Europe, asylum seekers, the work of the Commissioner for Human Rights, political participation of Roma, the situation of women, recognition and teaching of the genocide, the question of stereotypes and prejudice, the *Dosta!* campaign to combat that prejudice, and so forth.

Profile of MG-S-ROM members

Note: those members who are Roma are indicated by an asterisk (*). At the beginning of 2010 they numbered seven out of 31 states represented. There are currently 17 women out of 31 members, and so they constitute a majority on the committee. Twenty-three members belong to a governmental body, two are from bodies combating discrimination, and six from NGOs.

Table 2: Profile of MG-S-ROM members, 2010

Member state	Representative	Function
Albania	Ms Blerina Tepelena	Technical Secretariat of Roma Ministry of Labour, Social Affairs and Equal Opportunities
Austria	Ms Christa Achleitner	Federal Chancellery Department for National Minority Affairs
Belgium	*Has been represented in the past.*	
Bosnia and Herzegovina	Mr Samir Šlaku	Ministry for Human Rights and Refugees of Bosnia and Herzegovina
Bulgaria	Ms Elitsa Slavcheva	Chief Expert, European Affairs and International Cooperation Directorate Ministry of Labour and Social Policy
Croatia	Ms Milena Klajner	Former Head of the Office for National Minorities of the Government of Croatia
Czech Republic	Mr Czeslaw Walek	Deputy Minister of Human Rights and Minorities
Estonia	Ms Anne-Ly Reimaa	Undersecretary of Estonian Ministry of Culture Department of Cultural Diversity
Finland	Mr Henry Hedman*	Member of the Advisory Board on Romani Affairs
France	Ms Laure Michelet	Office of European and International Affairs (BEI) General Directorate of Social Action (DGAS) Ministry of Labour, Social Relations, the Family, Solidarity and Urban Affairs
Germany	Ms Inga Pöhle	Federal Ministry of Interior of the Federal Republic of Germany, Division M II 4, National Minorities; measures to promote mutual understanding; tracing services
Greece	Ms Louiza Kyriakaki (Chairperson)	Ministry of Interior, Decentralisation & E-Government Directorate of Development Programmes & International Organisations
Hungary	Dr Melinda Horvath	Deputy Head of the Department of Roma Integration Ministry of Social Affairs and Labour
Ireland	Ms Sinéad Leyden	Executive Diversity & Equality Law Department of Justice, Equality & Law Reform
Italy	Mr Pietro Vulpiani	National Office against Racial Discrimination (UNAR) under the aegis of the Council of Ministers, Rights and Equal Opportunities

Latvia	Ms Ilze Brands-Kehris	Director – Latvian Centre for Human Rights (LCHR)
Moldova	Mr Nicolae Radiţa*	Chairman NGO Roma National Centre
Netherlands	Mr Peter Jorna	Member of the Forum association, then independent expert since the beginning of 2010
Norway	Ms Tove Skotvedt	Senior Adviser Department of Sámi and Minority Affairs Ministry of Labour and Social Inclusion
Poland	Ms Małgorzata Różycka	The Chancellery of the Prime Minister Office of the Plenipotentiary of the Prime Minister for International Dialogue
Portugal	Mr Carlos Nobre	Deputy for Roma communities High Commissariat for Immigration and Intercultural Dialogue (ACIDI, I.P.)
Romania	Mr Dezideriu Gergely* (1st vice-chairperson)	National Council for Combating Discrimination
Russian Federation	Mr Sergey Tolkalin	Deputy Director Department for Humanitarian Cooperation and Human Rights Ministry of Foreign Affairs
Serbia	Mr Petar Antić* (2nd vice-chairperson)	Deputy Minister of Human and Minority Rights Agency for Human and Minority Rights of the Republic of Serbia
Slovakia	Mr Ján Hero*	Member of the Board Through the Children to the Family – NGO
Slovenia	Ms Tjaša Plohl	Government Office for National Minorities
Spain	Ms Isabel Alonso Luzuriaga	Head of Programme Area Sub-directorate General of Social Programmes, Directorate General of Social, Family and Child Policy, Ministry of Health and Social Policy
Sweden	Ms Emma Sterky	Deputy Director Ministry of Integration and Gender Equality
Switzerland	*Has been represented in the past.*	
"the former Yugoslav Republic of Macedonia"	Ms Mabera Kamberi*	State Adviser Department for Strategic Planning Ministry of Labour and Social Policy
Turkey	Mr Serkan Bozkurt	Culture and Tourism Assistant Expert Ministry of Culture and Tourism
Ukraine	Mr Petro Grygorichenko*	All Ukraine NGO "Congress of Roma of Ukraine"
United Kingdom	Mr Ian Naysmith	Race Equality and Diversity Division Department for Communities and Local Government

Targeted action

A flexible, cross-sectoral project

For the purpose of co-ordinating and following up on the action taken, a process which has tracked the measures mentioned above, in September 1996 the Committee of Ministers launched a project on Roma/Gypsies in central and eastern Europe. A special budgetary account was opened for it, with funding from the Demosthenes programme, but it was also able to receive earmarked contributions from states or foundations. In 1998 the scope of the project was broadened to all the member states, and in 2002 it was named the "Project on policies for Roma, Gypsies and Travellers in Europe". It functions through voluntary contributions from certain member states, particularly Finland (the main contributor) and from the Netherlands, the United Kingdom, Slovakia, Norway, Sweden, Slovenia and others. In conjunction with this project, the OSI also sponsors courses at the Council of Europe for young Roma, and financial help is provided to enable Roma to attend international events.

The project aims to assist and support governments in defining and implementing policies on Roma: it gives backing and an international profile to Roma projects in the member states. A number of major priorities have been set: assistance activities for the preparation and implementation of national programmes for Roma; meetings prior to the creation of ERTF; support for the setting-up of Roma NGOs; activities in the field of education and health; organisation of study visits, seminars and workshops, etc. The Roma and Travellers Division is responsible for implementing the project. Over the years, a great many activities have been organised,[19] focusing on priority subjects such as the training of school and social/health mediators, combating human trafficking, promotion of networks of women and young Roma, raising awareness of anti-Gypsyism, questions of freedom of movement and migration, etc. As noted in the activity report submitted to the Committee of Ministers for the first two-year period (1996-98) (CM(98)161):

> Nearly all the activities within the Project are carried out in partnership with other actors: government departments, Roma organisations, other NGOs and other international organisations (especially the OSCE/ODIHR Contact Point for Roma and Sinti Issues). This makes it possible to carry out, or to support, a large number of activities on the basis of a relatively small financial commitment and a very reduced Secretariat in Strasbourg.

> In selecting activities to be undertaken or supported within the Project, a major criterion is that there should be real prospects for follow-up. The aim is to provide an international input into an ongoing process or programme within the state or states concerned. Where a government is actively seeking to develop policies towards Roma that are in line with Council of Europe principles and standards, assistance is offered. Another important principle is that events organised with governments should normally involve active Roma/Gypsy participation.

---

19. These are mentioned in the Information Bulletin launched in 1995 and also on the Council of Europe/Roma and Travellers Division website: www.coe.int/t/dg3/romatravellers/default_EN.asp.

The project has an important place, and illustrates the logic underlying the Council of Europe's work. The Committee of Ministers emphasised this when examining the above-mentioned activity report (No. (98)875):

> As a result of the growth in activity, it can be said that the Council of Europe is now widely recognised as having developed a significant and constructive role in co-operation with the countries concerned on Roma/Gypsies issues. Moreover, the flexibility and rapid response of the Organisation's working methods have been widely welcomed.

The Committee of Ministers, "given that the Project is still very active, and is continuing to attract voluntary contributions", decided to extend the period of operation of the special account for a further three years and "to open up the Project on Roma/Gypsies in central and eastern Europe to all member states, so as to enable it to support occasional activities elsewhere in Europe".

The Forum of European Roma Young People

At the same time, following the organisation in April 1995 of a training course for Roma youth organisation leaders, the Council of Europe's Directorate of Youth and Sport organised a seminar for young Roma in September 1996. This led to the creation of the Forum of European Roma Young People (FERYP), for the purpose of promoting young Roma NGOs in Europe, supporting the representation of young Roma in the European institutions, and promoting co-operation and training for young Roma NGO leaders. The FERYP has organised, or helped organise, numerous activities over the years, including training courses for defining and developing projects, discussion seminars, the development of links with other youth organisations, political involvement, and promotion of the young Roma women's movement. Furthermore, the Youth Directorate encourages the opening up of every new youth-related activity to participation by young Roma.

A decade later, the invitation to a course held in May 2006 stated:

> Today FERYP has around 5,000 members – Roma youth associations and individuals – in more than 10 European countries. Among the core working strategies of FERYP is empowerment of young Roma through training.
>
> Why this study session?
>
> Violation of the Roma community's human rights and access of Roma to human rights throughout Europe are major concerns for many social and political players at all levels.
>
> Among the day-to-day challenges faced by young Roma in their community is a lack of awareness of their human rights and civil responsibilities.
>
> Various organisations and institutions (both Roma and non-Roma) at local and European level are working on Roma rights advocacy, and many are using human rights education (HRE) for young Roma as a means of addressing the above-mentioned issues and improving their situation.
>
> This study session is therefore for young Roma familiar with HRE and who use it in their work or are motivated to use it in their own environment, in order to achieve the aim pursued.

FERYP will implement this project in co-operation with the Council of Europe's Directorate of Youth and Sport, so as to be able to draw on the Council's experience and expertise in the area of human rights education for young people.

A Roma women's network

Another joint project concerns Roma women and access to health care, conducted in conjunction with the Office of the OSCE High Commissioner on National Minorities and the European Monitoring Centre on Racism and Xenophobia. The International Roma Women's Network (IRWN) created in February 2003 played a part in determining the priorities which were to have a major impact when the Committee of Ministers recommendation on health questions, discussed in an earlier chapter, was being prepared.

Roma under the Stability Pact

A joint project was launched in 2001 with the European Commission and implemented in conjunction with the OSCE, entitled "Roma under the Stability Pact". Its purpose was for the states of South-East Europe to devise and adopt comprehensive national strategies covering a series of fields – education, housing, social questions, health, employment, citizenship, and participation in public life. The programme comprised three elements: addressing the most acute crisis situations; policy development on Roma affairs; and participation of Roma in civil society. Co-operation was renewed in 2003. As with the first programme, close co-operation was established with the OSCE, a partner in the project.

The aim of this new project was to consolidate the action already undertaken to encourage states to devise and adopt comprehensive national strategies. It provides for assistance activities in the implementation of national programmes for Roma, and training courses designed to help them play a more effective part in implementation. Other joint programmes, to which we shall return, were launched subsequently.

Roma who are refugees, displaced and repatriated

In the sphere of refugees and displaced persons, joint activities were developed in 2003 with the UNHCR. These relate both to reception and integration of refugees and to voluntary return to the place of origin.

The Council of Europe Development Bank

Mention should also be made of the activities of the Council of Europe Development Bank (CEB), set up in 1956. It is the oldest of the European international financial institutions and the only one with an exclusively social mission, namely to develop a policy of solidarity under the auspices of the Council of Europe. It becomes involved, primarily through loans, in the funding of social projects and can provide a response to emergency situations in its 40 member states.

It is subject to the authority of the Council of Europe, but is financially independent.

In 2005, at the 3rd Summit of Heads of State and Government (Warsaw), the latter emphasised the importance of the CEB's activities on behalf of populations in distress and of social cohesion. They also called on the bank to contribute, through its own means of action, to the consolidation of a free, democratic and solidarity-based European society.

The CEB takes action primarily by granting reimbursable loans on request from states, local and regional authorities and public or financial institutions (see the CEB website: www.coebank.org).

As a CEB information bulletin states:

> In every European country, the Roma minority is the most disadvantaged group of the population, characterised by the highest unemployment rate, poor health, low education level and insalubrious housing conditions.
>
> It is the CEB's policy to:
>
> – support the efforts of governments and/or local authorities by means of medium/long-term investment loans on favourable conditions for social integration projects benefiting Roma
>
> – promote the participation of Roma in the design and implementation of projects
>
> – develop comprehensive programmes for Roma including education, housing, health and job creation.
>
> The CEB has been actively involved in activities related to the improvement of living conditions of Roma communities in recent years.

For example, since 1999 almost 30 million euros have been allocated to projects concerning Roma: approximately 26 million in loans and 4 million in grants. Between 2000 and 2010 loans have been granted to Bulgaria, Hungary and Spain. Grants have been approved primarily for projects concerning the former Yugoslavia (including Kosovo refugees) and Bulgaria.

The CEB, which is closely linked to the activities of the Council of Europe, is developing co-operation with the World Bank, the Roma Education Fund, the European Commission, and UN agencies such as the United Nations Children's Fund (UNICEF), UNDP and UNHCR.

9. The Education of Roma Children in Europe project: implementing a Committee of Ministers recommendation

In this overview of 40 years of activity concerning Roma, now that we have seen how a frame of reference emerged from the resolutions and recommendations of the Committee of Ministers, the Parliamentary Assembly and the Congress, and how co-ordinating and monitoring mechanisms were introduced, it would be instructive to show how some activities have developed. School education is an ideal example: this is a priority for all partners, and projects in this field – among the first to be undertaken by the Organisation – have been developed over a long period of time.[20] However, the example offered here is not suggested as a point of reference, since experience in such fields is not transposable. It is above all the illustration of a course of action that may trigger other activities, inasmuch as the processes which have been established make it more likely that the objectives laid down will be achieved.

The reality: a difficult situation

Difficult living conditions have left a deep mark on Roma communities. Rejection in various forms is the dominant element in relations between Roma and their immediate environment: housing problems, uncertain health, eviction, refusal of access to public places, etc. Tensions soon turn into conflict, especially in periods of economic hardship and unemployment; the result is harsh treatment of Roma in a permanent climate of insecurity.

In 1997, the MG-S-ROM adopted a memorandum for the Committee of Ministers entitled "Roma children educational policy paper: strategic elements

---

20. The author has also written a number of other documents referred to here, including the framework document for implementation of the Education for Roma Children in Europe project in 2002, and *L'éducation des enfants roms en Europe : Le contexte de mise en œuvre de la Recommandation CM/Rec(2009)4 du Comité des Ministres aux Etats membres sur l'éducation des Roms et des Gens du voyage en Europe* ["Education of Roma children in Europe: Background to implementation of Recommendation CM/Rec(2009)4 of the Committee of Ministers to member states on the education of Roma and Travellers in Europe"], which serves as the basis for the explanatory memorandum for the 2009 recommendation; consequently, some of the points made here borrow from other documents to which reference should be made for greater detail.

of education policy for Roma children in Europe". The MG-S-ROM members, delegates from their states, clearly recognised the difficult situation in their analysis:

> 1. Policies pursued by the state authorities toward Roma populations throughout their history in Europe and aimed at solving the so-called "Gypsy problem", have meant so often, the eradication of Roma identity and lifestyle. The school institution and the schooling of Roma children thus became a central means of achieving the goals of assimilation.
>
> 2. Majority-minority relations, so often hostile and based on stereotyped and prejudiced views of Roma people, have helped to maintain the disadvantaged position of Roma in society. Unequal status, discrimination and social exclusion which were, and are, characteristic of these hostile relations, have had a direct and an indirect impact on schooling, creating a school environment in which Roma children feel alienated.
>
> ...
>
> [Whatever strategies have been developed] neither of these strategies produced significant results. The negative features of the schooling of Roma children persisted: non-existent or temporary schooling, low school attendance, a high drop-out rate and a low percentage of students completing even primary-level education. Thus, illiterate and semi-literate young Roma continued to add to the broad social strata of unskilled, semi-skilled and unemployed Romanies, so perpetuating the marginalisation and inequality of the Romani community in society.

An initial link was thus established between the general situation and the situation regarding education. There is also a second connection between the two: the long-standing adaptability of the Roma has been severely tested and their strategies for adjusting proactively to their environment are no longer appropriate. The problems that Roma have in surviving as a minority cultural group are increasing. Any activity or occupation requires a minimum amount of knowledge to cope with present administrative requirements. Illiteracy is no longer a protection against the onslaught of other cultures channelled through the school and its processes of learning but has become a severe disadvantage in an environment where use of the written word is now a daily necessity.

Not having been to school is a severe disadvantage not only for economic reasons but also for social and psychological reasons. The latter include dependence on social services, a situation at odds with the Roma's legitimate pride in being able to shape their own future and that of their children. Provision of schooling can empower Roma while providing savings for the public sector: the costs of suitable schooling are substantially lower than the costs of social assistance perpetuated by inappropriate policies.

In other words, the future of Roma communities depends in large part on how their children are provided with schooling. Proactive adjustment to their environment in the social and economic fields now entails acquisition of basic knowledge enabling them to understand and analyse a constantly changing reality. In the field of culture, this same basic knowledge can be used as a tool for those who wish to preserve, assert and further develop an original identity.

Parents are aware of this and are more and more willing to send their children to school. This is therefore the second connection between the general situation and the situation regarding education: a transformation in working and living conditions in today's societies has led to the need for schooling and parents' determination that their children should receive it. However, at the present time, the gap is tending to widen between Roma children and neighbouring children in many cases, and situations which are currently bad will soon become serious.

Institutional origins

Most of the resolutions and recommendations adopted over the past four decades make reference to the problems of providing schooling for Roma children and young people and the need to improve the conditions for such schooling as well as access to their rights in the field of education. This is the case in Recommendation 563 (1969) of the Parliamentary Assembly and Resolution (75) 13 of the Committee of Ministers. Resolution 125 (1981) from the Standing Conference of Local and Regional Authorities of Europe clearly calls for the preparation of information dossiers for teachers on the history and culture of Roma as part of intercultural education. Then, in Resolution 249 (1993), the Standing Conference called on the Council for Cultural Co-operation:

> to step up the work pursued over the last 10 years with publications for the purposes of education and information in the field of schooling and training for Gypsy children and young people; ... to organise training seminars for teachers and other staff.

That same year, the Parliamentary Assembly, in Recommendation 1203 (1993), put the emphasis on teacher training and use of school mediators. The Committee of Ministers responded favourably and gave the Council for Cultural Co-operation appropriate instructions.[21] The CLRAE refined its requirements further in 1995 (Resolution 16 and Recommendation 11), emphasising:

> the possibility given to Rroma (Gypsy) communities to effectively exercise their fundamental right to education, having access to high-quality education at all levels, participating fully in the educational process and enjoying respect for their special needs;
>
> ...
>
> structures providing a good level of education for Rroma (Gypsy) communities, while at the same time endeavouring to optimise the multicultural context and encouraging links between schools in areas with different cultures in order to share the experiences of each minority culture.

---

21. The Council for Cultural Co-operation consisted of states that had signed the European Cultural Convention – one of the first Council of Europe conventions, opened for signature in 1954, including to non-member states. So far 50 states have signed it: 47 Council of Europe member states, as well as Belarus, the Holy See and Kazakhstan. The Steering Committee for Education implements education projects under the European Cultural Convention; it is therefore implementing the Education for Roma Children in Europe project.

In 1998, in its General Policy Recommendation No. 3 on combating racism and intolerance against Roma/Gypsies, the European Commission against Racism and Intolerance (ECRI) recommended that member states:

> vigorously combat all forms of school segregation towards Roma/Gypsy children and to ensure the effective enjoyment of equal access to education;
>
> ...
>
> introduce into the curricula of all schools information on the history and culture of Roma/Gypsies and to provide training programmes in this subject for teachers.

This was when the MG-S-ROM was preparing the memorandum for the Committee of Ministers, "Roma children education policy paper: strategic elements of education policy for Roma children in Europe" (MG-S-ROM (97)11). The decision-making procedure ran its course, and the Committee of Ministers adopted Recommendation No. R (2000) 4 on the education of Roma/Gypsy children in Europe, described in detail in an earlier section. The recommendation crystallised and articulated converging demands from different Council of Europe bodies as well as various states and NGOs. It represents a policy formulation of approaches found in studies and reports and is thus the keystone locking together many different building blocks, each of which has contributed to the common edifice.

Growth of knowledge

Already, with the request from the Standing Conference in Resolution 125 (1981), and well before the adoption of the above recommendation, the Education Directorate had begun to develop practical activities – among the very first at European level. They started in 1983 with the first European teacher training seminar and the preparation of a survey, *Gypsies and Travellers*, covering all 21 member states at the time and published in 1985. In 1994 this became *Roma, Gypsies, Travellers* in an expanded edition encompassing the whole of Europe. It should be mentioned that, as early as 1983 when the first edition was being prepared, the author of this book took the initiative of creating a network of 30 or so experts, in order to analyse the dynamics of project implementation. The experts were sent a questionnaire. This network was expanded to some 45 people for the second edition. A new edition was published in 2007: *Roma in Europe*.[22] The book, since its inception, has been intended to foster a better understanding of Roma by describing on the one hand the richness of their culture and lifestyle and, on the other, the mistreatment that they have suffered in the course of their long history. Its two parts, "Sociocultural data" and "Sociopolitical data" satisfy this two-fold need for information. Initially meant for teaching staff, the book soon came to be considered a useful reference work for trainers, community workers, social workers, people with political and administrative responsibilities, and anyone wanting information on Roma. For Roma organisations it has been a means of disseminating the general information needed by those around them. The book also lays down the foundations for a programme of appropriate, sensi-

---

22. Liégeois J-P. (2007), *Roma in Europe*, Council of Europe Publishing, Strasbourg. For translations, see Council of Europe website: www.coe.int.

tive and concerted action and has served as a guide for numerous programmes and activities ever since the 1985 edition.

The following were the first European seminars for teacher training:[23]

- "Training of teachers of Gypsy children", Donaueschingen, Germany, 1983 (DECS/EGT (83)63);
- "Schooling for Gypsies' and Travellers' children: evaluating innovation", Donaueschingen, Germany, 1987 (DECS/EGT (87)36);
- "Gypsy children in school: training for teachers and other personnel", Montauban, France, 1988 (DECS/EGT (88)42);
- "Towards intercultural education: training for teachers of Gypsy pupils", Benidorm, Spain, 1989 (DECS/EGT (89)31);
- "School provision for Gypsy and Traveller children: distance learning and pedagogical follow-up", Aix-en-Provence, France, 1990 (DECS/EGT (90)47).

Other seminars have followed over the years, and it is important to understand in detail the multiple roles played by these European meetings in terms of strategy, providing:

- guidance: by bringing together a range of relevant partners from a number of countries, including government officials and representatives of or experts from Roma communities, to assess current action and plan future activities, a sphere of dialogue has been created, allowing the Council of Europe and its partners to develop working guidelines;
- induction: the seminars are intended to highlight best practice, preferably developed in the country where the meeting is being held, and to develop discussion and working guidelines on the basis of this practice in order that other countries may become aware of and make use of it. The seminars' key role in this is to be sustained by dissemination of the results;
- meeting places: local visits and meetings with people directly affected by the issues discussed are important to foster exchanges between specialists so that they can learn of and study achievements and innovations in other states;
- educational tools: participants draw up exchange programmes between various member states;
- reference: summaries, conclusions and recommendations from seminar proceedings all provide information that can be used directly in other activities, in particular situation analysis, development of best practice, etc;
- information-gathering: seminars are good places to gather information for a better understanding of projects using best practices in the regions and states where they are organised;
- training: it is obvious that the seminars have a crucial role to play in training. Such in-service training by its very nature – flexibility and

---

23. The references given for the seminars are those for the reports published on them.

adaptability, short sessions and a broad range of training modules – is particularly suited to play the role required of it. The multiplier effect and multiple functions of each seminar should not overshadow this essential training function.

The seminars are not meant to be just training courses (which can be organised by member states) or ad hoc meetings. Given how infrequently they are held and the opportunities that they offer to bring together a wide range of knowledge and experience and compare a variety of activities, the European seminars have to act as a platform for new discoveries and future ideas, create momentum, open up avenues and foster innovation. They must complement each other and gradually lead to the acquisition of knowledge in priority fields and to a comprehensive and coherent body of knowledge at European level. The resulting recommendations and guidelines have proved helpful as a basis for both reflection and action, not only for teachers but also for the various partners concerned with the educational situation of Roma children.

Mention may also be made of the discussions, before Recommendation No. R (2000) 4 on the education of Roma/Gypsy children in Europe was adopted, on the teaching of history and the design of history textbooks, including the project Democracy, Human Rights, Minorities: Educational and Cultural Aspects (1993-97) and its pilot project Local History and Minorities: with special reference to the Gypsy Minority, implemented in co-operation with the Roma minority. The same project contained a component titled "A programme of case studies concerning the inclusion of minorities as factors of cultural policy and action". Of the 20 or so studies, three relate to Roma:

- "Self-government of the Gypsies in Hungary seen in the light of the experience of the Sami self-government in Norway" (DECS/SE/DHRM (96)17);
- "Romani culture: the Secondary School of the Arts and the Romathan Theatre, Košice, Slovakia" (DECS/SE/DHRM (96)18);
- "Roma policy: Gypsy national self-government and local self-governments", Hungary (DECS/SE/DHRM (96)23).

Since 1997, the Education for Democratic Citizenship project (DECS/EDU/CIT (99)58) has included the establishment of "sites of citizenship" for Roma in Bulgaria, Ireland, Portugal and Spain. Their purpose has been to encourage participatory democracy at local level. These activities, whose lessons are still relevant since they are genuinely exploratory and forward-looking, have in the majority of cases resulted in reference publications on a range of complementary subjects, thus creating a comparative body of knowledge at European level and avoiding duplication.[24] Over the course of 20 years all these activities have thus helped to develop experience that has been conducive to proper implementation of the recommendation.

---

24. Some of these activities (seminars, publications, programmes) are listed in Council of Europe (2006), *Education of Roma children in Europe: texts and activities of the Council of Europe concerning education*, Council of Europe Publishing, Strasbourg.

The Council of Ministers recommendation

In Recommendation No. R (2000) 4, the Committee of Ministers recognises:

> that there is an urgent need to build new foundations for future educational strategies toward the Roma/Gypsy people in Europe, particularly in view of the high rates of illiteracy or semi-literacy among them, their high drop-out rate, the low percentage of students completing primary education and the persistence of features such as low school attendance;
>
> ...
>
> that the disadvantaged position of Roma/Gypsies in European societies cannot be overcome unless equality of opportunity in the field of education is guaranteed for Roma/Gypsy children;
>
> ...
>
> that the education of Roma/Gypsy children should be a priority in national policies in favour of Roma/Gypsies;
>
> ...
>
> that policies aimed at addressing the problems faced by Roma/Gypsies in the field of education should be comprehensive, based on an acknowledgement that the issue of schooling for Roma/Gypsy children is linked with a wide range of other factors and pre-conditions, namely the economic, social and cultural aspects, and the fight against racism and discrimination.

The recommendation then offers "guiding principles of an education policy for Roma/Gypsy children in Europe" and details priorities in terms of structures; curricula and teaching materials; teacher training and recruitment; information research and assessment; and consultation and co-ordination. Shortly after the adoption of this recommendation, the Standing Conference of European Ministers of Education, at its October 2000 session, adopted the theme of "Educational policies for democratic citizenship and social cohesion: challenges and strategies for Europe". In their final declaration, the ministers asked the Council of Europe to consider the question of Roma/Gypsies and, in their resolution on the activity programme for 2001-03, to conduct work "on educational policies for and the educational needs of Roma/Gypsies in all its dimensions, drawing on relevant experience in member states".

A working framework

The Education of Roma Children in Europe project was conceived in 2001, based on the conclusions of a meeting of experts and the guidelines laid down by the Steering Committee for Education (CD-ED-BU (2002)13). The project was to serve as a source of inspiration and a tool for managing and co-ordinating a range of activities initiated both by member states and by and within the Council of Europe. To ensure that it would meet its goals, the project was presented in a framework document to the Steering Committee for Education in 2002 (CD-ED-BU (2002)30).

This framework document was fundamental in setting up the project, covering background, philosophy, implications, relationship to other projects, structure and progress of activities, activity management, etc. It offered an understanding of the processes involved and how they fitted into an overall strategy. Its aim was to organise activities as part of a coherent whole. It enabled time, energy and money to be saved at a critical period for Roma communities, when the effects of a difficult situation called for an urgent response but not one that would entail any decline in the standard of work.

The document covered:

1. intersectoral and inter-institutional co-operation;

a. intersectoral co-operation: a forward-looking assessment within the different sectors of the Council of Europe was carried out to obtain information on activities in the field of education and see whether these could be directly linked to the project's own activities, thus increasing the latter's potential and its role as a catalyst. Activities were to be aimed at young people, projects on the situation of minorities in education, development of the Route of Roma Culture and Heritage and the *Dosta!* campaign to combat stereotypes, etc;

b. inter-institutional co-operation: building bridges with the European Commission and the OSCE's Contact Point for Roma and Sinti Issues, as well as the United Nations Educational, Scientific and Cultural Organization (UNESCO) and international NGOs active in the provision of schooling for Roma children, particularly the Roma Education Fund;

2. seminars, and exchange of views and experience: such meetings can play multiple roles (described previously);

3. development of structural projects;

a. compendium of best practice: criteria for defining "best practice" put forward by Roma; data collection and analysis. Publications: a directory, a European compendium of selected projects, a policy brochure, standards for schooling of Roma children, a "guide" to help Roma teachers and school mediators/assistants grasp the background to their work;

b. design of teaching material: review of existing material (catalogue of available material); adaptation of existing material after evaluation and selection; new material, where needed, suitable for use throughout Europe (history, language, culture, politics, etc.). This material may take the form of brochures or educational fact sheets.

Implementing the recommendation in these areas is a realistic and economical way of stepping up activities at both national and European levels as part of existing education programmes whilst also strengthening networks.

Clear guidance: the example of educational fact sheets

Among the material produced by the project – such as a teaching kit for children at pre-school level to help them prepare for primary education and a guide for Roma school mediators – its educational fact sheets offer a practical illustration of the approach described above. This component of the project is a direct response to a number of the points advocated in Recommendation No. R (2000) 4:

> The curriculum, on the whole, and the teaching material should therefore be designed so as to take into account the cultural identity of Roma/Gypsy children. Romani history and culture should be introduced in the teaching material in order to reflect the cultural identity of Roma/Gypsy children. The participation of representatives of the Roma/Gypsy community should be encouraged in the development of teaching material on the history, culture or language of the Roma/Gypsies.
>
> ...
>
> It is important that future teachers should be provided with specific knowledge and training to help them understand better their Roma/Gypsy pupils. The education of Roma/Gypsy pupils should however remain an integral part of the general educational system.

Moreover, numerous official documents and reports stress that the training of education staff is a priority that must go hand in hand with, or even precede, development of other activities. They also note the lack of reliable teaching material. This component of the project was designed with intercultural education in mind in order to give teachers the necessary training to deal with culturally diverse classes.

It was decided to produce educational fact sheets on the modular principle to allow co-ordinated distribution characterised by:

- flexibility of use for training (in training colleges, for distance learning); the same documents can also be used by teachers as teaching aids in their work with pupils. In addition, the fact sheets may be used as education packs elsewhere, such as in museums of Roma culture or for exhibitions;
- their versatility for teachers, mediators, inspectors and other persons directly concerned by educational provision for Roma children or who do not work directly with Roma children but would like to acquire some relevant knowledge to pass on to other pupils;
- their adaptability to different systems and levels of training: the fact sheets are not teaching units but reference documents that can be used in different courses; they provide intercultural content for courses and make it possible to introduce rudiments of a history, a language and a culture which form part of Europe's heritage;
- their expandability inasmuch as the fact sheets form not a finite whole but rather a flexible body that can and must be constantly expanded in the light of teaching requirements and local context. The set of fact sheets is open-ended and has a tree structure; in other words, a common trunk of knowledge supports and provides background for the whole, and thematic and geographical branches (for particular states) offer a structure onto which new fact sheets can be grafted: more detailed consideration of particular themes, or local examples useful for schools. It must also be possible to incorporate feedback

through amendments to the fact sheets (corrections and additions in the course of reading and translation, enabling new readers to add their contributions).

At a time when access to knowledge has been made easier by the new information and communication technologies, the overall fact sheet project has been able to take advantage of these new methods and organise knowledge in a structured whole to guarantee its quality and, as well as giving it a higher profile, make it easier to understand through a comprehensive approach. In this respect, the production and use of fact sheets is an educational choice – and act – in a training process that represents more than just its content.

The way in which the fact sheets are to be produced has been laid down in an introductory fact sheet meant as much for people who may offer new fact sheets as for the people who are going to use them. Useful topics for training education staff have been clarified through a number of seminars attended by participants with complementary skills: students and teacher trainers being trained and teacher-researchers able to provide training of trainers and work on the content of training. These meetings have been used to define the nature and priorities of training content in three fields: history, culture and language. Other meetings have allowed further work on specific training content. Lastly, before the fact sheets were finalised, seminars were held to test the quality of this material in real-life situations.[25]

There are several types of fact sheet: "cross-disciplinary" or general fact sheets to foster a better understanding of issues in a broadly European context, and, for curriculum or local-interest purposes, national and regional fact sheets. Thus a basic theme such as the Nazi period in Roma history is covered both by "European" fact sheets and by fact sheets on particular states, each complementing the other. Some fact sheets may highlight a particular event of general significance in Roma history, such as their period of slavery in the Romanian principalities or the Great Gypsy Round-up in Spain.

Specific instructions in an introductory fact sheet provide an outline of what is to be produced: objectives, readability (wording, subheadings, boxes, illustrations, bibliography, ideas to explore, etc.) and format (word count). Lastly, the overall structure is explained: when put together, the fact sheets will make up an encyclopaedia of Roma history, culture, politics and language, and a hypertext function for browsing between the fact sheets using keywords will allow a dynamic, entertaining, attractive and rewarding approach.

---

25. Reports on most of the seminars are available on the Council of Europe website: www.coe.int. The finalised fact sheets are intended to be available in English, French and Romani, but upon application to the Council of Europe, they can also be published in other languages – for example, on the initiative of the various states' education authorities. Some of these other versions are already available on the Council of Europe website.

Essential teaching: the Romani language

The learning and teaching of Romani by way of implementation of Committee of Ministers Recommendation No. R (2000) 4, and also the above-mentioned Recommendation CM/Rec(2008)5 on policies for Roma, forms part of a programme of work. As early as 1954, the European Cultural Convention was making language recommendations, and the Council of Europe has been pursuing activities to promote linguistic diversity and language learning in the educational field ever since. Activities to promote Romani thus come within the programme of the Language Policy Division, whose work covers a large number of languages, including minority and migrant languages. Its achievements in the field of Romani are summed up on the Council of Europe's website as follows:

> A *Curriculum Framework for Romani* (CFR) has been developed to support the teaching of Romani. It was designed for practitioners as well as for manual designers and policy deciders. The CFR concerns age groups 4-16 and can be adapted to local contexts and needs. After a piloting phase a revised version was published in 2008.
>
> To supplement the CFR, additional tools were produced to help more specifically teachers of Romani: two *European Language Portfolio* models (for age groups 6-11 and 11-16) accompanied by a *Handbook for teachers*.
>
> ...
>
> With a view to introducing the CFR and launching a piloting phase, a seminar involving 10 countries (representatives of ministries with responsibilities for Romani in the curriculum, and Roma educators) was organised in May 2007 by the Language Policy Division in Strasbourg.
>
> ...
>
> A piloting phase was launched subsequently to the seminar. Projects presented by participants are included in the seminar's report.

This report is the "Curriculum Framework for Romani: seminar for practitioners and decision makers".

Another seminar in 2008, "Teaching Romani: the Curriculum Framework for Romani and the European Language Portfolio", was used to review the outcome of the previous phase and improve development of Romani teaching aids. According to the Council of Europe website, the European Language Portfolio is defined as follows:

> The European Language Portfolio (ELP) is a document in which those who are learning or have learned a language – whether at school or outside school – can record and reflect on their language learning and cultural experiences.
>
> ...
>
> It contains a Language passport which its owner regularly updates. A grid is provided where his/her language competences can be described according to common criteria accepted throughout Europe and which can serve as a complement to customary certificates.

...

The ELP also contains a detailed Language biography describing the owner's experiences in each language and which is designed to guide the learner in planning and assessing progress. Finally, there is a Dossier where examples of personal work can be kept to illustrate one's language competences.

A curriculum framework for Romani has been laid down as a result of this work, and a review of teaching practices and teacher training in various states has been undertaken.[26]

Historical recognition: Roma genocide

Activities (production of fact sheets, publications, dissemination of information) have stressed the importance of recognising the Roma genocide in teaching: its antecedents, events during the Nazi regime, extermination, and the aftermath. The project has therefore made provision for significant activities in this respect, especially as it took almost 50 years for the issue to emerge and become the subject of consistent research and 60 years for the general public and the education sector to take any notice of it. At the ministerial seminar organised by the Council of Europe in October 2002, Simone Veil underlined this fact:

> People do not, unfortunately, know about the way in which Gypsies were hunted down and exterminated. The voices of surviving Gypsies, whether or not they were deported, have not often been heard, because of their lifestyle and the lack of associations able to defend their interests. Yet it is quite wrong, and indeed scandalous, that there should be such widespread ignorance of their tragic fate.[27]

The resulting work was linked to implementation of Committee of Ministers Recommendation Rec(2001)15 on history teaching in 21st-century Europe. Teaching material was produced, participation in meetings, seminars and symposia was encouraged, and a "Roma genocide" website was developed,[28] where it is now possible to find the above-mentioned fact sheets, a downloadable virtual library and valuable bibliographies as well as an interactive map with links to information on the history of places of remembrance and on museums of Roma history and culture. Roma genocide was also linked with the European Roma route – important in educational terms – and activities that could be developed in various countries by schools or NGOs.

---

26. The curriculum documents for Romani are available on the Council of Europe website: www.coe.int. The Council of Europe holds the copyright for the *Curriculum Framework for Romani*, the *European Portfolio Language* models and the *Handbook for teachers*. Translation into national/official languages and into varieties of Romani is encouraged, subject to permission from the Council of Europe, in order to promote widespread dissemination and use of these tools.
27. Council of Europe (2002), *Day of Remembrance: Ministerial Seminar proceedings*, Council of Europe Publishing, Strasbourg, p. 39.
28. website: www.romagenocide.org.

A strategy

Willingness to act must be accompanied by the necessary means to act, and it is important for these means to be provided over a sustained period if activities are not to be short-term and ad hoc. When implementing Recommendation No. R (2000) 4, the Bureau of the Steering Committee for Education (CC-ED-BU (2002)13) said that the project:

> will guide member states in setting up a global and comprehensive programme that takes into account all (and not a selection of) measures and specific needs identified to integrate Roma into mainstream education. The programme should be sustainable, backed by secure funding from the ministries and be implemented uniformly throughout the education system.

In addition, the organisation and management of work plays a vital part. Thus the framework document suggests implementing activities by including:[29]

- a working framework, support and flexibility;
- complementarity and interrelationship;
- building on assets;
- fostering innovation;
- working in networks;
- hyperprojects: an analytical approach;
- a European dimension.

But planning on this basis, however sound it may be, is not enough if it fails to uphold certain principles integral to a comprehensive and structural approach. The educational situation of a cultural group must be put in perspective as part of a long-term history and a contemporary political context; provision of schooling for Roma children must therefore be considered in the light of both Roma and non-Roma policies. Individual parameters cannot be studied in isolation or used on their own to draw practical conclusions. Any assessment of teaching is also an assessment of policy.

These principles have been discussed at greater length in the book *Roma in Europe* (in the chapter on "Reflection and action"):[30] an activity has to be broken down into its component parts to take account of the dynamics of different communities as well as the various sociopolitical and socioeconomic parameters, which call for a realistic approach.

It must also be stressed that in these fields there is no all-purpose solution. Voluntary initiatives may possibly merge with official ones, but they cannot be officially planned. A patchwork of micro-developments and

---

29. These approaches are described more fully in the framework document (CD-ED-BU (2002)30).
30. Jean-Pierre Liégeois, op. cit; they have been adapted to education in *L'éducation des enfants roms en Europe – Le contexte de mise en œuvre de la Recommandation CM/Rec(2009)4 du Comité des Ministres aux Etats membres sur l'éducation des Roms et des Gens du voyage en Europe*.

micro-projects may therefore be the best way of responding to a wide range of situations and aspirations (this is where short-term, ad hoc efforts come in), but they must take place within a framework of regular consultation, co-ordination and overall structural assistance. Even the most exemplary activities will therefore result not in prescriptions but in tendencies, and, as mentioned at the beginning of this chapter, they will not necessarily come together where we might expect: convergence is more likely to occur in processes (consultation, reliance on internal dynamics, and other processes outlined below) than in results (specific achievements). The emphasis is on the following principles of:

– flexibility in diversity;
– precision in clarity;
– reliance on internal dynamics;
– dialogue;
– co-ordination;
– study and reflection;
– information and documentation.

The preparation and development of activities to implement Recommendation No. R (2000) 4 was guided by these principles. To understand their importance, reference should be made to the documents that shaped and supported the project and to the resulting publications, which might serve as a model for activities in other fields.[31] While the administrative stage of the project came to an end in 2009 with the organisation of a final conference, work has continued with the adoption, referred to in a previous chapter, of Committee of Ministers Recommendation CM/Rec(2009)4 on the education of Roma and Travellers in Europe, which updates the 2000 recommendation.

Priorities have been laid down, the project implementation strategy has begun to bear fruit, working tools have been tried out and proved reliable, and activities have led to practical results. In the past few years a start has been made on preparing a programme, and this programme should now be consolidated by moving it from the pilot stage to full-scale application following a positive appraisal from the various partners. A new period of work should allow established activities to expand in scope and depth. One of the basic goals of Recommendation CM/Rec(2009)4 is to organise and strengthen activities over the next few years.

A task force for Roma education

Following the project's final conference, organised in May 2009 by the Education Directorate of the Council of Europe, and a human dimension

---

31. The list of publications is available, mostly in downloadable form, from the Council of Europe website's education section, under the heading of the "Education of Roma/Gypsy Children in Europe" project.

meeting held by OSCE/ODIHR in 2009, the two organisations decided to establish an instrument for present and future co-operation in the shape of an international task force for the education of Roma.

The participants at the final conference, together with the representatives of a number of organisations present, including OSCE/ODIHR, UNESCO, OSI, the Roma Education Fund and the ERTF, emphasised the vital part to be played by international organisations in determining and implementing European and transnational policies.

As underlined at the outset and throughout this Council of Europe project, the role of this task force with regard to establishing strategy is to contribute more effectively to implementation of education goals whilst saving time and resources and avoiding duplication of work.

10. Consolidating the approach through law

Roma are now the most rejected and marginalised minority in Europe, as confirmed by all reports, whether from official or NGO sources. The General Conclusions of the European Conference against Racism (EUROCONF (2000)7 final) and the political declaration adopted by the ministers of Council of Europe member states in October 2000 at the concluding session of this conference (EUROCONF (2000)1 final) are unequivocal in this respect. In the General Conclusions:

> The European Conference underlines the necessity for participating States to pay particular attention to and adopt immediate and concrete measures to eradicate the widespread discrimination and persecution targeting Roma, Gypsies, Sinti and Travellers, including through the establishment of structures and processes, in partnership between the public authorities and representatives of the Roma, Gypsies, Sinti and Travellers.

In their political declaration, governments committed themselves "to develop effective policies and implementation mechanisms and exchange good practices for the full achievement of equality for Roma/Gypsies and Travellers".

Even before the growing rejection of Roma that marked 2007 and the following years, the Deputy Secretary General of the Council of Europe, Maud de Boer-Buquicchio, spoke on 8 April 2006 (International Roma Day) on the need for radical action:

> Europe also has a duty to protect the Roma community from the systematic, regular and repetitive racism its members continue to be victims of across Europe on an almost daily basis. Sometimes this persecution takes the form of violent acts committed by deranged individuals or groups, which is terrible. Very often, it takes form of official acts, which is even worse. ... [We need] to overcome not only years, but generations of accumulated injustice and accumulated pain.

In their Recommendation CM/Rec(2008)5 on policies for Roma and/or Travellers in Europe, the Committee of Ministers emphasised:

> that Roma and Travellers have faced, for more than five centuries, widespread and enduring discrimination, rejection and marginalisation all over Europe and in all areas of life; and were targeted victims of the Holocaust; and that forced displacement, discrimination and exclusion from participation in social life have resulted in poverty and disadvantage for many Roma and Traveller communities and individuals across Europe.

In August 2008, the Council of Europe Commissioner for Human Rights, Thomas Hammarberg, stated that "today's rhetoric against the Roma is very similar to the one used by Nazis and fascists before the mass killings started in the thirties and forties. Once more, it is argued that the Roma are a threat to safety and public health". The Parliamentary Assembly's Committee on Legal Affairs and Human Rights, in its February 2010 report,[32] said that it was:

> shocked by recent outrages against Roma in several Council of Europe member states, reflecting an increasing trend in Europe towards anti-Gypsyism of the worst kind.
>
> 3. Taking advantage of the financial crisis, extremist groups capitalise on fears deriving from the equation made between Roma and criminals, choosing a scapegoat that presents an easy target, as Roma are among the most vulnerable groups of all.
>
> 4. This situation is reminiscent of the darkest hours in Europe's history.

Not only the increased rejection of Roma but also the specific nature of discrimination against them has attracted attention. Thus a 2007 decision of the European Court of Human Rights pointed out that:

> as a result of their turbulent history and constant uprooting the Roma have become a specific type of disadvantaged and vulnerable minority ... they therefore require special protection.

And in Recommendation CM/Rec(2008)5 the Committee of Ministers emphasised that anti-Gypsyism is:

> a specific form of racism and intolerance, leading to hostile acts ranging from exclusion to violence against Roma and/or Traveller communities.

Given the convergence and serious nature of these conclusions, together with the fact that states are very often slow to do anything to improve the situation, there has been a growing call for legal instruments and procedures to penalise failure to respect the fundamental rights of Roma. This approach was initiated years ago on an ad hoc basis, and most of the texts adopted make reference to legal instruments. Some cover specific aspects, such as the first Recommendation No. R (83) 1 of the Committee of Ministers, described above, on stateless nomads and nomads of undetermined nationality: it recommends that member states give effect to principles of non-discrimination with regard to such matters as links with a state and residence and movement of nomads. Over the following years, the Ad hoc Committee of Experts for Identity Documents and Movement of Persons (CAHID) worked on these issues. The work of the Ad hoc Committee of Experts on the Legal Aspects of Territorial Asylum, Refugees and Stateless Persons (CAHAR) also had implications for Roma. The Steering Committee for Equality between Women and Men, which in September 1995 organised the first hearing of Roma women, also did so as part of its work to combat

---

32. "The situation of Roma in Europe and relevant activities of the Council of Europe", report by the Committee on Legal Affairs and Human Rights, rapporteur: József Berényi, 26 February 2010 (Doc. 12174). This report was discussed in the chapter on the Parliamentary Assembly.

racism, xenophobia and intolerance, and this meeting highlighted the twofold discrimination suffered by Roma women, as women and as Roma.[33]

Let us now look at a number of structural activities with an important legal element which have been consolidated over recent years and which are particularly appropriate for consideration of the Roma's situation.

The work of the European Commission against Racism and Intolerance and recognition of anti-Gypsyism as a specific form of racism

The European Commission against Racism and Intolerance (ECRI) was set up in 1993 at the 1st Summit of Heads of State and Government of the Council of Europe (mainly concerning, as we have seen, the question of minorities). Its statute was redefined by Committee of Ministers Resolution Res(2002)8, which states:

> ECRI shall be a body of the Council of Europe entrusted with the task of combating racism, racial discrimination, xenophobia, anti-Semitism and intolerance in greater Europe from the perspective of the protection of human rights, in the light of the European Convention on Human Rights, its additional protocols and related case law. It shall pursue the following objectives:
>
> – to review member states' legislation, policies and other measures to combat racism, xenophobia, anti-Semitism and intolerance, and their effectiveness;
>
> – to propose further action at local, national and European level;
>
> – to formulate general policy recommendations to member states;
>
> – to study international legal instruments applicable in the matter with a view to their reinforcement where appropriate.
>
> ...
>
> In the framework of its country-by-country approach, ECRI shall monitor phenomena of racism, racial discrimination, xenophobia, anti-Semitism and intolerance, by closely examining the situation in each of the member states of the Council of Europe. ECRI shall draw up reports containing its factual analyses as well as suggestions and proposals as to how each country might deal with any problems identified.

Members of ECRI are independent and impartial, and there is one member for each member state. In an innovative country-by-country monitoring procedure, country reports are published only after a process of dialogue with each country concerned, making it possible to monitor and identify changes in those countries' situations. In addition to preparing regular reports for each country, ECRI works on general themes of particular significance in combating racism and xenophobia and adopts general policy recommendations in

---

33. "Hearing of Roma/Gypsy Women of West, Central, and Eastern Europe", report, EG/TSI (95)2. The repercussions of the hearing were all the more important as a European Roma women's network was set up as a result.

these fields. There are 13 of these recommendations (the first was published in 1996 and the latest in 2011), which deal with issues such as anti-Semitism, education, policing and sport. Recommendation No. 3 on combating racism and intolerance against Roma/Gypsies, adopted in March 1998, directly concerns the situation of Roma:

> Noting that Roma/Gypsies suffer throughout Europe from persisting prejudices, are victims of a racism which is deeply-rooted in society, are the target of sometimes violent demonstrations of racism and intolerance and that their fundamental rights are regularly violated or threatened;
>
> ...
>
> recommends the following to Governments of member states:
>
> ...
>
> – bearing in mind the manifestations of racism and intolerance of which Roma/Gypsies are victims, to give a high priority to the effective implementation of the provisions contained in ECRI's general policy recommendation N° 1, which requests that the necessary measures should be taken to ensure that national criminal, civil and administrative law expressly and specifically counter racism, xenophobia, anti-Semitism and intolerance;
>
> – to ensure that discrimination as such, as well as discriminatory practices, are combated through adequate legislation and to introduce into civil law specific provisions to this end, particularly in the fields of employment, housing and education;
>
> – to render illegal any discrimination on the part of public authorities in the exercise of their duties;
>
> – to ensure that suitable legal aid be provided for Roma/Gypsies who have been victims of discrimination and who wish to take legal action;
>
> – to take the appropriate measures to ensure that justice is fully and promptly done in cases concerning violations of the fundamental rights of Roma/Gypsies;
>
> – to ensure in particular that no degree of impunity is tolerated as regards crimes committed against Roma/Gypsies and to let this be clearly known among the general public;
>
> – to set up and support specific training schemes for persons involved at all levels in the various components of the administration of justice, with a view to promoting cultural understanding and an awareness of prejudice;
>
> – to encourage the development of appropriate arrangements for dialogue between the police, local authorities and Roma/Gypsy communities;
>
> – to encourage awareness-raising among media professionals, both in the audio-visual field and in the written press, of the particular responsibility they bear in not transmitting prejudices when practising their profession, and in particular in avoiding reporting incidents involving individuals who happen to be members of the Roma/Gypsy community in a way which blames the Roma/Gypsy community as a whole;

- to take the necessary steps to ensure that rules concerning the issue of *de jure* and *de facto* access to citizenship and the right to asylum are drawn up and applied so as not to lead to particular discrimination against Roma/Gypsies;
- to ensure that the questions relating to "travelling" within a country, in particular regulations concerning residence and town planning, are solved in a way which does not hinder the way of life of the persons concerned;
- to develop institutional arrangements to promote an active role and participation of Roma/Gypsy communities in the decision-making process, through national, regional and local consultative mechanisms, with priority placed on the idea of partnership on an equal footing;
- to take specific measures to encourage the training of Roma/Gypsies, to ensure full knowledge and implementation of their rights and of the functioning of the legal system;
- to pay particular attention to the situation of Roma/Gypsy women, who are often the subject of double discrimination, as women and as Roma/Gypsies;
- to vigorously combat all forms of school segregation towards Roma/Gypsy children and to ensure the effective enjoyment of equal access to education;
- to introduce into the curricula of all schools information on the history and culture of Roma/Gypsies and to provide training programmes in this subject for teachers;
- to support the activities of non-governmental organisations, which play an important role in combating racism and intolerance against Roma/Gypsies and which provide them in particular with appropriate legal assistance;
- to encourage Roma/Gypsy organisations to play an active role, with a view to strengthening civil society;
- to develop confidence-building measures to preserve and strengthen an open and pluralistic society with a view to a peaceful co-existence.[34]

Other general policy recommendations are of fundamental importance for Roma, such as Recommendation No. 7 on national legislation to combat racism and racial discrimination, and Recommendation No. 10 on combating racism and racial discrimination in and through school education.

Most states have so far been covered by three reports, and fourth reports are gradually being drawn up for a number of countries. The fourth-cycle reports currently in progress cover five priority areas: the legal and institutional framework, discrimination in various fields, racist violence, racism in public discourse, and vulnerable/target groups for racism. Roma often figure in these periodic (five-year) country reports,[35] often to a considerable

---

34. Although much of the text is quoted here in view of its importance, it is worth reading it in its entirety on the Council of Europe website, where it is available in over 30 languages. A compilation of ECRI's 12 recommendations can also be downloaded in nine languages.
35. Roma are mentioned in 117 of the 135 reports available by May 2010. All reports can be accessed online, and reference should also be made to press releases and statements, which often mention the Roma issue.

extent. ECRI has also published several compendia of examples of best practice, one of which covers Roma: "Practical examples in combating racism and intolerance against Roma/Gypsies" (CRI (2001) 28). This publication makes reference to Recommendation No. 3 and presents measures and examples that may assist with its implementation. The examples are grouped together in three main fields: empowering Roma to participate in decision-making and politics; education and youth; and policing and justice.

ECRI's annual reports, which offer an overview of major trends during the year in question, regularly address the issue of Roma. The 1997 report, which refers to the preparation of the above-mentioned Recommendation No. 3, explains:

> Noting that Roma/Gypsies suffer throughout Europe from persisting prejudices, are victims of a racism which is deeply-rooted in society, are the target of sometimes violent demonstrations of racism and intolerance, and that their fundamental rights are regularly violated or threatened, ECRI aims to encourage by this future recommendation a series of measures with a view to combating manifestations of racism and intolerance and discriminatory practices against Roma/Gypsies.

From 1998 to 2002, the same facts were noted every year. The 2002 report emphasised that:

> Roma/Gypsies are particularly the target of racism in many countries. They suffer from prejudices and discrimination in many fields of social and economic life and are also often the object of violent acts of racism and intolerance.

Discrimination was more acute in 2003:

> Roma/Gypsies are a target for racism throughout Europe, to the extent that they do not, in our society, enjoy equal rights, which is however, a fundamental human right. Most members of Roma/Gypsy communities are victims of numerous and varied human right violations.

And they began to form the subject of special round tables organised by ECRI in various states. The 2004 report offered some important details:

> Roma/Gypsies/Travellers are singled out as a particular target for racism throughout Europe. During its second round of country-by-country reports, ECRI monitored the situation with regard to racism and intolerance in 43 member states of the Council of Europe: the problems encountered by Roma/Gypsies are covered in 32 of the 43 reports and in 10 of these reports, ECRI considered that they were issues of particular concern. This finding applies to countries in western Europe as much as to those in eastern Europe. It can be said that most members of the Roma/Gypsy community are victims of numerous and varied human rights violations and that racism and racial discrimination are in many cases central elements of these violations.

In 2007, the report stressed that there had been an appreciable increase in discrimination against Roma in Europe:

> Roma and Travellers throughout Europe are the victims of anti-Gypsyism, which takes the form of racist remarks, discrimination and sometimes violence against Roma and Travellers. This trend, far from being reversed, has recently become

more pronounced with the adoption by some member states of measures facilitating the expulsion of members of these communities and with the tone of public debate on the adoption of such measures. Sustained, intensified efforts must be made to combat the particular forms of exclusion and segregation to which Roma and Travellers are subjected, in particular in schools.

In 2008:

anti-Gypsyism continued to be a worrying problem, with extreme forms of racism and discrimination being experienced by Roma and Travellers in some Council of Europe member states, including instances of raids and attacks against their settlements. Public opinion continued to be openly hostile towards Roma and Travellers in many European countries, sometimes encouraged by political figures who incited racial hatred against this group often for electoral purposes. In parallel, there was greater public awareness of the discrimination and social exclusion faced by Roma and Travellers in many areas including housing, education and employment, partly as a result of increased activism by organisations representing this minority. Programmes in favour of Roma and Travellers adopted and implemented by member states continued to improve the situation in some respects. However, in order to be efficient, such programmes need to be fully implemented and their impact duly monitored and assessed.

At its 50th plenary session in December 2009, ECRI discussed options for combating racism and xenophobia more effectively at a time when tensions were being exacerbated with regard to migrant and minority populations.

In June 2011, ECRI adopted its General Policy Recommendation No. 13 on combating anti-Gypsyism and discrimination against Roma. The text covers a number of fields, including education, employment and housing.

Contribution of the Commissioner for Human Rights of the Council of Europe

In Resolution (1999) 50 adopted in May 1999, the Committee of Ministers decided to establish the office of Commissioner for Human Rights. This independent person is elected for six years by the Parliamentary Assembly from a list of three candidates provided by the Committee of Ministers. The resolution (Article 3) states that:

The Commissioner shall:

a. promote education in and awareness of human rights in the member states;

b. contribute to the promotion of the effective observance and full enjoyment of human rights in the member states;

c. provide advice and information on the protection of human rights and prevention of human rights violations. When dealing with the public, the Commissioner shall, wherever possible, make use of and co-operate with human rights structures in the member states. Where such structures do not exist, the Commissioner will encourage their establishment;

d. facilitate the activities of national ombudsmen or similar institutions in the field of human rights;

e. identify possible shortcomings in the law and practice of member states concerning the compliance with human rights as embodied in the instruments of the Council of Europe, promote the effective implementation of these standards by member states and assist them, with their agreement, in their efforts to remedy such shortcomings;

f. address, whenever the Commissioner deems it appropriate, a report concerning a specific matter to the Committee of Ministers or to the Parliamentary Assembly and the Committee of Ministers;

g. respond, in the manner the Commissioner deems appropriate, to requests made by the Committee of Ministers or the Parliamentary Assembly, in the context of their task of ensuring compliance with the human rights standards of the Council of Europe;

h. submit an annual report to the Committee of Ministers and the Parliamentary Assembly;

i. co-operate with other international institutions for the promotion and protection of human rights while avoiding unnecessary duplication of activities.

The Commissioner is in constant dialogue with member state authorities, makes recommendations, promotes awareness of human rights and publishes a variety of documents. The first Commissioner Alvaro Gil-Robles, during his term of office from October 1999 to March 2006, paid regular attention to the Roma issue. The reports produced after his visits to various countries are proof of this, and an overview is provided in the European report that he put out in 2006 on the human rights situation of Roma, Sinti and Travellers in Europe.[36] Recommendations were put forward in the fields of housing, education, employment and health and also concerned racially motivated violence and relations with law-enforcement authorities, while others covered asylum, displacement and trafficking in human beings. In his final report (CommDH(2006)17, 29 March 2006), the Commissioner stressed the importance of thematic reports "analysing structural or recurring human rights challenges identified in several Council of Europe member states during official visits", and he added that he had managed to produce only one such report, right at the end of his term of office – the report on Roma.

On 8 April 2006, to mark International Roma Day just one week after he had taken office, the new Commissioner Thomas Hammarberg drew attention to the situation of Roma in a statement which is here reproduced in full, since it provides a summary of the various aspects of the situation and demonstrates that throughout his term of office the Commissioner would pay close attention to the situation of Roma:

> On the eve of the International Roma Day, we should remember the long history of discrimination and persecution of the Roma, including the *porrajmos*. Through years the Roma have suffered persistent ignorance and prejudice from the

---

36. Alvaro Gil-Robles, Commissioner for Human Rights, "Final report on the human rights situation of the Roma, Sinti and Travellers in Europe", for the attention of the Committee of Ministers and the Parliamentary Assembly, 15 February 2006, CommDH(2006)1.

majority population. In Europe today, all too many Roma women, men and children continue to experience multiple discrimination in their daily lives. They are also often hidden from the public view by unemployment and isolation in Roma settlements or special schools.

International and European human rights standards clearly provide for equality before the law and prohibit discrimination on the grounds of ethnicity. There is no place for racism in a democratic society. Governments have a positive duty to bring about equality of opportunity for all. Improved access to housing, education, employment and health care is key for many Roma.

National action plans are one means of addressing these issues and I am aware that new plans have been drawn up in connection with the Decade of Roma Inclusion, 2005-2015. I will follow the implementation of these strategies during my country visits. Moreover, in a growing number of countries, the establishment of low-threshold complaints bodies such as specialised ombudspersons and anti-discrimination tribunals has already made it easier for the Roma, among others, to access genuine justice.

The institutions and monitoring bodies of the Council of Europe have strived to uphold the full enjoyment of human rights by Roma. This is definitely a priority for the Commissioner for Human Rights and will continue to be so under my mandate. Co-operation with the European Roma and Travellers Forum and other bodies representing Roma will be important.

We should also bridge the knowledge gap. Europeans must learn more about Roma, their history and the diversity of their identities. Roma should be visible in all walks of life. Local authorities have to engage in an active process of mutual integration. In many European municipalities, policies of inclusion and raising awareness have yielded promising results. It is through living, working and learning together that we can eradicate our ignorance and prejudice.

The realisation of Roma inclusion will reinforce everyday democracy and the rule of law. It is the only way to reach a society of substantive equality where everyone has the right to participate and to be heard.[37]

Indeed, the Commissioner decided to include protection of the human rights of Roma and especially enforcement of the non-discrimination principle for the latter among his thematic priorities. Thus he regularly encouraged awareness among the general public by publishing his "Viewpoints": articles dealing with subjects which the Commissioner has encountered and which he felt it was important to address. Their intention was not to cover every aspect of the subject in question but to raise vital issues and suggest options for practical action. A significant number of "Viewpoints" dealt with Roma and tackle a range of issues. A list of titles and dates is given below:

- Forced eviction of Roma families must stop [4 September 2006]
- Roma job seekers are discriminated against [2 April 2007]

---

37. "Europeans must learn more about Roma", statement by Thomas Hammarberg, Council of Europe Commissioner for Human Rights, 8 April 2006, on the occasion of International Roma Day, CommDH/Speech(2006)2.

- Hate crimes – the ugly face of racism, anti-Semitism, anti-Gypsyism, Islamophobia and homophobia [21 July 2008]
- The key to the promotion of Roma rights: early and inclusive education [31 March 2008]
- The shameful history of anti-Gypsyism is forgotten – and repeated [18 August 2008]
- Roma representatives must be welcomed into political decision-making [1 September 2008]
- Anti-Gypsyism continues to be a major human rights problem in Europe – governments must start taking serious action against both official and interpersonal discrimination of Roma [27 April 2009]
- Many Roma in Europe are stateless and live outside social protection [6 July 2009]
- European migration policies discriminate against Roma people [22 February 2010]

Only a few brief extracts are given here. On 2 April 2007 the Commissioner stated that:[38]

> The seriousness of anti-Ziganism demonstrates that we cannot eradicate it through measures aiming at formal equality alone. Roma must reach effective equality of opportunity with everyone else and this clearly requires positive measures to compensate for long-term discrimination and prejudice. Otherwise the situation of many Roma will get worse rather than better.
>
> Special measures are justified when they pursue a legitimate aim and are proportionate to the objective. Governments should draw up dedicated strategies which can effectively bring about equality of opportunity for Roma in employment, education, housing and health care.
>
> There is a shameful implementation deficit on Roma rights. The issue has been put on the agenda of all major international organisations and national governments in Europe, for example through national action plans – but this has not had much impact. Policies have lacked adequate resources, co-ordination and involvement of local authorities.

On 27 April 2009:

> We know that the Roma population – whether citizens, displaced persons or migrants – is worse off than any other group in Europe in relation to key social indicators on: education, health, employment, housing and political participation.
>
> ...
>
> At the same time, we have to conclude that progress is slow. We have learned that there is no single reform or action which would cause a quick change for the better. Though, for example, a strong investment in education, including pre-schooling, for Roma children is essential, the results would still depend on other

---

38. Full texts of all the documents cited are available on the Council of Europe website and on the Commissioner's website: www.commissioner.coe.int.

improvements, such as ensuring better housing conditions and enhanced health care. A comprehensive but also participatory and sustained programme is needed.

What is absolutely essential is to combat anti-Gypsyism. The continued negative attitudes of many in the majority population is a deep problem. Without changes in these all the programmes will fail.

And on 22 February 2010:

Discrimination of Roma in migration policies has met with little or no opposition in almost every country. This may not be surprising in view of the lingering anti-Gypsyism in large parts of Europe.

However, it is high time to review the approach.

To push Roma families between countries, as now happens, is inhumane. It victimises children – many of whom were born and grown up in the host countries before they were deported.

As part of his continuing dialogue with member state authorities, the Commissioner makes targeted visits to examine one or more specific issues concerning human rights protection in the various member states. After the visit, a report may be published containing conclusions and recommendations for improving the human rights situation in the country concerned. Human rights protection for Roma is the subject of conclusions and recommendations in a large number of reports. Following his visit, the Commissioner may also send letters to prime ministers and ministers of the interior of member states. The Roma issue features in these letters and sometimes is the subject itself of these communications, for example with regard to forced returns to Kosovo, treatment of Roma by the police, or other acts of discrimination.

As part of his thematic work, the Commissioner has also carried out important research in the field of human rights protection for Roma and has brought out, together with the OSCE High Commissioner on National Minorities, a study on recent Roma migration in Europe.[39] A study on the human rights situation of Roma and Travellers in Europe was published in February 2012.

Summary indicators are to be found in the Commissioner's annual reports. Already in the first report covering 2006 (CommDH(2007)3) Roma are mentioned on several occasions, with a sub-section addressing their issues. In 2007, the situation of Roma was again among the priority themes, especially with respect to housing and evictions (CommDH(2008)10Rev). The 2008 annual activity report (CommDH(2009)12) deals at length with the Roma under its thematic priorities and makes reference to the rise in discrimination:

Roma and Travellers in Europe continue to suffer systematic discrimination in all major social sectors in most of the Council of Europe member states. The Commissioner observed and expressed his particular concern about a strong trend of anti-Gypsyism that continued unabated or was even strengthened in certain member states in 2008

---

39. Claude Cahn and Elspeth Guild, "Recent migration of Roma in Europe", CommDH(2009)37, 22 April 2009.

...

> The human rights of Roma in Europe are linked to the effective general protection of minorities by member states. Roma are a pan-European minority with a particularly long history of continued discrimination and intolerance, occasionally amounting to persecution – a minority that comprises approximately 10 million people. The Commissioner pointed out in his speeches and other publications the essential role national action plans may play in the effective implementation of human rights standards. He also invited member states to ratify or further promote the implementation of the Framework Convention for the Protection of National Minorities and the European Charter for Regional or Minority Languages.

In his 2009 report (CommDH(2010)8), the Commissioner emphasised concerns relating to discriminatory treatment of Roma, especially those forced to migrate, and found that the general situation remained difficult:

> Extremist groups and parties are more active and threatening. Groups such as Roma, already very vulnerable, are more and more targeted and suffer particularly violent attacks. Mainstream political parties and the majority population display a weak and confusing reaction to these trends.

...

> Roma and Travellers continued to be subject to racism and pervasive discrimination across all social sectors in most Council of Europe member states in 2009. Progress in tackling poverty among Roma and enhancing their socio-economic status continued to be slow. The Commissioner identified anti-Gypsyism as a crucial cause for such slow progress and focused extensively on combating this phenomenon throughout the year. In a Viewpoint he published on 27 April ("Anti-Gypsyism continues to be a major human rights problem in Europe – governments must start taking serious action against both official and interpersonal discrimination of Roma"), the Commissioner underlined that no programme aimed at improving the situation of Europe's Roma populations can be successful without resolute action to combat anti-Gypsyism. States must therefore promote Roma culture, knowledge of Roma history and effectively combat hate speech.

Judgments of the European Court of Human Rights: recognition of discrimination suffered by Roma

The European Court of Human Rights, according to the information brief on its website:

> is an international court set up in 1959. It rules on individual or state applications alleging violations of the civil and political rights set out in the European Convention on Human Rights. Since 1998 it has sat as a full-time court and individuals can apply to it directly.

> In almost 50 years the Court has delivered more than 10 000 judgments. These are binding on the countries concerned and have led governments to alter their legislation and administrative practice in a wide range of areas. The Court's case law makes the Convention a powerful living instrument for meeting new challenges and consolidating the rule of law and democracy in Europe.

...

> The European Convention on Human Rights is an international treaty under which the member states of the Council of Europe promise to secure fundamental civil and political rights, not only to their own citizens but also to everyone within their jurisdiction.

The Court consists of one judge for each state, appointed for six years by the Parliamentary Assembly from a list of three names provided by the state concerned. The judges are totally independent. Applications can be lodged by states, but in actual fact virtually all applications are lodged by individuals who have brought their cases directly to the Court alleging one or more violations of the European Convention on Human Rights. Cases can be referred to the Court simply by sending in a duly completed application form, and the procedure is free of charge. At present, the Court receives some 30 000 applications every year. For an application to be admissible, domestic remedies must first have been exhausted (in the various courts up to the highest level) and the rights violated must be rights enshrined in the Convention. States are under an obligation to execute judgments delivered by the Court, and domestic legislation will have to be amended if proved to be out of line with the Convention.

Article 14 ("Prohibition of discrimination") is particularly relevant to the situation of minorities:

> The enjoyment of the rights and freedoms set forth in this Convention shall be secured without discrimination on any ground such as sex, race, colour, language, religion, political or other opinion, national or social origin, association with a national minority, property, birth or other status.

As one judge put it, when analysing the Court's case law:

> The word "secured" in Article 14 ECHR implies the placing of an obligation on the Contracting States. This obligation is not only a simply negative one in the sense of a mere abstention to intervene, but includes positive actions of the state. Thus a discrimination within the meaning of Article 14 ECHR may occur even when a person or group is treated without proper justification less favourably than another, although the more favourable treatment may not be called for by the Convention.[40]

With this in view, a number of protocols have been added to the Convention. Particularly important here is Protocol No. 12, which entered into force in 2005. This took up and strengthened the above-mentioned Article 14 and was wholly given over to discrimination. Article 1 ("General prohibition of discrimination") provides that:

> 1. The enjoyment of any right set forth by law shall be secured without discrimination on any ground such as sex, race, colour, language, religion, political or other opinion, national or social origin, association with a national minority, property, birth or other status.
>
> 2. No one shall be discriminated against by any public authority on any ground such as those mentioned in paragraph 1.

---

40. Kemper G. (1995), "Aliens, immigrants, Gypsies and other Travellers", Council of Europe, *Exclusion, equality before the law and non-discrimination*, Council of Europe Publishing, Strasbourg, p. 134.

Since it is important for Roma to be able to lodge applications, the Roma and Travellers Division jointly organises, together with the Court, study sessions for lawyers dealing with Roma cases: 2010 saw the 14th session of this kind. The Roma and Travellers Division has also published a handbook for lawyers defending Roma and Travellers: *Ensuring access to rights for Roma and Travellers: the role of the European Court of Human Rights*.[41] This handbook explains the procedure for lodging an application with the Court and provides a summary of cases handled by the Court under specific articles of the Convention. Some cases concern Roma and others do not, but the latter may have direct implications for the situation of Roma. The Roma's situation makes them particularly vulnerable: the very fact of belonging to an ethnic group makes them a target for extreme right-wing groups, and central government owes them protection; some local authorities isolate Roma families in ghettos or put them on unsanitary sites where their health is at risk. All these situations are covered by the Convention and its additional protocols. The handbook has a chapter showing which articles are most frequently involved in Roma cases:

> They are: Article 2 (right to life), Article 3 (freedom from torture), Article 5 (right to liberty), Article 6 (fair trial), Article 8 (respect for private and family life), Article 14 (freedom from discrimination), and Article 4 of Protocol No. 4 to the Convention (prohibition of mass expulsions). Of course, other articles, for instance Article 10 (freedom of speech) and Article 11 (freedom of association), may apply in individual cases as well, but for the sake of brevity, they are not discussed further here. The Court's case law interpreting these articles is an important tool in combating prejudice and mistreatment of Roma, and in protecting their rights. Citations of cases involving Romani applicants are included, where applicable. In some instances, examples of situations that are common to Roma are offered to illustrate the principles, even though they may not yet represent actual cases before the Court.

As pointed out in a Court fact sheet from April 2010:

> Roma victims of discrimination have been able to turn to the Council of Europe's European Court of Human Rights, relying mainly on Article 14 of the European Convention on Human Rights, which prohibits discrimination in relation to the other rights and freedoms protected by the Convention. As we look back on 60 years of the Convention, some of the cases which the Court has had to decide provide telling examples of the challenges faced by Roma. Behind each case were individual applicants who persevered in their fight to assert their rights and were ultimately rewarded by a judgment in Strasbourg in their favour.

---

41. Council of Europe, 2009, available online from the Council of Europe/Roma and Travellers Division website. In 1998, the Gypsy Research Centre of the Université René-Descartes (Paris), with the co-operation and support of the Council of Europe and the European Roma Rights Centre (ERRC) in Budapest, organised a seminar in Strasbourg to draw up a programme of work for Roma rights. This meeting was used to lay down working guidelines and set up specific projects to be developed over time: studies and research, information through a database for legal experts and lawyers, and training through the publication of handbooks and the organisation of seminars for professionals.

Applications expressly relating to Roma have been lodged and declared admissible since 1996. The Court's first finding against a state concerned the ill-treatment by police and illegal pre-trial detention of three Roma; the judgment was based on violations of Article 3 of the Convention (right to an effective official investigation), Article 5, paragraph 3 (right to be brought promptly before a judge and to trial within a reasonable time), Article 5, paragraph 4 (right to an effective remedy regarding the lawfulness of detention), Article 13 (right to an effective remedy) and Article 25, paragraph 1 (right to an effective remedy, right to lodge an individual application with the European Court of Human Rights). The second case concerned an application relating to police brutality after the death of a Rom in police custody; the Court found the state guilty of violating Article 2 (death of the applicant's partner and lack of an effective investigation) and Article 13 (right to an effective remedy).[42]

By June 2010, the Court had delivered some 20 judgments concerning Roma. They cover 10 or so states in various parts of Europe and are indicative of a high level of discrimination widespread across Europe. In addition to the first two cases mentioned above, others have concerned, to cite only a few examples:

- living conditions of Roma villagers following involvement of police officers in the murder of several Roma and destruction of their homes (Nos. 41138/98 and 64320/01, judgment of 12 July 2005, violation of Article 14 taken in conjunction with Articles 6 and 8);

- placing of Roma children in "special schools" (No. 57325/00, judgment of 13 November 2007, violation of Article 14 read in conjunction with Article 2 of Protocol No. 1);

- police violence against a Roma boy (No. 42722/02, judgment of 4 April 2008, violation of Article 14 taken in conjunction with Article 3);

- denial of survivor's pension due to non-recognition of a traditional Roma marriage (No. 49151/07, judgment of 8 December 2009, violation of Article 14 taken together with Article 1 of Protocol No. 1).[43]

Looking at how the Court's case law has evolved, it would appear that the Court is very supportive of respect for minority rights (including Roma rights). In a report, "The protection of national minorities in the case law of

---

42. *Assenov and Others v. Bulgaria*, 90/1997/874/1086, judgment of 28 October 1998, and *Velikova v. Bulgaria* (App. No. 41448/98), judgment of 18 May 2000, respectively. The judgments are available online from the Hudoc database on the Council of Europe/European Court of Human Rights website: www.echr.coe.int/echr/en/hudoc.

43. References of other judgments not cited in the text: No. 38361/97, 13 June 2002; Nos. 43577/98 and 43579/98, 6 July 2005; No. 15250/02, 13 December 2005; No. 40116/02, 31 May 2007; No. 48254/99, 26 July 2007; No. 42722/02, 4 March 2008; No. 32526/05, 5 June 2008; No. 15766/03, 17 July 2008; Nos. 27996/06 and 34836/06, 22 December 2009; No. 14383/03, 7 January 2010; No. 15766/03, 16 March 2010; No. 37193/07, 25 March 2010; a number of applications concerning Roma are currently pending before the Court.

the European Court of Human Rights",[44] written by a judge and a lawyer at the Court, the authors stress the following:

> The Court appears to have "imperceptibly" and "indirectly" become the protector of national minorities. This protection is provided indirectly through the defence of individual rights, which can be enjoyed both individually and collectively.
>
> ...
>
> An examination of the Court's case law shows that the rights of national or other minorities are protected in particular by Articles 9 (freedom of thought, conscience and religion), 10 (freedom of expression) and 11 (freedom of association) of the Convention and Article 3 of Protocol No. 1 (right to free elections). These rights are central to all problems concerning minorities, as religion, language and traditions are all fundamental aspects of identity, and the possibility to exercise these rights in public or private, individually or collectively, is the means by which this identity can be acknowledged, transmitted and preserved.
>
> ...
>
> With a view to protecting rights which are "practical and effective as opposed to theoretical and illusory", the Convention bodies have always applied the theory of "positive obligations" to a wide range of provisions. This approach is particularly important when the case concerns minorities, especially national minorities, because states not only have a duty to tolerate such minorities without interfering with their rights but also to take a more proactive attitude towards them.

In its judgments, which are gradually coming to form an important corpus of case law, the Court makes reference to the fact that Roma are in a vulnerable position. In *D.H. and Others v. the Czech Republic* (App. No. 57325/00) it notes that:

> the vulnerable position of Roma/Gypsies means that special consideration should be given to their needs and their different lifestyle both in the relevant regulatory framework and in reaching decisions in particular cases ... as a result of their turbulent history and constant uprooting the Roma have become a specific type of disadvantaged and vulnerable minority.

States are further urged to respect their way of life. In *Chapman v. the United Kingdom* (App. No. 27238/95) the Court stressed that "there is thus a positive obligation imposed on the Contracting States by virtue of Article 8 to facilitate the Gypsy way of life".

One example of practical follow-up for enforcement of the Court's judgments is to be found in the comments published on a particular case in a 2009 annual report from the Committee of Ministers on the Court's judgments:[45]

---

44. Françoise Tulkens, a judge at the European Court of Human Rights and President of the Second Section, and Stefano Piedimonte, a lawyer in the Research Division and Library of the Registry of the European Court of Human Rights, 7th meeting of the Committee of Experts on Issues relating to the Protection of National Minorities (DH-MIN), March 2008. The quotations given here are very reductive, and it is advisable to read the whole of this insightful and balanced text.
45. Committee of Ministers (2010), "Supervision of the execution of judgments of the European Court of Human Rights – Annual report, 2009", Council of Europe Publishing, Strasbourg, p. 180.

57325/00

Judgment of 13/11/2007, final on 13/11/2007

Discrimination in the enjoyment of the right to education due to the applicants' assignment to special schools between 1996 and 1999 on account of their Roma origin (Violation of Art. 14 in conjunction with Art. 2 of Prot. No. 1).

...

The legislation at the origin of this case has been repealed in 2005 and the current legislation provides that children with special educational needs, including socially disadvantaged children, are to be educated in ordinary primary schools. The effectiveness of these measures in practice has been contested before the CM [Committee of Ministers] by a specialised NGO (European Roma Rights Centre), according to which further progress remains needed to achieve real school desegregation.

In April 2009, the Czech authorities provided detailed information on the measures taken to increase the inclusiveness of education and improve Roma children's academic achievements. In June 2009, they submitted an action plan of further measures underway or envisaged. These measures include surveys aimed at identifying the causes of the problems and finding the most appropriate solutions; training and awareness-raising measures for teachers and Roma children's parents; better targeting of the counselling system; development of a National Plan of Inclusive Education.

The CM has requested information on the findings of the surveys and on the other measures taken to implement the action plan, having regard in particular to Recommendation No. R (2000) 4 of the CM to member states on the education of Roma/Gypsy children in Europe.

Statistical data remain also expected on the impact of the new Schools Act in practice, as well as information on awareness-raising of all actors concerned, including information on how the European Court of Human Rights' judgment has been disseminated to the competent authorities, apart from its translation and publication on the website of the Ministry of Justice.

Lastly, it is important to mention that in the course of its various judgments the Court has gradually clarified its appreciation of the facts. We may take as an illustration the Court's judgment of 13 June 2002 concerning Application No. 38361/97:

The applicant alleged that her son had been ill-treated by police officers and had died as a result, that the police had failed to provide adequate medical treatment for her son's injuries, that the authorities had failed to carry out an effective investigation, that her son's detention had been unlawful, that she did not have an effective remedy and that there had been discrimination on the basis of her son's Roma/Gypsy origin.

The applicant relied on Articles 2, 3, 5, 13 and 14 of the Convention.

The Court held unanimously that there had been a violation of Articles 2, 3, 5 and 13 of the Convention. But, by six votes to one, the Court ruled that there had been no violation of Article 14, whose importance was mentioned above.

One of the judges, Judge Bonello, then registered an extremely detailed partly dissenting opinion, from which it is worth quoting a few passages:

> 1. I concurred with my colleagues in all the votes but one. I could not subscribe to the majority view that, in the present case, there has been no infringement of the prohibition against discrimination (Article 14).
>
> 2. I consider it particularly disturbing that the Court, in over 50 years of pertinacious judicial scrutiny, has not, to date, found one single instance of violation of the right to life (Article 2) or the right not to be subjected to torture or to other degrading or inhuman treatment or punishment (Article 3) induced by the race, colour or place of origin of the victim [The Commission held, in 1973, that "differential treatment of a group of persons on the basis of race might therefore be capable of constituting degrading treatment when different treatment on some other ground would raise no such question" (*East African Asians v. the United Kingdom*, Commission's report of 14 December 1973, Decisions and Reports 78-A)]. Leafing through the annals of the Court, an uninformed observer would be justified to conclude that, for over 50 years democratic Europe has been exempted from any suspicion of racism, intolerance or xenophobia. The Europe projected by the Court's case law is that of an exemplary haven of ethnic fraternity, in which peoples of the most diverse origin coalesce without distress, prejudice or recrimination. The present case energises that delusion.
>
> 3. Frequently and regularly the Court acknowledges that members of vulnerable minorities are deprived of life or subjected to appalling treatment in violation of Article 3; but not once has the Court found that this happens to be linked to their ethnicity. Kurds, coloureds, Muslims, Roma and others are again and again killed, tortured or maimed, but the Court is not persuaded that their race, colour, nationality or place of origin has anything to do with it. Misfortunes punctually visit disadvantaged minority groups, but only as the result of well-disposed coincidence.
>
> ...
>
> 13. So long as the Court persists in requiring in human rights disputes a standard of proof that 50 years experience has shown it to be as unreal as it is unrealistic and unrealisable, it will, in effect, only continue to pay lip-service to the guarantees it then makes impossible to uphold. The way forward, in my view, lies in a radical and creative rethinking of the Court's approach, leading to the removal of the barriers which, in some important human rights domains, make the Court an inept trustee of the Convention. The Court has often risen to the challenge in spectacularly visionary manners, and ought, in matters of ethnic discrimination, to succumb with pride to its own tradition of trail blazing.
>
> ...
>
> 18. The Court has thus at its disposal a notable arsenal of weapons with which to break the stalemate that has not allowed it, throughout 50 years of activity, to censure one single act of racial discrimination in areas of deprivation of life or inhuman treatment. Ideally it should reconsider whether the standards of proof should not be the more juridically justifiable ones of preponderance of evidence or of a balance of probabilities. Alternatively it should, in my view, hold that when a member of a disadvantaged minority group suffers harm in

an environment where racial tensions are high and impunity of state offenders epidemic, the burden to prove that the event was not ethnically induced shifts to the government.[46]

The Court subsequently confirmed in certain cases that there had indeed been a violation of Article 14. Clear evidence of this is to be found in another case concerning Roma (App. No. 57325/00, judgment of 13 November 2007) in the dissenting opinion of Judge Borrego, who nevertheless believes that the Court is embarking too quickly on this course:

> In 2002 Judge Bonello said that he found it "particularly disturbing that the Court, in over 50 years of pertinacious judicial scrutiny, has not, to date, found one single instance of violation of the right [guaranteed by] ... Article 2 or ... Article 3 induced by the race ... of the victim" (*Anguelova v. Bulgaria*, judgment of 13 June 2002, no. 38361/97, dissenting opinion). While I agree with Judge Bonello's criticism that the absence, five years ago, of a single case of racial discrimination concerning the core Convention rights was disturbing, the judgment in the present case has now got the Court off to a flying start. The Grand Chamber has in this judgment behaved like a Formula One car, hurtling at high speed into the new and difficult terrain of education and, in so doing, has inevitably strayed far from the line normally followed by the Court.

We can thus see that the case law that is gradually evolving and the frame of reference gradually being created on the basis of the European Convention on Human Rights are both to the advantage of Roma.

The European Social Charter

The European Social Charter, which safeguards social and economic rights, is held up as the "natural complement" to the European Convention on Human Rights, which safeguards democracy, human rights and the rule of law. Adopted in 1961, it was revised in 1996, which is why the latter text, which came into force in 1999, is now often referred to as the European Social Charter (revised). The Charter lays down rights and freedoms and establishes a supervisory mechanism to ensure that they are respected by the states parties. The rights guaranteed relate to daily existence: housing, health, education, employment, legal and social protection, free movement of persons, and non-discrimination. This list of fields alone suggests that this legal instrument is of particular relevance for Roma. Taking just the example of the free movement of persons – now crucial because of migration within Europe – the Charter secures the following rights: the right to family reunification, the right of nationals to leave the country, procedural safeguards in the event of expulsion, and simplification of immigration formalities for European workers.

Enforcement of the Charter and its monitoring procedure lies with the European Committee of Social Rights (ECSR), which has the task of

---

46. The entire document, together with other judgments and documents, can be consulted on the Council of Europe and European Court of Human Rights website: www.echr.coe.int/echr/en/hudoc.

determining whether or not law and practice in states parties are consistent with the Charter. By April 2012, 47 member states had signed the Charter, and 43 had ratified it. The ECSR consists of 15 independent members elected for a period of six years by the Committee of Ministers (eventually this role may fall to the Parliamentary Assembly). It adopts conclusions indicating whether or not the situation in individual countries complies with the Charter. In the case of collective complaints, it adopts decisions.

Practical experience shows that the Charter is particularly relevant to Roma and is being used to an ever-increasing extent. The first complaint (No. 15/2003), concerning a violation of Article 16 (the right of the family to social, legal and economic protection) was held to be admissible by the ECSR in June 2003. Under the monitoring procedure the ECSR forwarded its decision to the Committee of Ministers, which adopted a resolution on the state in question (ResChS(2005)11 of 8 June 2005). It is worth quoting passages from this resolution, which in this case concerns Greece, since the events referred to also occur in many other states of Europe:

> The Committee of Ministers,
>
> ...
>
> Having regard to the report transmitted by the European Committee of Social Rights, in which it found that the insufficiency of permanent dwellings, lack of temporary camping sites and forced evictions constitute a violation of Article 16 of the Charter for the following reasons:
>
> *"ii) As to the alleged insufficiency of permanent dwellings*
>
> 40. The Committee notes the allegation made by the complainant organisation that an estimated 100 000 Roma live in sub-standard housing conditions is corroborated by information from other bodies and was not convincingly denied by the government.
>
> 41. The government failed to provide information as to the estimated number of Roma living in what could be considered to be sub-standard housing. It provided information on the IAP which was adopted in 2001, the number of requests made for loans under the housing loans programme and information on measures taken or planned in the future. It acknowledged that the situation of Roma in certain settlements was unsatisfactory.
>
> 42. The Committee finds that Greece has failed to take sufficient measures to improve the living conditions of the Roma and that the measures taken have not yet achieved what is required by the Charter, notably by reason of the insufficient means for constraining local authorities or sanctioning them. It finds on the evidence submitted that a significant number of Roma are living in conditions that fail to meet minimum standards and therefore the situation is in breach of the obligation to promote the right of families to adequate housing laid down in Article 16.
>
> 43. In light of the excessive numbers of Roma living in sub-standard housing conditions, even taking into account that Article 16 imposes obligations of conduct and not always of results and noting the overarching aim of the Charter is to achieve social inclusion, the Committee holds that the situation is in violation of Article 16 of the Charter.

...

iii) As to the alleged insufficiency of temporary camping sites

46. The Committee notes that as a result of the terms of the 2003 Joint Ministerial Decision which concerns itinerant persons in general and the 1983 Ministerial Decision which expressly concerned the Roma, the conditions for temporary encampment as well as the conditions regarding the amenities are extremely strict and that in the absence of the diligence on the part of the local authorities on one hand to select appropriate sites and on the other the reluctance to carry out the necessary works to provide the appropriate infrastructure, Roma have an insufficient supply of appropriate camping sites.

47. The Committee therefore holds that the situation constitutes a violation of Article 16 of the Charter.

...

iv) As to the forced evictions and other sanctions

50. The Committee notes that the government provides no real information on evictions, (either statistics, or remedies for those unlawfully evicted or examples of relevant case law). It fails either to comment on or contradict the information provided by the ERRC on collective evictions of Roma both settled and itinerant without the provision of alternative housing and sometimes involving the destruction of personal property.

51. The Committee considers that illegal occupation of a site or dwelling may justify the eviction of the illegal occupants. However the criteria of illegal occupation must not be unduly wide, the eviction should take place in accordance with the applicable rules of procedure and these should be sufficiently protective of the rights of the persons concerned. The Committee considers that on these three grounds the situation is not satisfactory.

Having reiterated the monitoring committee's conclusions, together with the explanations and proposals from Greece, the Committee of Ministers noted that these proposals to improve the situation in compliance with the violated article had been implemented. In other cases, states have changed some aspects of their legislation in order to comply with the Charter. Collective Complaint No. 27/2004 concerned Italy, as summarised on the Council of Europe website:

The complaint, lodged on 28 June 2004, relates to Article 31 (right to housing) alone or in conjunction with Articles E (non-discrimination) of the Revised European Social Charter. The complaint alleges that the situation of Roma in Italy amounts to a violation of Article 31 of the Revised European Social Charter. In addition, it alleges that policies and practices in the field of housing constitute, *inter alia* racial discrimination and racial segregation, both contrary to Article 31 alone or read in conjunction with Article E.

It was declared admissible and the Committee of Ministers adopted Resolution ResChS(2006)4 of 3 May 2006, in which it "looks forward to Italy reporting, on the occasion of the submission of the next report concerning the relevant provisions of the Revised European Social Charter, that the situation has improved, and keeping the Committee of Ministers regularly informed of all progress made."

In a long appendix, the Italian authorities expand on the fact that they are trying to improve the situation and conclude thus:

> For all the above-mentioned reasons, the Italian delegation asks the Committee of Ministers to adopt a resolution which takes into account the progress achieved at local level as also recognised by the competent institutions of the Council of Europe, which also takes note of the work in progress on the drafting of a comprehensive strategy at national level and of the creation of a National Office against Discrimination.
>
> The Committee of Ministers will be kept regularly informed about further steps taken by Italian authorities to improve the present situation.

Complaint No. 31/2005, declared admissible and resulting in a Committee of Ministers Resolution ResChS(2007)2 of 5 September 2007, concerned Bulgaria:

> The complaint, lodged on 22 April 2005, relates to Article 16 (right to social, economic, and legal protection) alone or in combination with Article E (non-discrimination) of the Revised European Social Charter. It is alleged that the situation of Roma in Bulgaria amounts to a violation of the right to adequate housing.

Complaint No. 44/2007 once again concerned Bulgaria; it was declared admissible in December 2007, but the ECSR decided to strike the case from the list because "the complainant organisation … lacks the capacity to take part in further proceedings in respect of this complaint":

> The complaint registered on 8 August 2007 relates to Article 13§1 (the right to social and medical assistance) alone or in conjunction with Article E (non-discrimination) of the Revised European Social Charter. It is alleged that Bulgarian legislation as from 01/01/2008 will no longer ensure the right to adequate social assistance to unemployed persons without adequate resources. This will notably affect Roma and women.

Complaint No. 46/2007 also concerned Bulgaria. Declared admissible, it was the subject of a Committee of Ministers Resolution (ResChS(2010)1) on 31 March 2010:

> The complaint registered on 22 October 2007 relates to Article 11 (right to health) and Article 13 (right to social and medical assistance) alone or in conjunction with Article E (non-discrimination) of the Revised European Social Charter. It is alleged that legislation excludes a large number of Roma persons from health insurance coverage, that government policies do not adequately address the specific health risks affecting Romani communities, and that there is widespread discriminatory practices on the part of health-care practitioners against Roma in the provision of health services.

Complaint No. 48/2008 again concerned Bulgaria. Declared admissible, it led to a Committee of Ministers Resolution (ResChS(2010)2) on 31 March 2010:

The complaint registered on 28 March 2008 relates to Article 13§1 (the right to social and medical assistance) alone or in conjunction with Article E (non-discrimination) of the Revised European Social Charter. It is alleged that Bulgarian legislation as from 01/01/2008 will no longer ensure the right to adequate social assistance to unemployed persons without adequate resources. This will notably affect Roma and women.

Complaint No. 49/2008 concerns Greece; it was declared admissible in September 2008 and a decision was forwarded to the Committee of Ministers in December 2009. It is taking its course:

The complaint was registered on 28 March 2008. It is alleged that the Greek Government continues to forcibly evict Roma without providing suitable alternative accommodation. It also alleges that the Roma in Greece continue to suffer discrimination in access to housing in violation of Article 16 of the European Social Charter (Right of the family to social, legal and economic protection) alone or in conjunction with the non-discrimination clause in the preamble.

Complaint No. 51/2008 concerns France. It was declared admissible in September 2008 and a decision was forwarded to the Committee of Ministers in December 2009. It is taking its course:

The complaint was registered on 17 April 2008. The complainant organisation pleads a violation of Articles 16 (right of the family to social, legal and economic protection), 19 (right of migrant workers and their families to protection and assistance), 30 (right to protection against poverty and social exclusion) and 31 (right to housing), read alone or in conjunction with Article E (non-discrimination), on the grounds that Travellers in France are victims of injustice with regard to access to housing, *inter alia* social exclusion, forced eviction as well as residential segregation, sub-standard housing conditions and lack of security. Furthermore, France has failed to take measures to address the deplorable living conditions of Romani migrants from other Council of Europe member states.

Complaint No. 58/2009 concerns Italy. It was declared admissible in December 2009 and is taking its course:

The complaint was registered on 29 May 2009. The complainant organisation pleads a violation of Articles 16 (the right of the family to social, legal and economic protection), 19 (right of migrant workers and their families to protection and assistance), 30 (right to protection against poverty and social exclusion) and 31 (right to housing), read alone or in conjunction with Article E (non-discrimination) of the Revised Charter. The complainant organisation alleges that the recent so-called emergency security measures and racist and xenophobic discourse have resulted in unlawful campaigns and evictions leading to homelessness and expulsions, disproportionately targeting Roma and Sinti.

Complaint No. 61/2010 concerns Portugal:

The complaint was registered on 23 April 2010. The complainant organisation pleads a violation of Articles 16 (the right of the family to social, legal and economic protection), 30 (right to protection against poverty and social exclusion) and 31 (right to housing), read alone or in conjunction with Article E (non-discrimination) of the Revised Charter. The ERRC maintains that the sum of housing-related injustices in Portugal (including problems of access to social housing, sub-standard quality of housing, lack of access to basic utilities, residential segregation of Romani communities and other systemic violations of the right to housing) violates these provisions.

Of the 61 collective complaints lodged between 1998 and 2010, a significant number relate to Roma: we have mentioned 10, representing 17% of the total, but Roma also figure in other complaints concerning homeless people, migrants, children in difficulty, and discrimination in the various fields covered by the Charter.

In addition to handling and following up complaints, the ECSR has a reporting procedure. Annual reports from states parties provide an opportunity to review cross-cutting issues, including the situation of Roma, and to ascertain compliance with the Charter by the states having ratified it, especially states that have been the subject of an admissible complaint and a Committee of Ministers resolution. The ECSR then drafts conclusions for each state.[47] Thus, in the 2006 conclusions, Roma were mentioned for 25 states, especially in relation to Article 16 (right of the family to social, legal and economic protection) but sometimes in connection with other articles as well.

The collective complaints procedure, which came into force some years ago, has proved vital for Roma, since states were not voluntarily addressing the Roma issue in their reports. The fact that approved organisations are able to lodge complaints has considerably raised the profile of this issue. As the President of the ECSR explained in January 2010:[48]

> The Additional Protocol providing for a system of collective complaints which entered into force in 1998 in order to reinforce the traditional reporting procedure, has proven to be a new and innovative procedure. This has since been confirmed in practice as the collective complaints procedure both increases the efficiency of the Charter's supervisory mechanism and contributes to the implementation of the rights it lays down. The procedure also enables the European Committee of Social Rights, the body that is competent to assess from a legal standpoint compliance of national law and practice with the obligations arising from the Charter, to further clarify and refine the position it had adopted with regard to certain rights within the reporting procedure, and to contribute to jurisprudential developments regarding the rights laid down by the Charter.

The 10 complaints described previously were lodged by international NGOs, the majority of them by the ERRC.

By studying complaints and the findings of violations, it is possible to see which rights have been violated (right to housing, right to social protection, etc.) and accordingly observe that some rights have so far tended to escape attention. This is particularly the case for education. It is obviously one of

---

47. The national reports and the ECSR's conclusions can be found on the Council of Europe website.
48. "Newsletter of the European Committee of Social Rights (ECSR)", No. 2, January 2010.

the fields covered by the Charter, and a fact sheet has been produced on the subject:[49]

> The Charter is a major European treaty on social rights which secures, *inter alia* the right to education from primary to higher education and the right to vocational training through a range of provisions, i.e. Articles 9 (right to vocational guidance), 10 (right to vocational training), 15§1 (right to vocational training for persons with disabilities) and 17§1 (right of children to assistance, education, and training). It guarantees an accessible and effective primary and secondary education and vocational training system, as well as equal access to higher education.
>
> ...
>
> Particular attention must be paid to ensure that vulnerable groups benefit from the right to education and have equal access; for example children from minorities, children seeking asylum, refugee children ... Where necessary equal access to education for these children should be guaranteed through special measures. However special measures for Roma children must not involve the establishment of separate/segregated schooling facilities.

It is worth noting that, in the order of importance for complaints, which runs from 1 to 3, complaints concerning Roma matters are often classified as 1, that is, according to the Council of Europe website "High importance: new case law or decisions which make a significant contribution to the clarification or modification of the case law".

---

49. "The right to education under the European Social Charter", information document prepared by the Secretariat of the European Social Charter, 17 November 2006.

11. Beyond prejudice to culture and partnership

The Council of Europe has been consolidating its experience in the field of Roma policies for several decades: through the adoption of framework provisions by various bodies, presence of Roma in conventions and charters concerning minorities, minority languages and protection of human rights and social rights, and the introduction of co-ordinating and monitoring tools to link activities throughout the Organisation. This has allowed for a comprehensive and structural approach that transcends the boundaries created by an administrative structure.

Before looking to the future, it is important to present three activities that differ in nature but share the distinctive feature of crystallising a number of basic elements with regard to both strategy, as analysed in the chapter on education for Roma children, and the development of an intercultural approach. The first of these activities aims to go beyond prejudice and stereotyping, the second to promote the emergence and existence of Roma culture in Europe, and the third to establish a political partnership.

Going beyond prejudice: *Dosta!*

It is obvious that the Roma's situation is largely determined by the fact that the people around them know nothing or next to nothing about them. Misconceptions have accumulated over centuries, and it is these misconceptions that underlie attitudes to Roma. These attitudes in turn give rise to negative behaviour – both individual and official – which, as history has shown, can range from rejection to confinement to assimilation. Reality is overlaid by invention, and Roma are judged not for what they really are but for what they are constrained to be for political purposes: the image of Roma that is presented is used to justify the measures taken regarding them, and these measures then reinforce that image.[50]

Most of the above-mentioned resolutions and recommendations adopted by the Committee of Ministers, the Parliamentary Assembly and the Congress stress the significance of these social misrepresentations and the need to correct them. At the Warsaw Summit in May 2005, the heads of state and government of member states confirmed their "commitment to combat all

---

50. On the question of the functions and consequences of prejudice and stereotyping, see the chapter on "The imaginary Gypsy: manipulated images", in Jean-Pierre Liégeois, *Roma in Europe*, op. cit.

kinds of exclusion and insecurity of the Roma communities in Europe and to promote their full and effective equality."

ECRI, in its General Policy Recommendation No. 3 on Roma, stated in the preamble that "Roma/Gypsies suffer throughout Europe from persisting prejudices".

On 8 April 2006, International Roma Day, the Deputy Secretary General of the Council of Europe dwelt on this fact:

> Silence has always been an accomplice of crime and persecution and in this respect Europe has a debt to its Roma ... We have a duty to educate. It would be difficult to find an example of more deeper rooted, more widespread and more persisting prejudice than the one against Roma which continues to blind so many of our fellow Europeans. The only way out is to teach – about Roma, about tolerance, about acceptance and about respect.

The Commissioner for Human Rights frequently returns to the subject, as recorded in CommDH/Speech(2006)2:

> Through years the Roma have suffered persistent ignorance and prejudice from the majority population. ... We should also bridge the knowledge gap. Europeans must learn more about Roma, their history and the diversity of their identities. ... It is through living, working and learning together that we can eradicate our ignorance and prejudice.

And in his Viewpoint of 2 April 2007:

> The seriousness of anti-Ziganism demonstrates that we cannot eradicate it through measures aiming at formal equality alone. Roma must reach effective equality of opportunity with everyone else and this clearly requires positive measures to compensate for long-term discrimination and prejudice. Otherwise the situation of many Roma will get worse rather than better.

To combat the weight of prejudice and its consequences, the Council of Europe launched a joint programme with the European Commission in the Balkans for 2006-07: Advancing Equality, Tolerance and Peace: Equal Rights and Treatment for Roma. The programme included an awareness-raising campaign called *Dosta!* Go Beyond Prejudice, Meet the Roma! The word *"dosta"* means "That's enough!" The campaign initially covered five states: Albania, Bosnia and Herzegovina, Montenegro, Serbia and "the Former Yugoslav Republic of Macedonia". It was subsequently extended to Moldova and Ukraine and in 2008 was opened to other member states. Other states gradually joined: Romania, Croatia and Slovenia in 2008, Latvia in 2009, Italy and Bulgaria (as well as several French municipalities) in 2010, Greece and Kosovo in 2011. Slovakia and Spain may join the campaign in 2012.

As the campaign literature states:

> Roma rights are violated every day in Europe. Roma workers are refused jobs, their children are refused places in school. Their community is often considered marginal and traditional, meaning they are more likely to suffer social exclusion.

> In reality, Roma can be considered as the first European people, since they "broke" European borders much before any international treaty or convention existed.

They travelled all around Europe enriching their culture with the culture of the visited countries, as well as enriching European cultural heritage.

...

The Council of Europe is Europe's guardian of human rights, and it is our duty to make sure everyone's rights are respected. *"Dosta!"* is therefore an awareness-raising campaign aiming to fight the discrimination which Roma suffer from because of widespread anti-Gypsyism.

...

"Dosta" means that we want to stop prejudices and stereotypes not by denouncing them but by breaking them, showing who the Roma really are. ... Being European citizens means that Roma have not only duties but also rights and aspirations like everybody else, and therefore their citizenship and human rights must be recognised. Furthermore, Roma culture is a rightful part of Europe's cultural heritage: it has always contributed to the enrichment of European societies. It is now time to recognise this contribution.

When the campaign was launched in Italy (Rome) on 7 June 2010, the Deputy Secretary General of the Council of Europe stated:

The *Dosta!* campaign is an invitation to learn about our neighbours, our fellow citizens, our fellow Europeans. It shows Roma as they are, in their daily routines, in their family, with their friends, at work, in school, at home, with their hopes and with their problems. It shows the richness of their culture and the harshness of their daily lives.

On this occasion, Fanny Ardant, who has supported the campaign as its patron, emphasised that:

In an era marked by human rights, a focus on minorities by institutions and democratic progress, recognition of Roma rights no longer needs to be declared but must be defended. For what remains to be done is the most difficult part: changing attitudes and showing good will. We must stop talking and thinking in terms of clichés and prejudices.

...

Roma are a threat only to conformists, the right-thinking, the timid and, above all, the fearful. All the better for the fearful, as fear is the worst guide and the most effective weapon for certain policies of a kind already experienced in the past. There is some dangerous talk in political circles and in the media that tends to pander to the public and indulge in sensationalism and disinformation or shift debate to find a scapegoat.

The following principles underlie the campaign:

- The campaign addresses very deep-rooted beliefs and prejudices. This campaign is considered as the first step of a long process to be continued through future projects.
- The campaign architecture addresses national, regional and local partners, who "translate" and multiply the campaign message. The local dimension is taken into account and specific co-operation at local level is encouraged.

– The campaign messages are the same for all European countries.

– The campaign is conceived as a tool for the Roma representatives, the majority population and the governments for changing the status quo. It is built up with the contribution of the Roma, through the Council of Europe Roma network, but also with the contribution of the European Roma and Travellers Forum. The participation of the Roma in all the processes related to them is a key issue for the success of any event aimed at granting their access to social and human rights.

– The campaign targets "society at large", by identifying target groups that are most likely to "cascade" and multiply the message, such as journalists, teachers in primary and secondary education, youth, members and organisers of civil society organisations, or members of local and regional parliaments.

Co-ordination is provided by the Roma and Travellers Division, and synergies have been created with various Council of Europe bodies through their participation in various complementary activities. These bodies include the Congress, the Directorate of Education, Eurimages, the European Youth Centre, and the Directorate of Communication. The campaign involves governments and local authorities, Roma and non-Roma NGOs, national television broadcasters and other media, cinema directors, photographers, performers and numerous volunteers.

The tools produced can be used for activities to help the Roma's neighbours know more about them and work towards understanding, recognition and respect, and include:

- official launches and press conferences in every state that joins the campaign;
- an interactive website for the exchange of ideas and comments;[51]
- TV spots, devised with a Roma student association in 25-second and 50-second formats in a number of different languages, as well as a radio spot;
- production of videos by young Roma;
- Roma cinema fortnights;
- the launch of a CD with five performances of the European anthem in Roma languages;
- poster and photo competitions to overcome anti-Roma stereotypes, and the creation of visuals for use in documents;
- school project competitions on Roma culture;
- media training on Roma culture and ethical reporting;
- training of teachers and school assistants;
- training of Roma mediators in public health matters;
- arts and youth festivals against discrimination;

---

51. Website: www.dosta.org.

- collections of testimonials from key figures;
- the distribution of a media pack containing a DVD video kit with interviews of well-known figures, video statements, a Euronews report on Roma and the TV spots for the *Dosta!* campaign, as well as a "toolkit". The media pack is distributed to the press at major Council of Europe events relating to Roma.

In addition, the *Dosta!* prize to reward local authorities which have run projects to uphold and protect Roma rights was launched in 2007 and has been awarded regularly since. All municipalities in the 47 member states can take part. In 2007, the prize was awarded to three cities in South-Eastern Europe: Vitez and Banja Luka in Bosnia and Herzegovina and Novi Sad in Serbia. The President of the Congress, Ian Micallef, emphasised the key aspects at the ceremony to award the 2008 prize:

> I know that many interesting and innovative projects of a high quality have been submitted, and that the jury had a tough time making the decision. Indeed, this is why there are two joint-first prizes, but I must especially congratulate all the winners – Mostar and Prijedor of Bosnia and Herzegovina, Volos of Greece and Lom of Bulgaria – and welcome them to Strasbourg.
>
> This year's winning projects have, amongst other things, sought to improve Roma living standards, especially with regard to decent housing and health care, to educate children and provide mediation and counselling services – in particular with regard to using the administration and public services, which is often a real stumbling block. They also endeavoured to create all-important employment opportunities through vocational training and, last but certainly not least, ensure the active participation of the Roma community and its representatives in municipal life.
>
> It is important to point out that municipalities sometimes undertake this kind of work in favour of their Roma population in a national climate and with a background of public opinion that is not at all favourable to Roma rights and in fact can be quite the opposite. This makes the municipalities' commitment to Roma human rights all the more remarkable and praiseworthy and shows that the local level is where democracy starts and can show the way.
>
> The Congress is convinced that building a truly cohesive community where all citizens – members of a minority or not – feel involved, respected and listened to is one of the most important tasks facing local authorities, and that it necessarily includes the need – no, the obligation to raise public awareness on Roma rights and culture, and to fight against the stereotypes and prejudices towards them.

One key result of the campaign has been the preparation and distribution of a "toolkit" which outlines the project's background and its political and theoretical foundations before offering practical guidance on campaign planning and situation analysis, including how to set and achieve goals in terms of strategy, planning and tactics. The toolkit also provides a list of suggestions to help develop the campaign in the state or region concerned: preparation of fact sheets for journalists, a list of experts, a website profile, promotional material, photo gallery, testimonials, public relations strategy, organisation of press conferences, simulation exercises, etc. It further offers testimonials from well-known figures and links to the websites of the Council of Europe and other institutions.

The campaign is of two-fold importance: firstly, it is a comprehensive and cross-disciplinary response to the numerous recommendations appearing in the texts adopted by Council of Europe bodies, and, secondly, by tackling deep-seated prejudices, it is an important vehicle of change in moving towards respect and recognition of Roma, and unrecognised populations in general, especially as it reaches young people at an age when it is still possible to affect the way they perceive society.

Route of Roma Culture and Heritage

How the project came into being

The Council of Europe has been developing the European Cultural Routes programme since 1987. After the initial period, activities were refocused by Committee of Ministers Resolution (98) 4 and more recently by Resolution CM/Res(2007)12. The latter lays down the foundations for this project in its preamble:

> Considering that the main aims of European cultural co-operation are to promote the European identity in its unity and its diversity; to preserve the diversity of Europe's cultures; to encourage intercultural dialogue and to facilitate conflict prevention and reconciliation;
>
> Considering that highlighting the influences, exchanges and developments which have formed the European identity can facilitate awareness of a European citizenship based on the sharing of common values;
>
> ...
>
> Noting that the identification of European values and a common European cultural heritage may be achieved via cultural routes tracing the history of peoples, migrations, and the spread of the major European currents of civilisation in the fields of philosophy, religion, culture, the arts, science, technology and trade;
>
> Aware that such routes lend themselves to long-term European co-operation programmes in the fields of research, heritage enhancement, culture and the arts, cultural and educational youth exchanges, cultural tourism in Europe and sustainable cultural development.

The resolution then sets out the rules, eligibility criteria and priority fields of action for developing the routes.

A "Roma Cultural Route" was proposed as early as September 1992: the very concept of a cultural route, the values that it conveys and the nature of the activities that can be developed around it chime perfectly with Roma vitality. The project fully reflected the concept and also fostered an appreciation of the Roma's historical and cultural presence in Europe, promoting a better understanding and bringing to light events which have been systematically neglected by national histories despite being part of those histories for centuries.

The importance of a cultural route is emphasised in the conclusions of the October 1992 symposium Gypsies in the Locality, an event at the root of a resolution on Roma (see the chapter on the Congress):[52]

> This suggestion could engender a considerable number of opportunities and campaigns, and is in line with the working principles and priorities which the colloquy participants put forward. Its implementation can be flexible in so far as such a route can take in numerous existing activities of the kind mentioned during the colloquy (museums, theatricals, cultural centres, publications, historical research work, conferences, etc.), and it is wholly desirable and appropriate that our work should be directed along a Gypsy route, which would bring Gypsy culture and history into the limelight, and enable large-scale information campaigns to be brought within reach of the general public. Such a route, which could be developed over several years, would also bear the stamp of the Council of Europe awarded for quality activities and so provide essential support for intensifying international relations and reinforcing the desired networks. It would without doubt facilitate the emergence and consolidation of Gypsy cultural centres in a number of states and regions of Europe.

An exploratory report on the subject was produced in 1993, and four years later, in 1997, the MG-S-ROM asked for the idea to be studied in greater detail. This request resulted in a second document.[53] Both reports showed the usefulness, relevance and feasibility of instituting a Roma cultural route by cross-referencing data from institutions and the field to create a sound basis. A framework for discussion was thus mapped out, and practical proposals were put forward based on an analysis of projects, the findings of a special survey and the priorities of a group of Roma experts.

The results of the 1993 exploratory study were presented at the meeting of the Advisory Committee on the Council of Europe Cultural Routes in 1994. The minutes of this meeting (meeting report ICCE (94) 13) reveal the importance attached to the project and the possibility that it might be developed to draw in the whole of the Organisation:

> it was felt inappropriate to reduce a theme of such great interest to a Cultural Route. Instead, it should be the subject of a general Council programme. That did not mean that certain activities connected with the theme could not be handled (in) the form of a Route. Indeed, given that Gypsies were a central (policy) concern for the Council of Europe, a project conducted at Council of Europe level could be so devised as to include collaboration by the Cultural Routes Project, taking into account the cultural and educational aspects of the subject and the need to involve the Gypsies themselves in any action taken.

---

52. Council of Europe (1994), *Gypsies in the locality*, Studies and Texts No. 38, Council of Europe Publishing, Strasbourg, p. 154.
53. Council for Cultural Co-operation, "A Council of Europe Gypsy Cultural Route, Exploratory study", document ICCE (93)9, 1993, then Group of Specialists on Roma/Gypsies, "A Council of Europe Gypsy Cultural Route (continued)", document MG-S-ROM (97)12, 1997. Both reports were brought together in a single publication in 2004: "Roma Cultural Route", DGIV/EDU/ROM(2004)8.

Expressions of interest grew in number and can be found in texts adopted by the Congress, in the conclusions of various hearings and in a variety of reports. In 2003, a meeting was held at the Brno Museum of Roma Culture in the Czech Republic to propose activities based on a network of museums of Roma culture: the idea was to develop the educational aspect of the cultural route through activities implementing the Education of Roma Children in Europe project described in a previous chapter.[54]

Finally, in 2008, a decisive discussion based on two meetings with experts and cultural stakeholders took place on the initiative of the Directorate of Culture. It was to result in the launching of the Route of Roma Culture and Heritage in 2009 in Slovenia. An introduction is provided on the Council of Europe website:

> The objective of the Route of Roma Culture and Heritage is to increase the knowledge of people in Europe about Roma history, culture, values and lifestyle, to encourage the contribution of Roma to Europe's cultural life and diversity and ultimately contribute to giving a positive value to an image of Roma which are, more often than not, perceived in a negative and stereotyped way.
>
> To achieve this, the Cultural Route will first develop as a network of organisations (associations, museums, documentation and cultural centres, art and education institutions, festivals, etc.) which work together towards developing a common set of activities.[55]

In 2011, the network involved partners in seven states:

> The route will originally link places where founding organisations are based, and will eventually grow as new partners join in. The route will also seek to empower Roma themselves to be presenters ("ambassadors") of their own culture through face-to-face encounters and the media.

Promoting the culture

All too often, Roma issues are regarded as being synonymous with problems. One great advantage of a cultural approach is the ability to get away from this bleak view of Roma communities as "problematic" and instead give them credit for their dynamism and grant them the positive recognition that is their due. In other words, a cultural route is synonymous with combating rejection, intolerance and racism. For the Roma themselves, it is also a vehicle for recognition and promotion of their culture, synonymous with their pride in this culture, and a highly symbolic project.

To speak of a "Roma route" is only logical. The history of the Roma consists of the routes they have travelled rather than the physical traces they have left behind, and what survives is the very essence of culture in their social relations, language and other practices, and in what others see from the outside, such as their music, dancing and way of life. Employing the term "European"

---

54. A report on this meeting was published in the document combining the two previous reports: "Roma Cultural Route", DGIV/EDU/ROM(2004)8.
55. Reference should be made to the website for details of project structure, partner organisations, activities and activity timetable, etc: www.coe.int/t/dg4/cultureheritage/culture.

is also clearly justified for transnational communities who have no territory of their own and whose social and cultural ties have been forged across frontiers by people who for centuries have been citizens of Europe as a whole.

Because the Roma have a culture that has had to be on the move, they have not been builders of cities, sites or monuments. Nor, as providers of services for those around them, have they really left behind any products allowing their history to be easily traced, or even, since they are bearers of an oral tradition that extends right up to the present day, any written traces of their own. The idea of a European cultural route is therefore both obvious and something of a challenge because although Roma culture is strong, it is intangible. Such a route is, in any case, a necessity at the present time and ties in with the recent tendency of both UNESCO and other international bodies to recognise intangible culture.

In the case of this route, priorities and needs – as well as projects that could be linked together – existed before the proposal was actually put forward. In other words, the European Roma cultural route was both an appropriate response to existing needs and a proposal able to structure and consolidate individual activities by linking them together and promoting them. The situation augurs well for future progress: it is not a matter of coming up with an idea and then looking for the building blocks of a programme but rather a matter of bringing together the many building blocks that already exist in a programme that can cement them together.

To launch such a route is to actively implement the aims of the Council of Europe in the fields of education and human rights: providing tools for respect, recognition and cultural development encourages mutual understanding between communities which are too often in conflict with each other and helps to bring about an improvement in the situation. The Council of Europe is thus enabling a culture that forms part of a shared heritage to emerge onto the European stage and is encouraging exchange by strengthening intercultural dialogue across the whole of Europe.

Considerable potential

The specific proposals made from 1993 onwards in the reports and discussions preceding the launch described a variety of themes that might be addressed through a European route. The following were among the suggestions for highlighting the value and relevance of such a route:

- The first major Roma migrations from the easternmost marches of Europe to western Europe might be signposted. Records exist marking the advance of Roma across Europe and providing evidence of their enduring presence and centuries of co-existence with neighbouring communities.

- Such a route could draw on key historical moments and major sites associated with Roma, including pilgrimages, tragic sites such as the concentration camps, and centres of the arts, such as parts of Andalusia for flamenco, Hungary and elsewhere for both similar and different types of music and song. This would bring home the history and existence of Roma and thus lead to greater recognition.

- Focal points for the route already exist, such as information centres, museums, cultural associations, theatres, arts schools, etc., which could form networks to facilitate exchange and the organisation of joint projects. The dynamism associated with a network can raise the profile of individual activities, each of which forms part of a whole, and allows more effective organisation, avoiding repetition and duplication while meeting actual needs (thus frequent calls have been made for a "European Gypsy cultural centre", but using the proposed route to link cultural sites where Roma have already left their mark would create a remarkable cultural centre in the more realistic – and pluralistic – form of a European Roma cultural network).

- Museums have been set up in several European states. A network would allow exchange of material and travelling exhibitions and would be of interest to non-specialist museums ready to accept temporary exhibitions on Roma communities. Joint publication of catalogues would also be a way of strengthening the work of museums and making their treasures more widely available. A knowledge of Gypsy arts and crafts would do much to promote recognition of their contribution to European culture. One section of exhibitions could show the influence of Gypsy art and culture on other artists (musicians, singers, painters, writers, etc.).

- In the fields of music, song, literature and the visual arts, the development of a route would make it possible to introduce little-known artists and promote their work. It is extremely important to collect and anthologise Roma/Gypsy poetry, song and music from all over Europe as a matter of urgency. The present time of upheaval makes such action a matter of priority, and it fits in perfectly with the European cultural route as both an objective and a product.

- It is essential to link cultural activities with the education sector: general provision of information for pupils and, more specifically, direct collaboration with secondary schools specialising in arts and crafts (music, visual arts, making and repair of musical instruments, and modern and traditional decorative arts: jewellery, iron work, copper work, woodwork, etc.).

- There is a large Roma presence in many folk festivals in Europe; raising its profile would enable different communities to become more aware of it and increase mutual understanding whilst encouraging an appreciation of Roma culture and creative talents through the cross-cultural nature of the festival. Various aspects of the arts are represented in festivals, which mark the entire history of Europe. In this respect, more and more cultural meetings, festivals, "heritage weeks" and the like are being organised. Building bridges between such events would allow them to have a greater influence, complement one another and make some of what has been produced (exhibitions, lectures, etc.) more widely available.

- The emphasis might be put on visual and audiovisual material, such as photographs and videos, to reach a larger audience. Photography, for example, creates imagery that is expressive and understood by everyone; it is readily accessible, both technically and financially, and easy to exchange, transport, reproduce, exhibit and publish. Photography alone could be a very important area of work for publicity.

- A network of producers of newsletters and books, along the lines of a "European bookshop", could be conceived not as being in a particular location but as a network to publicise and make available important, rare and little-known documents such as printed matter, films, video documents, music scores and photographs, and possibly to produce news publications.

- The introduction of European prizes sponsored by the Council of Europe and awarded to particular events or products associated with the cultural route could encourage action and have considerable symbolic value.

- For all these activities and for each field of work, it is extremely important to produce an up-to-date directory of performing groups, museums, available exhibitions and so on, so that the people who are developing the cultural route (artists and all the other partners) are aware of each other and anyone requiring their services for the purposes of an exhibition, a festival or a publication can contact them easily.

The launching of such a route reflects the fundamental mandate of the Council of Europe in what have always been its priority fields (human rights, democracy, education, minorities, etc.) and offers practical and positive ideas and action which set an example in a situation where minority issues are all too often considered only in negative terms. This pilot project is to provide historical redress and cultural support for a community which has been waiting for it for centuries.

A European political partnership

Growth of an idea

After a few earlier attempts, a Roma political movement began to emerge in several European countries from the 1920s onwards, engaging in various activities and developing programmes and policy positions. But the movement was stopped in its tracks by the Second World War, during which Roma suffered surveillance, imprisonment and extermination. Political action was resumed in the 1950s in many states, and the World Gypsy Community was established at international level, to be replaced in 1967 by the International Gypsy Committee. This committee, which consisted of a federation of organisations in a number of states, was active on a number of fronts, including lobbying institutions regarding the situation of Roma. One of its first delegations visited the Council of Europe in 1969, the same year that the Parliamentary Assembly adopted the Organisation's very first recommendation on Gypsies.

Not long afterwards, from 8 to 12 April 1971, the committee held a meeting in the vicinity of London which is considered to be the first World Romani Congress. The committee became the International Rom Committee, and 8 April, the opening day of the congress, was declared International Roma

Day. A flag and an anthem were adopted, and working committees were set up.[56] Later the committee was to become the International Romani Union, which is still active today.

The idea of a European political organisation for Roma made its appearance in 1986, when it was discussed at a meeting called by the Central Council of German Sinti and Roma. It was subsequently the subject of other meetings and proposals, including at the Council of Europe in 1991 with a hearing of the Standing Conference of Local and Regional Authorities in Strasbourg: "The Gypsy people and Europe: continuation of the tradition in a changing Europe". Roma participants from 12 states took part, and the conclusions suggest that member states help Roma organisations establish a major European association to represent them with regard to public authorities and European institutions. The hearing also recommended that organisations representing Roma communities at European level be granted consultative status with the Council of Europe. The same year (1991), the International Romani Union floated the idea of a European Committee of the Romani Union and proposed that a Conference for Harmonisation, Assistance and Co-operation of Roma Associations be held on a regular basis. Two years later, in Resolution 249 (1993), the Standing Conference called "on Rom/Gypsies themselves ... to set up a European association to represent Gypsy communities which will serve as a political interface for governments and European bodies".

In 1994, in the course of a meeting in Strasbourg, Roma delegates, supported by the other participants, set up the Standing Conference for Co-operation and Co-ordination of Romani Associations in Europe. In 1996, this body met at the same time as the very first meeting of the recently established group of government specialists for Roma, the MG-S-ROM, allowing constructive discussion and a variety of proposals from Roma on defining the group's terms of reference and activities. It was then felt that the body should have a permanent observer at MG-S-ROM meetings.[57]

Political resolve

In 2001, the projects and aspirations of various bodies were endorsed by political resolve at government level: in January that year the Finnish President, Tarja Halonen, speaking before the Parliamentary Assembly, proposed that "serious consideration be given to the need to create for the Roma some kind of consultative assembly to represent them on the pan-European level". The Parliamentary Assembly welcomed this proposal and, in order to discuss it and study it in more detail, Finland organised a seminar in Helsinki in October 2001 attended by representatives of various Roma organisations, members of the MG-S-ROM, other experts and the Finnish authorities. At the end of the seminar, the Roma participants made a statement:

> we, representing Romani people from 13 European countries, would like to once more express our support and interest in developing the idea further. Therefore,

---

56. For more detail on the development of this movement, see the chapter on "Roma/Gypsy organisations" in Jean-Pierre Liégeois, *Roma in Europe*, op. cit.
57. Ibid.

we propose that a working group be established for a period of 6-12 months to carefully look at all the details and work out outlines for the consultative body. The working group should be composed of representatives of Roma experts, representatives of IRU, RNC, representatives of some governments, as well as representatives of the EU, Council of Europe and the OSCE.

The following day, at a meeting also held in Helsinki, the MG-S-ROM supported the proposal of the Roma representatives, and in November the Committee of Ministers of the Council of Europe was informed by the Finnish Secretary of State for Foreign Affairs that:

> Given its broad membership and extensive expertise in human rights, the Council of Europe provides in our view the most appropriate framework for such a body. An ad hoc group will study in detail the various aspects related to establishing such a body. My Government looks very much forward to working together with all interested parties in order to develop this initiative.

The ad hoc working party met from December 2001 onwards, chaired by the Chair of the Parliamentary Assembly's Committee on Legal Affairs and Human Rights. To help plan the programme of work, the first meeting addressed the:

– aims and objectives of the representative/consultative body;

– details of its structure (size, composition and representativeness);

– functions and working methods;

– sources of finance for its management;

– nature of its official links with the Council of Europe.

The second meeting, in February 2002, was used to study various examples of Roma representation in Europe and determine the objectives of the body that might be set up. A third meeting in March made progress on matters concerning the body's composition, size and structure and its links with Council of Europe directorates. In May, a fourth meeting returned to objectives, composition and functions, and finally a fifth meeting in September drew up a final report on the creation of a pan-European Roma consultative forum. The report was submitted to the MG-S-ROM at its October 2002 meeting. A seminar was held at the same time to follow up on the previous year's Helsinki seminar, and the Committee of Ministers was informed of the progress of discussions. The Committee of Ministers decided to take action by forwarding the matter to the Rapporteur Group on Social and Health Questions (GR-SOC). The GR-SOC then suggested setting up a working party to study the question of a possible forum, and in January 2003 it laid down the terms of reference for this working party (GR-SOC(2003)4 revised):

> 1. The working party shall examine the proposals concerning a European Forum for Roma as well as all related issues ... As a preliminary question, it shall, in particular, examine whether the proposals are appropriate and compatible with the principle of non-discrimination as contained in Article 14 of the European Convention on Human Rights.

2. In carrying out its work, the working party shall seek information about the relevant activities on Roma carried out in the Council of Europe, in the member states and in other international organisations. It shall take account of the opinions with respect to the proposals made on the Forum for Roma by the Specialist Group on Roma/Gypsies and other bodies interested in the subject. It shall also endeavour to obtain contributions from member states, international bodies and experts on the subject. For this purpose it may organise hearings.

In April 2002, the Parliamentary Assembly supported the idea and recommended that the Committee of Ministers:

support the initiative of setting up a European Roma consultative forum, democratically established, that can articulate and transmit the voice of Romany individuals and communities and serve as an advisory body to the Committee of Ministers, the Parliamentary Assembly of the Council of Europe and institutions of the European Union.

In October 2002, at a seminar on participation of Roma in Europe, the Deputy Secretary General of the Council of Europe in turn supported the idea of a forum:

We are engaged in a rapidly accelerating dynamics. In January 2001 the Finnish President, Ms Halonen, speaking before the Parliamentary Assembly, proposed setting up a Forum to provide the Roma people with a voice and the possibility of participating in European standard-setting and decision-making. It is time we shelved paternalism and stopped taking decisions on their behalf. The time has come for the Roma to take charge of their own affairs.

The Forum should help the various Roma organisations to come together in pursuit of common goals. I would like to stress the importance which I attach to the role of Roma NGOs. Their co-operation and commitment to defending the interests of Roma populations in Europe will be essential to the future of the Roma community.

The Forum will also promote a better understanding of the Roma and their problems. There are multiple problems, including wretched living conditions (lack of decent housing, water, electricity and sanitation), very high levels of illiteracy and unemployment and lack of identity papers. These problems obviously require national solutions, but I think the Forum could help highlight the difficulties facing Roma people in their daily lives and launch dialogue with the Council of Europe on the requisite measures to tackle this situation.

I was pleased to note that each of the national delegations to the Forum will comprise one man and one woman; gender equality is a principle to which we are very strongly attached. A Forum intended as the democratic expression of Roma populations would betray its own principles if it failed to grant women their rightful place in constructing the future of the Roma people.

In conclusion, I would like to appeal to young Roma people to take responsibility for the destiny of the Roma populations. Their future belongs to them. This Forum should be an opportunity for young Roma to form a new generation aware of its rights and obligations, integrated in the society in which it lives and proud of its identity.

The working party, the GT-ROMS, met eight times in 2003 and eight times in 2004. The matters addressed included a consideration of existing bodies for Roma participation, a subject on which all member states were surveyed (and 25 replied). Consideration was also given to the forum's advisory functions, structure, composition (size, method of representation, etc.), working methods, legal status, funding, and links with the Council of Europe as well as member states and other bodies.

Hearings were held while these questions were being addressed, and these included officials from the OSCE, the European Commission, the Parliamentary Assembly, the Congress, ECRI and the Framework Convention for the Protection of National Minorities. The Commissioner for Human Rights also attended, as did representatives of Roma organisations. From this it emerged that there was agreement on such a forum and a shared interest in setting it up, but some states had reservations, since the body's profile might in some cases be incompatible with domestic legislation on minorities and their political representation. In the course of discussion, the model was proposed of an international association independent of the Council of Europe, having a consultative role and linked to the Council of Europe by a partnership agreement. The signing of this agreement would be conditional on the forum's respecting basic general principles such as representativeness, transparency and democracy. A number of delegations in the GT-ROMS voiced support for an association rather than a Council of Europe body, emphasising the importance of an independent forum which would genuinely represent Roma aspirations. This opinion was shared by the Roma organisations present, which endorsed the idea of an association.

It was this proposal that was discussed and finalised at the working party's subsequent meetings. It was then the Roma's responsibility to draw up a plan for the association while the GT-ROMS worked on a draft agreement for partnership with an international association. The question of the forum's composition (representation of Roma from different states, presence of European Roma organisations as members, etc.) was also considered at length. In January 2004, the GT-ROMS submitted a progress report to the GR-SOC confirming that there was no existing equivalent of the planned forum and that, with regard to consultation, the latter therefore provided added value in the current situation. The members of the working party believed that a project based on the idea of an international association that would sign a partnership agreement with the Council of Europe could be discussed in future work. The GR-SOC welcomed these results and invited the working party to continue its work on the basis of the proposals that it had made.

The working party continued its work in spring 2004 by, amongst other things, preparing guidelines for the forum and producing a draft partnership agreement. It examined the draft statutes drawn up at a meeting of Roma representatives. In May 2004, the Committee of Ministers welcomed "the significant progress made with respect to the Finnish initiative ... concerning a European Forum for Roma and Travellers, which would take the form of an NGO" (CM(2004)70 final). The GT-ROMS then finalised the guidelines and partnership agreement and studied the financial implications with the relevant

Council of Europe bodies. This item was finalised in September 2004, and the working party submitted its final report to the GR-SOC containing guidelines for the forum, a draft statute and a draft partnership agreement. The working party proposed that the GR-SOC should recommend that the Committee of Ministers authorise the Secretary General of the Council of Europe to sign the partnership agreement. It was also recommended that, once the agreement had been signed, the forum should be invited with observer status to the various meetings that might concern Roma. The GR-SOC approved these recommendations in November 2004 and recommended that the Committee of Ministers adopt the items put forward.

Finally, at their meeting of 3 November 2004 (CM(2004)179), the Ministers' Deputies, taking note of the final activity report of the GT-ROMS, adopted the guidelines, took note of the present version of the statute, and:

> 4. authorised the Secretary General to sign the Partnership Agreement between the Council of Europe and the European Roma and Travellers Forum
>
> ...
>
> 5. encouraged their rapporteur groups to invite a representative of the Forum to their meetings as an observer whenever engaging in a debate of particular concern to the Roma and Travellers;
>
> 6. decided to invite the European Roma and Travellers Forum to send a representative as an observer to the meetings of the Steering Committees and Expert Committees, the list of which appears in the Appendix to the Partnership Agreement.

The documents appended to the Committee of Ministers decision offered the following guidelines (these recommendations, which were to be incorporated into the statute, give a better idea of the forum's nature and purpose):

> The member states of the Council of Europe, conscious of the particular situation and the vulnerability of the Roma and Traveller population in Europe, have decided to draw up these guidelines concerning the establishment by the Roma and Travellers of a consultative Forum to further their interests. The Forum would enjoy special relations with the Organisation should it be created in accordance with the guidelines.
>
> *Constitution, title and members*
>
> The European Forum for Roma and Travellers (hereinafter "Forum") shall be established in the form of an international association, a non-profit-making legal entity governed by the legislation in force in France. The Forum shall have its seat in Strasbourg, France. The working languages shall be English, French and Romani.
>
> The members of the Forum shall be international, transnational/subregional and national NGOs or other existing national structures for Roma and Traveller participation, where appropriate.
>
> *Aims*
>
> The aim of the Forum would be to oversee the effective exercise by Roma and Travellers of all human rights and fundamental freedoms as protected by the legal

instruments of the Council of Europe as well as by other relevant inter-national legal instruments. It shall promote the fight against racism and discrimination and facilitate the integration of these population groups into the European societies and their participation in public life.

For this purpose, the Forum shall propose, in order to contribute to the improvement of the conditions of the said populations, the implementation of initiatives at the most adequate levels, primarily with regard to housing, health, education and employment. It shall propose measures to combat any discrimination that Roma and Travellers may meet in relation to the freedom of movement. It shall also propose measures with a view to overcoming the specific difficulties these populations may face due to their nomadic lifestyle.

Functions

The Forum could deliver opinions and make proposals to decision-making bodies in Europe at international, national, regional or local level in order to influence decision-making processes likely to affect Roma and Travellers whether directly or indirectly. It is to promote a dialogue between the Roma and Traveller communities and governments and to encourage the exchange of best practices as well as the implementation of national policies in the field of Roma and Travellers in a European framework.

Composition

1. The Plenary Assembly of the Forum shall be composed by a maximum of 75 delegates.

2. The Committee of Ministers considers that the task of determining the exact composition of the Forum shall be primarily assigned to the founders of the Forum, it being understood that the criteria for the selection of the first Forum will be defined and subject to examination by the Committee of Ministers. In order for the partnership agreement to be concluded, they shall be in conformity with a certain number of criteria laid down by the Committee of Ministers in these Guidelines. These criteria include the respect of the general principles of the Council of Europe and of agreed principles of representativity, transparency, geographical specificity and gender equality.

...

The organisations that become members of the Forum, and that select delegates to it, will have to respect the general principles of the Council of Europe and also to respect principles of representativity, transparency, geographical specificity and gender equality. Eligible organisations are those that have aims that are compatible with those of the Forum, i.e. Roma and Traveller organisations aiming to promote the interests of Roma and/or Travellers.

Administrative organs

The management bodies of the Forum shall be a Plenary Assembly and an Executive Committee. The Forum shall be serviced by a Secretariat.

Finance

Subject to the budgetary decisions which the Committee of Ministers takes each year, the Forum will receive an annual contribution awarded by the Council of

Europe ... The Forum shall, with a view of gradually becoming financially self-sustaining, actively seek funding from other sources, such as other international organisations, member states of the Council of Europe (voluntary contributions) or any other private or public source intended to further the Forum's aims in general or a specific purpose not contrary to the Forum's Statute.

...

Relations with the Council of Europe

Relations between the Forum and the Council of Europe shall be formalised by a partnership agreement whereby the Council will undertake to use the Forum as a consultative body while contributing to the practical means enabling it to perform this role.

The Council of Europe's approval of the agreement, which would be subject to the Forum's compliance with these broad guidelines concerning its manner of constitution (proper representation) and the principles of its functioning (transparency and democracy), will take the form of a document signed by the Secretary General on behalf of the Council of Europe and by the President of the Forum, mandated for this purpose in accordance with the relevant provision of the Statute of the Forum.

The forum registered as an association in September 2004, and the partnership agreement was signed on 15 December 2004, as described in the official press release:

Council of Europe signs partnership agreement with Roma and Travellers Forum

Strasbourg, 09.12.2004 – The Council of Europe is to sign a partnership agreement on 15 December with a body representing the continent's Roma and Travellers population. The European Roma and Travellers Forum has the status of an international non-governmental organisation (INGO), with the mandate to represent Roma communities all over Europe. The partnership agreement will allow the Forum to play a bigger role in decision-making processes inside the 46-nation Council of Europe, which will provide the Forum with staff and offices at its Strasbourg headquarters.

Council of Europe Secretary General Terry Davis said, "This Forum is the result of a personal initiative by President Tarja Halonen of Finland. At the Council of Europe we are proud that both Finland and the representatives of Roma and Travellers have entrusted us with bringing President Halonen's initiative to fruition. Now we must ensure that both international and national authorities not only hear the voices of Roma and Travellers, but also listen to them."

The signing ceremony will take place in Strasbourg, between Mr Davis, representing the Council of Europe, and Rudko Kawczynski, Interim President of the Roma Forum. It will be attended by representatives from the Roma and Travellers community, and international organisations including the European Commission, UNHCR, OSCE-ODIHR, the World Bank and the Open Society Institute. The President of Finland, Tarja Halonen, will also be present.

On the day that he signed the agreement, the Secretary General of the Council of Europe noted that:

> The title of the Agreement which we are signing today speaks for itself. It is about partnership. ... [with] the creation of the Forum, Roma and Travellers will now have a voice at the pan-European level. For the first time in their history, they will be able to influence the decision-making which affects them.

The following day Rudko Kawczynski, Acting President of the ERTF, stressed that:

> 15 December 2004 is truly an historic day: at last we have been recognised by Europe as a whole, for the first time in 700 years. ... This agreement will enable us to take part in all Council of Europe activities, although our top priority will clearly be human rights. We are counting on the Council of Europe for greater efforts to combat the all-too-frequent discrimination and "anti-Roma" attitudes that we experience. ... The rule of law must put a stop to racism, violence and discrimination. In other words, we no longer want to be Europe's losers.

During 2005, members of the ERTF were appointed under its statute by the process of selecting national organisations in the various states and electing delegates. The forum was then able to begin work, and its first session was held from 13 to 15 December 2005.

As an international NGO, the ERTF is therefore an independent body, linked to the Council of Europe through a partnership agreement which provides for special relations with the latter's various bodies, allowing it to attend meetings, hearings and similar events and providing it with expertise to achieve its aims. Its rules of procedures and rules for electing delegates must comply with the principles of representativeness, transparency and democracy and seek to ensure gender equality and the involvement of young people. By encouraging this initiative, adopted by all the relevant political partners after dozens of meetings over a four-year period, the Council of Europe has enabled Roma representatives to work with a higher profile and position themselves more effectively, as well as have top-level contacts in national and international bodies, in order to put forward their ideas, suggest initiatives and ensure that they are implemented. The objective has been to provide both administrative back-up and a recognised political platform. As the introduction to the ERTF on the Council of Europe website states:

> The idea behind the initiative ... was to create for the Roma an international body having close and privileged links with the Council of Europe.

The ERTF will give the Roma and Travellers the possibility to participate in and influence decision-making processes in issues concerning them, openly and officially, through a special relationship with the Council of Europe. This will be the first time that national and European Roma organisations from all over Europe will be able to discuss together and formulate jointly their hopes and concerns. These are the unique features of the forum which distinguish it from any other international organisation.[58]

---

58. See www.coe.int/t/dg3/romatravellers/ertf_EN.asp. For the statute, programme of events, news items, policy statements, etc., please consult the forum's website: www.ertf.org/. On the hazards and difficulties of establishing political bodies for Roma, see the chapter on "Roma/Gypsy organisations" in Jean-Pierre Liégeois, *Roma in Europe*, op. cit.

As pointed out by the Deputy Secretary General of the Council of Europe on 24 February 2010, at the opening of the ERTF's fifth plenary assembly:

> This heightened political attention to the problems of Roma communities should be seen as an opportunity for a qualitative and quantitative change in Europe's policy towards its Roma population. Public awareness must also develop further.
>
> In the Council of Europe, we are ready and looking to the Forum for a reliable, resolute and responsible partner.
>
> Against this background, I am very pleased to note that we have delegates with us today who come from recently established national umbrella organisations representing Roma and Travellers communities in several Council of Europe member states. I hope that similar organisations will be set up in other countries as rapidly as possible. In this way, the Forum will enjoy the largest possible representation and legitimacy to speak on behalf of the 10 to 12 million Roma and Travellers in Europe.
>
> The active participation of these umbrella organisations in the Forum will increase the channels of communication not only between Strasbourg and member states, but also among Roma organisations in each member state.
>
> ...
>
> What the Council of Europe expects from the Forum is to ensure that Roma have a real voice at the European level. A voice which is heard, not only listened to. In this respect, you can clearly count on the Council of Europe. We count on you to contribute actively, and we will feed this input into the process of Council of Europe activities, including those related to monitoring and assistance.

After the first five years, the processes developing around the ERTF are aimed at promoting within it a spirit of democratic pluralism representing the diversity of Roma communities in Europe and increasing the support and encouragement that it can provide to grassroots Roma NGOs to improve their position in negotiating with the public authorities in the states where they are based – states that are responsible for Roma policies. The ERTF has thus been able to strengthen its role as an interface between local, regional and national Roma organisations and communities on the one hand and, on the other, the European bodies which, through their resolutions and recommendations, inquiries and regular monitoring can impel states to comply with their obligations.

12. Issues for the future

From discovery to action

If we look at Council of Europe activities related to Roma over the past 40 or so years we find continual progress, each period being marked by a distinguishing feature.

The resolutions and recommendations in the first period reflect the discovery of the Roma issue and the wish to bring it to the attention of local and national authorities. The terminology used and the topics addressed, particularly with reference to "nomadism", are characteristic of an approach to issues that were still unfamiliar. But these initial documents were already drawing attention to matters whose relevance was to be confirmed, and would indeed increase, in the following decades in the form of rejection, migration, discrimination and problems of access to social rights.

The second period was marked by a better understanding of the historical, linguistic and sociocultural realities of Roma communities and an acknowledgment of their richness. This trend coincided with the emergence and recognition of the minority phenomenon in Europe, confirmed by the adoption of the Framework Convention for the Protection of National Minorities and the European Charter for Regional or Minority Languages. Questions of language and culture were thus seen as being on a par with, and sometimes even more important than, social questions.

When population movements came together with the emergence of minorities to give European states a multicultural image, the policy response had to be guided by the intercultural approach which began with the creation of the Council of Europe and was subsequently theorised, especially in the field of education. This was an approach that was increasingly accepted as necessary. This third period saw the introduction of a body of standard-setting texts, exemplified in the case of Roma by the series of recommendations adopted by the Committee of Ministers on complementary themes: education, economic situation and employment, movement, housing, health and general policies. A frame of reference was established, reflecting a transition from the awareness of the earlier periods to a political resolve to improve a situation that was now known and above all recognised. Indeed, one of the major changes in this period was that the situation was acknowledged, and often expressly recognised, to be the result of previous, inappropriate policies. Beyond this acceptance of failure, there emerged a political determination to improve the situation, resulting in the adoption of benchmark resolutions and recommendations.

Finally, in recent years we have seen the beginnings of a fourth period, characterised by a determination to move from theory to action through practical pilot projects such as Education of Roma Children in Europe, the *Dosta!* campaign and the Route of Roma Culture and Heritage. At the same time, Roma, who had initially gone relatively unnoticed, began to figure more systematically in the monitoring of implementation of a number of treaties, such as the Framework Convention and the European Charter for Regional or Minority Languages. Concurrently, the Commissioner for Human Rights and ECRI, which act as discrimination watchdogs for states, drew greater attention to the Roma's situation, whilst increasing use was made of the European Convention on Human Rights and the European Social Charter, resulting in a body of case law quickly being built up.

Variable implementation of existing provisions

The present, extremely complex situation is dictated by a number of parameters that operate in combination and reinforce each other. Each one of these parameters is both influential and hard to change. The upshot is discrimination and exclusion, which, because they are everyday occurrences, tend not to attract attention. Routine dulls any sense of surprise, and we end up with a failure of democracy. In the chapter on the history of Roma in Europe, reference was made to press reviews as indicators, mentioning the consequences of the type of information purveyed. The same idea may be taken up to illustrate this failure of democracy: you have only to read the comments beneath articles on Roma published on the Internet. An overwhelming majority, and sometimes all of them, are delighted by the treatment meted out to Roma, especially when they are rejected by local authorities or government policies, and the comments suggest the Roma are responsible for the situations that they are suffering. The prejudice and stereotyping that underlie such remarks are so rudimentary that the discriminatory and racist nature of these comments goes unnoticed not only by the people making them but also by the people reading them.

Discrimination by omission

Implementation of adopted resolutions and recommendations takes place against this background and requires both a strategy, to which we shall return, and sustained attention, since Roma are very often totally neglected by programmes which are nevertheless intended to improve the situation in society as a whole. Although for some years now, reference has been made to forms of indirect discrimination as well as direct discrimination, not enough attention is being paid to what we may call discrimination by omission. The position of Roma in a country's social, cultural, geographical and historical space is such that they usually fall outside any support and development programmes or are even excluded from them because the qualifying criteria are not relevant in their case – to which must be added the weight of prejudice that influences the attitudes of political and administrative decision makers and those involved in social services. We have seen that, when the European Charter for Regional or Minority Languages was implemented,

Romani was sometimes forgotten. Thus, when the Framework Convention was implemented, the monitoring committee all too often found that the Roma minority was simply not considered.

At the same time there has developed a determination to introduce mainstreaming policies and universal programmes which assume that everybody will be able to benefit from the proposed action. Yet the present situation clearly shows that this assumption is wrong and that more attention should be given to marginalised communities. In other words, if specialist projects and structures are to be phased out, in whatever field, it is necessary to develop the skills of the people affected, together with monitoring and assessment tools for the relevant activities. Otherwise there is a considerable risk that, in attempting to combat discrimination through action, we may lapse into discrimination by omission. Selective oversight must be considered a form of discrimination, especially if it occurs in policy planning.

While mainstreaming is a policy objective, the practical conditions for its implementation require several stages, including, as already mentioned, skill improvement, sustained attention and the introduction of targeted activities. Thus Recommendation 1557 (2002) of the Parliamentary Assembly on the legal situation of Roma in Europe clearly addresses discrimination and its consequences, the lack of recognition of Roma as a minority and the consequent failure to enforce the Framework Convention and the European Charter for Regional or Minority Languages in the case of Roma, and their lack of civic rights in the political field. The Assembly therefore calls upon the member states:

> *b.* to elaborate and implement specific programmes to improve the integration of Roma as individuals and Romany communities as minority groups into society and ensure their participation in decision-making processes at local, regional, national and European levels
>
> ...
>
> *d.* to develop and implement positive action and preferential treatment for the socially deprived strata, including Roma as a socially disadvantaged community, in the field of education, employment and housing
>
> ...
>
> *e.* to take specific measures and create special institutions for the protection of the Romany language, culture, traditions and identity.[59]

It is worth recalling the response of the Committee of Ministers to the Assembly (CM/AS(2003)Rec1557 final, 13 June 2003), for example on matters relating to education:

> The Committee of Ministers finds that the approach suggested by the Assembly to elaborate and implement specific programmes to improve the integration of Roma and to ensure their participation in decision-making processes, is important in particular in the education field:

---

59. See Chapter 4 on the Parliamentary Assembly, where the text is quoted at length.

- by taking specific measures to improve equal opportunities and adapting curricula, teaching material, etc. for Roma pupils, without allowing their specificity to have a ghetto effect; and,

- by ensuring that Roma are actively involved as a community, through families, Roma experts and associations, in designing and implementing projects concerning them, particularly in the education field, on a genuine partnership basis.

...

As to the mention made of specific measures and special institutions for the protection of the Romany language and culture, the Committee of Ministers underlines that all the factors mentioned in this context have important educational implications reflected in the priorities mentioned in its Recommendation No. R (2000) 4 on the education of Roma/Gypsy children in Europe.

Committee of Ministers Recommendation CM/Rec(2008)5 on policies for Roma and/or Travellers in Europe emphasises this approach:

"With a view to ensuring full equality in practice, the principle of equal treatment shall not prevent any member state from maintaining or adopting specific measures to prevent or compensate for disadvantages linked to racial or ethnic origin." (EC Directive 2000/43/EC). "The law should provide that the prohibition of racial discrimination does not prevent the maintenance or adoption of temporary special measures designed either to prevent or compensate for disadvantages suffered by [Roma and/or Travellers] or to facilitate their full participation in all fields of life. These measures should not be continued once the intended objectives have been achieved." (ECRI General Policy Recommendation No. 7 on national legislation to combat racism and racial discrimination, paragraph 5).

...

The states concerned should consider amending their national legislation in an appropriate manner in order to enable positive action aimed at overcoming particular disadvantages experienced by Roma and/or Travellers and at giving equal opportunities for Roma and/or Travellers in society.

ii. Positive measures should be considered, for example, to enable Roma and/or Travellers to have an equal chance to access all levels of education and/or the labour market, and to be hired as advisers in different fields (education, health, housing, employment, etc.). Positive measures should also be taken to encourage Roma and/or Travellers to take up careers, *inter alia*, in education, media, state administration and the police.

In the same recommendation, the Committee of Ministers states that it is necessary to ensure "that the Roma and/or Traveller populations do not become invisible in generic policies".

Implementation gap

The gap between recommendation and enforcement – between the adoption of a text and its implementation – is underlined by families, NGOs and the officials launching the programmes on Roma. The Deputy Secretary General of the Council of Europe, at the launch of the *Dosta!* campaign in Italy on 7 June 2010, said that:

> Much of the Council of Europe's work is designed to help the authorities to manage sometimes very complex, sensitive and difficult situations, and to put in place adequate measures and policies. What we insist upon, however, is that any such measures are effective and respectful of the human rights and the human dignity of all involved – and this is regrettably not always the case.

In his opening address at the conference on Enhancing the Impact of the Framework Convention in Strasbourg, 9 October 2008, the Director General of the Directorate General of Human Rights and Legal Affairs at the Council of Europe, Philippe Boillat, outlined:

> First of all, the need to take decisive steps to bridge the sometimes all too obvious gap between the objectives set out in policies and legislative texts and the actual situation on the ground. The fact that legal frameworks are improving and that more attention is gradually being given to the problems raised by the Advisory Committee [on the Framework Convention] in its opinions is obviously a step in the right direction. Nevertheless, there is undeniably a gap between policies and the actual situation.
>
> Take for example the situation of Roma populations. The difference between the ambitious and generous proposals set out in national strategies concerning the Roma and the very different situation we see when visiting districts inhabited mainly by these populations is undoubtedly an issue of concern to all of us. The Roma are completely marginalised not only socially but also with regard to their most fundamental rights. One of the aims of this conference should be to do everything we can to overcome this divide!

Pierre-Henri Imbert, then Director General of Human Rights at the Council of Europe, emphasised a similar point in his opening speech to the seminar Exclusion, Equality before the Law and Non-discrimination, held in Taormina-Mare (Italy) from 29 September to 1 October 1994:

> A considerable discrepancy may be observed between the progress made in setting standards and creating institutions at international level and everyday realities at national level. This is why we must look beyond legal systems and concern ourselves with societies. It is they that must become "genuine and effective democracies", to paraphrase the expressions used in the Statute of the Council of Europe and the European Convention on Human Rights.
>
> Since the end of the Second World War extraordinary headway has been made in the international protection of human rights. At the same time, however, less progress seems to have been achieved "lower down", in our national societies – as though the shock wave caused by the discovery of the death camps had remained superficial, as though we were all, in one way or another, revisionists – through forgetfulness.
>
> This serves to show that, in spite of appearances, democracy and human rights do not go fully or automatically hand in hand.

> We need to realise that the advent of dictatorship is not the only threat to human rights. Danger can also lurk in a "peaceful" democracy without our even being aware of it.
>
> ...
>
> human rights abuses are not confined to violations of the law. Nor is the law the only means of ensuring respect for human rights, for it more often prescribes what should *not* be done than what should be done. Human rights are not an innate but an acquired possession: they are not "natural" ... they can be learned but not be decreed. It is also, indeed perhaps above all, mentalities that need to be influenced.
>
> ...
>
> The legal methods used to counter exclusion and discrimination will not be effective unless they are supplemented by other means of combating these evils of society. The legal approach must be accompanied by action in the fields of education and information. What we should try to achieve is a genuine human rights culture.

Once we have concluded that official provisions and policy recommendations have failed to have a proper impact, other options then open up.

A comprehensive and structural approach

The chapter on the Education of Roma Children in Europe project, describing implementation of the Committee of Ministers recommendation on education, stressed that there could be no intercultural education without a comprehensive intercultural policy: this fact was proved with the first European study on school provision for Roma children, produced in 1984, and was studied as early as 1983 in the first training seminar organised by the Council of Europe.[60]

The same chapter pointed out the need for, as confirmed by activities developed over several decades, foundations based on:

- a working framework, support and flexibility;
- complementarity and interrelationship;
- building on assets;
- fostering innovation;
- working in networks;
- hyperprojects: an analytical approach;
- a European dimension.

But planning on these foundations, however sophisticated, will not be enough if it fails to respect the logistical principles entailed by a comprehensive and structural approach.

---

60. "Training of teachers of Gypsy children", Donaueschingen, 1983 (DECS/EGT (83) 63).

These principles have been discussed at greater length in the chapter on "Reflection and action" in the book *Roma in Europe*:[61] an activity has to be broken down into its component parts to take account of the dynamics of different communities as well as the various sociopolitical and socio-economic parameters, which call for a realistic approach based on:

– flexibility in diversity;
– precision in clarity;
– reliance on internal dynamics;
– dialogue;
– co-ordination;
– study and reflection;
– information and documentation.

The strength and uniqueness of the Council of Europe in implementing its programmes is its ability to control the entire chain all the way from adoption of a resolution or recommendation by bodies such as the Committee of Ministers, the Parliamentary Assembly and the Congress to practical action in the field (by providing training for teachers and for the various social, legal and political stakeholders, producing education and information material, etc.). We have seen how this works in the field of education, for the *Dosta!* campaign and for the European cultural route. This control of the chain of action makes it possible to have a stronger impact but also entails special responsibility. Current studies often refer to the need for networking, monitoring, evaluation, communication and dissemination of information, sometimes with a bandwagon effect that can lead to excesses: form ends up becoming more important than content, when the two are obviously interlinked.

What action is needed?

Looking to the future, and drawing on the experience of the past few decades, we can put forward a few ideas on what is needed in terms of action.

---

61. Jean-Pierre Liégeois, op. cit. These principles were already to be found in the first edition of this book, *Gypsies and Travellers*, Council of Europe Publishing, Strasbourg, 1985. They have been amply confirmed since then, having been highlighted again, for example, in 2009, 25 years later, after a number of meetings held by the EU, which has adopted "The 10 Common Basic Principles for Roma Inclusion" appended by the EU Employment and Social Affairs Ministers on 8 June 2009 to their Conclusions on the inclusion of Roma. The fact that certain principles such as the "intercultural approach" were described by the EU in 2009 as "very innovative" is a good illustration of the lack of institutional memory that was mentioned in the introduction, when such principles have been clearly present and treated as priorities with regard to the Roma issue for over 30 years in Council of Europe work and official documents, and even since 1984 in the work of the European Commission: an entire section is devoted to this priority (and most of the other principles listed in 2009 are also covered) in the study *School provision for Gypsy and Traveller children*, published in five languages by the Office for Official Publications of the European Communities. This study served as the basis for the 1989 European Council resolution on school provision for Roma children.

A need for management

We may call it a "jigsaw strategy": actions and activities must be organised which are original and yet complementary, each occupying a unique and essential position in a uniform whole. This strategy can be used to proceed in stages; progress jointly and cautiously in a difficult context; make use of the opportunities that arise; draw upon multiple skills; incorporate flexibility and pluralism in the approach; respect the diversity of situations; avoid repetition as well as omission; respect democratic values and variety of choice; and support both local and community initiatives and ministerial programmes. But a project supervisor is still required in order to guarantee consultation and co-ordination, evaluation and continuity: this is one of the basic roles of the Council of Europe. In its choices, follow-up and evaluation, it must meet this need for management.

A need for comprehensiveness

We have seen that while the jigsaw strategy is a process, its result transcends it, inasmuch as the whole is greater than the sum of its parts. Each piece of the jigsaw has its own characteristics – a particular colour and a unique shape (the various activities pursued) – but each only comes into its own as part of the whole. In other words, each individual piece is unique and has value but it is only in relation to all the other pieces and the whole that they form that its role and importance can be fully understood. The image of a mosaic is an apt representation of the whole formed by the various activities: we have to have it all in front of us to appreciate the composition, see clearly what is missing and suggest additions and complements.

What we call "best practices" form part of a structured whole and cannot be separated from their social, cultural, educational and political background. In this respect, the links between the building blocks are as important as the building blocks themselves; every project, together with its results, forms part of a not only structured, but also dynamic, whole. If this factor is not taken into account, an unrealistic or utopian emphasis may be placed on a project's outcome in isolation from its environment. This is one of the reasons why it is necessary to introduce "specific programmes", as emphasised by the Committee of Ministers, to avoid what I have called "discrimination by omission".

A need for innovation

Any project sustained by an international process must be designed from the outset as both a model project and – even if the word is so overused as to often lose its meaning – a pilot project, that is, one which will pave the way for those following behind.

A trail must be blazed that is deemed reliable and feasible for all. The aim of developing activities is not to promote routines or practices that can be used in other contexts or programmes. It is important that innovation be a factor in choosing which activities should be supported in a European project. Activities which are supported must show originality and explore new territory. This approach has a number of advantages, such as:

– avoiding duplication with other programmes and initiatives;

- maximising the potential of activities for the communities affected by projects: it is important that these activities continue to serve as a model for everybody, generating respect and recognition for communities and also fostering fresh ideas and initiatives and making a contribution to reflection on society in general;
- allowing micro-projects to be developed: micro-projects and micro-developments should be used to respond to diverse situations and aspirations. It is important to work flexibly and in a range of ways. We know that development aid is a realm of uncertainty and that byways can lead to the various partners' objectives more reliably and ultimately faster than a motorway;
- directly involving research projects: innovation requires research, and promoting innovation means promoting research. No programme can now manage without support from research projects and action research, and innovation must go hand in hand with assessment.

It should here be stressed that action must be accompanied by research, in order not to fall into the trap of action for action's sake. The potential of research being carried out by a project's leaders must be demonstrated. Those engaged in action research need to undertake a critical analysis of their skills and develop methods of disseminating them with a view to evaluating and, if necessary, modifying practices in order to ensure that they meet their purpose. Although it is not applied research, action research is by its nature based on a process of adaptability: doing action research means carrying out evaluation in order to evolve.

A need for involvement

As pilot projects are developed and seminars are held, there is an exchange between teams which strengthens the links that build between people working in the same field in different countries. After a period of local work, teams get to the stage of setting up networks. At this stage some consideration must be given to the future. It is essential to step up:
- interrelationships and exchanges between projects belonging to the same network: these projects must form a coherent whole focused on a specific issue at European level;
- interrelationships and exchanges in each state with various projects in the same field: in other words, it is important that networks remain open to similar activities and experience, thus increasing the number of partners and their involvement, allowing more concerted action and opening up work to new ideas. It is important to widen the circle and aim at participation by as many people as possible if a pilot project is to have a broad enough base and be sufficiently adapted to the reality on the ground to be properly valid and legitimate, and if, as a pilot project, it is to deserve its name by leading to further reflection and fresh projects.

A need for information

Two keywords for the development of activities are "complementarity", to avoid duplication and repetition, and "interrelationship", to combine and mutually strengthen these activities. To this end, it is necessary to improve general information and mutual information.

We are currently seeing an increase in the number of projects, and this calls not only for careful administrative management but also for fast, effective and targeted information management.

Programme implementation can encounter organisational problems such as lack of contacts, absence of co-ordination, failure to set up actual networks of partners, complex timetables and complicated forms. These have distinctly pernicious consequences, which range from disruption to duplication of work and include the fact that it is mainly teams with sound financial and extensive technical resources that are able to put forward projects, which runs counter to equality of opportunity and the spirit of innovation. Equality of opportunity entails equal access to support programmes, especially European programmes.

A need for enlargement: adopting an across-the-board approach

In such a sensitive and difficult field as that concerning minorities and the development of intercultural policy, where there are many, often conflicting tendencies, interrelationships cannot be confined to exchanges between projects developed in the same community.

It is necessary to adopt an across-the-board approach that can open up activities relating to Roma. By definition, an intercultural policy is a policy involving and for the benefit of everybody, both minorities in the plural and the multi-faceted majority. To take the example of education, the whole range of programmes and activities in this field can and should be used to support intercultural education. Conversely, this means that activities developed in the intercultural field can inspire and generally underlie schooling for all children. Examples are easy to find as work on intercultural education is often marked by its high standard, innovative ideas and the commitment of those involved in it, although this is also true of housing, health, cultural development, etc.

A need for openness: time for synergy

Dissemination of "best practice" encourages exchange and pooling of ideas, plans, results and assessments. It is important to develop "synergies" – a term frequently employed in presentations of European projects but seldom put into practice – between these activities. Dictionaries define synergy as the working together of two or more actions to produce a combined effect greater than the sum of their separate effects. At a time when extensive programmes are being implemented throughout Europe, the need for synergy must be underlined: there is too much to do, too little time and too few resources not to make every possible effort along these lines, in particular by providing tools for teams to keep in touch in order to exchange and consolidate their knowledge and practices. At a time when the "sustainability" of activities beyond their initial period is being emphasised, it is essential to develop tools that can be used to ensure such continuation and extend project life. Co-operative exchanges are part of this.

Closer co-operation

In recent years closer co-operation has been developed between international organisations on the question of synergy.

There has been contact between the Council of Europe and the European Commission on Roma issues. Over the years, participation by the two institutions in meetings and activities organised by one or the other, or jointly, has increased. Since 2000, the Council of Europe's Roma and Travellers Division has been successfully running joint projects concerning Roma on a long-term basis. Thus the third joint programme on equal rights and treatment for Roma in South-Eastern Europe was completed in 2008. It aimed to encourage development of participatory monitoring and evaluation and improve the image of Roma in South-Eastern Europe (Albania, Bosnia and Herzegovina, "the Former Yugoslav Republic of Macedonia", Montenegro and Serbia) by using the *Dosta!* campaign to combat prejudice and stereotyping.

The fourth joint programme for Roma in Ukraine and Moldova was launched in January 2008. It was designed to help those countries better prepare, implement, monitor and promote their action plans for Roma (with a focus on health and education) and combat stereotyping. It made it possible to provide training for better planning, implementation and participatory monitoring of the action plan for Roma in Moldova at both local and national levels; to promote a more positive image of Roma in Ukraine and Moldova through the *Dosta!* Campaign; and to empower Roma communities in Moldova (and especially women and young people) by encouraging them to become actively involved in implementing national action plans through employment as classroom assistants and public health mediators.

Co-operation with the EU also occurs through participation in activities of the European Parliament, the European Economic and Social Committee, and the European Union Agency for Fundamental Rights (FRA), as noted in the latter's annual report for 2010:

> Valuable sources of information for this report also continue to derive from various institutions and mechanisms established by the Council of Europe. Examples of fruitful co-operation between the FRA and the Council of Europe include the common project on Roma migration and Roma movement that was finalised in 2009. In early 2010, the Agency concluded an agreement with the European Court of Human Rights to work on a joint project with the aim of publishing a case law handbook on European non-discrimination. Deliverables such as these add further strengths to a complementary relationship that provides the European landscape of fundamental rights protection with reliable data and solid findings.[62]

As mentioned in a previous chapter, a number of bodies have observer status at the meetings of the MG-S-ROM, the Council of Europe's committee of

---

62. Co-operation with the agency is not something new. See, for example, the study released by the European Monitoring Centre on Racism and Xenophobia (2003), *Breaking the Barriers – Romani Women and Access to Public Health Care*, European Communities, Luxembourg.

government experts. This has been the case ever since the MG-S-ROM was set up for the Contact Point for Roma and Sinti Issues of the OSCE/ODIHR, with which joint projects have been developed – for example, on history teaching and genocide, the situation in Kosovo, and pre-school teaching. The UNDP also has observer status at MG-S-ROM meetings, together with the International Organization for Migration, OSI and the World Bank. There has been growing co-operation with the UNDP on defining common indicators for monitoring implementation of Roma action plans. There is also co-operation on Roma issues with UNESCO, UNICEF and the UNHCR.

The Council of Europe Co-ordinator for Activities concerning Roma and Travellers liaises with outside institutions by organising the regular meetings of the ICG of international organisations and institutions: the Council of Europe, the OSCE/ODIHR, the European Commission, FRA, the European Parliament, UNDP, UNHCR and the World Bank. The ICG meets under each EU presidency to exchange information and co-ordinate activities.

A source of inspiration

As soon as Roma issues are addressed, they tend to be regarded as a "problem", in language shot through with negative overtones that convey the difficulty of "integrating" a group considered marginal.

Yet Europe today is witnessing two new phenomena. Firstly there are population movements due to migration. In western Europe, countries which used to be countries of emigration have in turn become countries of immigration. Now, some central and east European states have become countries of both emigration and immigration. The Parliamentary Assembly, in Recommendation 1917 (2010) on migrants and refugees: a continuing challenge for the Council of Europe, adopted in April 2010, emphasised the importance of a policy response to these population movements:

> 1. Migration continues to shape the European economy, culture and society.
>
> …
>
> 2. The challenges that particularly require the Council of Europe's attention range from reinforcing the rights and protection of migrants, refugees, asylum seekers and displaced persons to contributing to managing migration in a coherent and co-ordinated manner and developing greater responsiveness to new emerging trends.
>
> …
>
> The Council of Europe is a value-based organisation, which was created to protect the rights of all people within Europe. Migrants, refugees, asylum seekers and displaced persons are often some of the most vulnerable people in Europe. There is a need not only to strengthen their rights but also to ensure that these rights are guaranteed in practice.
>
> 4. The Council of Europe should focus on the areas where it can provide added value at pan-European level. Its major strength lies in its standards of human rights and the rule of law. It also has the advantage of combining experiences amongst its

member states, which include countries of origin, transit and destination. Whereas the European Union is concentrating on migration processes, the Council of Europe should make it its explicit priority to concentrate on the people involved in this process and examine issues of migration, asylum and displacement primarily through a human rights prism in the context of the migration process.

...

7. Drawing from wide experience across all relevant sectors of the Organisation, the Assembly considers it necessary to set up a transversal Council of Europe project on migrants, asylum seekers and displaced persons in Europe, with a key focus on the protection of their rights and promotion of their integration.

As for the question of Roma migration as exploited in national and regional politics, it is important not to let it disguise the fact that Roma families have been present for centuries in individual states. This exploitation has many pernicious consequences: the negative light cast on Roma migrants overshadows the problems of Roma who have been living in a country for centuries and are no better treated. Moreover, the political and administrative treatment of Roma migrants who are to be returned to "their state of origin" results in the additional rejection of Roma citizens of the rejecting state, since public opinion is quick to regard all Roma families, even those who have been in the country for hundreds of years, as "foreigners". Another pernicious effect is the sometimes negative reaction of long-established Roma families and NGOs towards new arrivals and towards the NGOs providing support for the latter, since the way these "foreigners" are talked about is prejudicial to long-established Roma and causes their situation to be neglected. This leads to either confusion or division, which does not reflect the historical and sociological reality and is detrimental to the persons and groups concerned. It is therefore essential to consider Roma as constituting a whole – one which is undoubtedly diverse but all of whose parts must be treated in accordance with human rights and anti-discrimination legislation, whatever the citizenship of individuals. Exploitation of the current image of "foreign" Roma makes it possible to return people and responsibilities to another state and at the same time disregard the situation of Roma already present.

In addition to migration, the second striking phenomenon is the emergence of minorities. The 1993 Vienna Summit, where the heads of state and government of Council of Europe member states met for the first time, focused on the issue of minorities. The heads of state and government here emphasised that "the national minorities which the upheavals of history have established in Europe should be protected and respected so that they can contribute to stability and peace". The decisions taken were followed by the adoption of major texts such as the framework which have become basic points of reference for most member states.[63]

The combination of these two phenomena, migration/mobility and the emergence of minorities, has given a new look to the social, cultural, demographic

---

63. It may be noted that of the Council of Europe's 47 member states, only four had failed to sign the Framework Convention as at 1 April 2012: Andorra, France, Monaco and Turkey.

and political landscape of Europe, which is now distinguished by multiculturalism. But this concept is simply an observation – a static description of a demographic reality. Through the processes of migration, the facts are constantly changing. To take account of this when implementing policies designed to tackle the situation in Europe in the 21st century means moving from the juxtaposition that is multiculturalism to the dynamic interaction that is interculturalism.

Roma offer a good example in this respect inasmuch as they combine the two features mentioned: they are sometimes on the move, sometimes migrants, and always a minority. Given their paradigmatic position, we may note that programmes to provide schooling for Roma children serve as a model in several fields, playing a key role that is at once indicative, inspiring and emblematic.

In the case of Roma there is already a European dimension, which provides the starting point for any discussion and action without first having to be constructed in order to be considered from an international or transnational angle. Consequently, the work that has been carried out for 40 years, and which has contributed substantially to reflection in such various fields as schooling, housing, language and cultural development, is all the more important. It has:

– demographic legitimacy: there are over 10 million Roma in Europe;
– geographical legitimacy: Roma live throughout Europe;
– historical legitimacy: Roma have been marginalised for centuries.

Their experience is instructive for other minorities, and also for all the issues surrounding established multiculturalism at national level. Acknowledging and publicising the fact that Roma can thus act as a driving force because of their vitality and the development of their activities is a way of improving and making more positive the often negative and stereotypical image that others have of them. They constitute an example for the right reasons rather than the wrong ones.

With this in mind, the Steering Committee of the Education of Roma Children in Europe project spelt out the importance of the project's repercussions for education in general by asserting that schooling for Roma in a European context should be recognised as a source of much needed renewal in the education field, and that an updating of approaches to teaching could and should be one of the project outcomes.

We can thus see what was expected of this project and the part played by a consideration of Roma children.

The foundations of a European approach

That Roma, who live all over Europe, receive virtually no support from the states of which they are citizens lends extra weight to the Council of Europe's role regarding them. It is the Organisation's duty to play a part in developing policies, in co-operation with member states, to:

- encourage innovative initiatives;
- propose and support positive and appropriate action;
- ensure that activities are co-ordinated and interrelated;
- ensure that the lessons which emerge are well publicised;
- promote exchange of experience.

It is clear that international mediation can and must be provided for what is a small financial outlay in terms of the positive impact produced. Such action would save both money and effort, since pooling of trials and results, which could be compared through a set of co-operative arrangements, is a necessary and appropriate response to the problems that have to be faced.[64] Ad hoc initiatives, divorced from overall considerations and from structural projects, will, despite best efforts in terms of time, funding and human resources, at best result in a few minor successes. But they will mostly be a costly duplication of previous experience and, in many cases, a repetition of errors that should have been known to lead to failure.

As the Parliamentary Assembly states in Resolution 1713 (2010) on minority protection in Europe: best practices and deficiencies in implementation of common standards, adopted in March 2010:

> The Assembly considers that it would be useful to disseminate as broadly as possible best practices in implementing the Framework Convention by States Parties in order to offer guidance to all member states wishing to overcome difficulties and to further improve the protection of persons belonging to national minorities and respect for diversity in their societies.

Co-ordination, analysis and evaluation, together with subsequent information and training activities, mean that concerted action at European level produces results that are much more than just the sum of the activities co-ordinated and evaluated. Apart from the fact that these activities may have a domino effect and lead to further action, the combination and complementarity of their efforts makes them more effective. In such circumstances, a state that might hesitate to take action on its own will readily do so if it is thereby contributing to a common undertaking.

It is up to the Council of Europe to provide the keystone needed to complete the edifice and guarantee its strength. The Council of Europe's contribution is intended not to replace existing programmes or take the place of the states responsible for enforcing adopted texts but to provide these states with the assistance that they may need to implement the commitments which they have made.

The foundations of Council of Europe work in 2010 are clearly laid down in a number of texts, chief among them being Committee of Ministers Recommendation CM/Rec(2008)5 on policies for Roma and/or Travellers in

---

64. Studies are beginning to emerge which show that the cost of exclusion – for example, the cost of no schooling – is much higher than the cost of positive and appropriate action. This is a new approach which is winning over more and more policy makers.

Europe. It has been stressed that this particularly detailed recommendation represents the culmination of a policy structure built up over years. It sets out clear guidelines for activities to be developed as part of a strategy whose various strands are specified; this is a benchmark recommendation from a decision-making body of the Council of Europe. It is consistent with the principles discussed above, giving them normative legitimacy, and deals with questions of monitoring, evaluation and sustainability of activities.

The Parliamentary Assembly has produced a second text, Resolution 1740 (2010) on the situation of Roma in Europe and relevant activities of the Council of Europe. It was noted in the chapter on the Parliamentary Assembly that this resolution is akin to a review of past work, taking a critical approach in both the text of the resolution and the rapporteur's explanatory memorandum, and seems to be opening up new avenues for the immediate future while indicating what is to be done. In this resolution, the Assembly calls on member states to implement adopted texts, and in Recommendation 1924 adopted on the same day, after stressing that "the Council of Europe, which has been a pioneer in promoting the protection of Roma, should renew its impetus in its long-standing commitment to ensure greater protection and social integration of Roma", invites the Committee of Ministers to "keep the issue of the situation of Roma in Europe high on its agenda".

In 2010 the Congress redefined its work. I have stressed the importance of the European Charter of Local Self-Government, now one of the Organisation's essential instruments, which was drawn up in 1985 and is the Council of Europe's basic text in the field of local politics. But in 2010 the Congress intends to refocus its work to give itself "a clearer and stronger political profile by focusing resources on the activities which constitute the Congress' political and institutional mission and are at the heart of the Council of Europe's mission". The impact of adopted texts is to become a priority, and reference is made to follow-up: "All adopted Congress documents should be subject to clear follow-up procedures focusing on the evaluation of the impact achieved" (Standing Committee, CG(18)16, 9 June 2010). The proposed institutional and operational changes fit in with the overall reform of Council of Europe activities during 2010, which the Congress describes as follows:

> The new Secretary General elect of the Council of Europe, Thorbjørn Jagland, undertook, with the support of member states, a profound reform of the Organisation whose purpose is to refocus the activities and mission of the Council of Europe around its core values: human rights, democracy and the rule of law.
>
> ...
>
> This thorough reform aims at revitalising the Council of Europe as a political body and an innovative organisation by concentrating its work on projects that offer the highest added value and present comparative advantages – to do what others cannot do.

As part of the reconfiguration of activities for Roma, a policy document was prepared for the Committee of Ministers in 2009. This thematic exchange of views, entitled "Facing the future: Council of Europe action in the field of Roma and Travellers" (CM/Inf(2009)23, 22 April 2009) stated that:

In that respect the MG-S-ROM and the Congress have envisaged closer cooperation in the future. Following a joint meeting held in March 2009, the Congress agreed to appoint a contact person for Roma and Travellers issues who will participate in future MG-S-ROM meetings. Both bodies will further discuss the possible creation of a network of municipalities having Roma and Traveller populations, which would help implement one of the recommendations of the Congress [see item 7. ii of Resolution 16(1995) of the Congress on "Towards a Tolerant Europe: the contribution of the Roma (Gypsies)"].

In the earlier chapter on the Congress, mention was made of its considerable body of work on the Roma and the vital role played by local authorities. The latter are central to practical action, for it is in their areas that the families in question live. It is in these areas therefore that both positive and negative relationships manifest themselves. Thus refocusing activities on the Council of Europe's core values can only improve the situation of Roma. In the same Congress document (CG(18)16, 9 June 2010), the overall reform of the Organisation is summed up as follows:

> In January 2010, when he launched his ambitious reform plan, Secretary General Thorbjørn Jagland spoke of three goals and four pillars. The goals were: to revitalise the Organisation as a political body; to concentrate work on fewer projects with added value and comparative advantages; to develop a flexible organisation that is more visible and more suited to the needs of European citizens. The four pillars were: governance; a review of activities to concentrate on impact and added value; appropriate structures and a focus on the European Convention of Human Rights.

No further proof of added value is needed in the case of the Roma: it has been amply demonstrated over the years and frequently emphasised throughout these pages, together with the attention paid to compliance with the European Convention on Human Rights. Equally, the "subsidiarity" principle, which is often cited at European level, especially by states wishing to avoid European intervention in some of their actions, cannot be cited at will in the case of Roma, since this principle provides that action must be taken at the lowest possible level, and by the proper authorities, unless it is considered that the matter can be resolved more effectively at a higher level, particularly European. Centuries of experience have more than proved that local and national policies have mostly been unsuitable and that co-operation extending from the most local stakeholders to the most European is now essential if the added value from this co-operation is to be properly felt.

The Secretary General has clarified his policies in his speeches to the Committee of Ministers concerning the reform. On 20 January 2010 he stated that:

> the Council of Europe is the only organisation which has the mandate and the necessary tools to effectively and comprehensively monitor the compliance with obligations related to the respect for human rights, democracy and the rule of law. The Court of Human Rights, as one, is a unique instrument never seen on any other continent at any time in history.
>
> ...

the Council of Europe is reaching out to all European countries and the fact that the organisation has monitoring tools, presence in the field, parliamentarians from all countries, unique contacts with local and regional governments, a close co-operation with NGOs, makes the Council of Europe a unique institution with an exceptional access to knowledge and information.

On 21 April 2010 he said that the Council of Europe "should be the reference organisation in Europe – and beyond – for human rights, rule of law and democracy" and he mentions the "most vulnerable groups, in particular Roma". On 11 May 2010 he noted that:

> Only the Council of Europe can bring all nations under the same binding standards with regard to human rights, rule of law and democracy. And only the Council of Europe will be allowed to monitor. And only the Council of Europe can bring everybody under the same Court.

Sustained attention has been given to the Roma question in the reform process. For example, during a visit to Finland on 8 and 9 June 2010, the Secretary General said:

> It is a pressing issue to advance the rights and living conditions of Roma throughout Europe. I am confident that with the support of Finland, we will be able to put this question at the top of our agenda.

And on International Roma Day in April 2010:

> I am particularly moved by the alarming calls of Roma organisations across Europe on the need to urgently respond to the continuing discrimination they face, as well as the failure of many national policies targeting the Roma. We cannot close our eyes to the evidence. Governments and international organisations have put in place a strong political and legal arsenal, but the Roma in Europe continue to suffer human rights abuses.

What next?

Following the four periods defined at the beginning of this chapter (discovery, recognition, development of a frame of reference, launching of activities), a new period is now beginning, marked by comprehensive, sustainable, practical action guided by precise management.

For 40 years, activities relating to Roma have been based on three priorities: protecting human and minority rights, combating racism and intolerance, and combating social exclusion. The framework texts have mostly been adopted. The elements of a strategy have been set out and tested. Bearing in mind the strategy's recommendations, we might focus on:

- close monitoring of activities, covering not only direct projects such as the European cultural route and educational activities but also the decisions of the European Court of Human Rights and the European Committee of Social Rights (ECSR) for the European Social Charter. The monitoring system must allow for political and technical support of activities requiring it;

- accurate evaluation using indicators to help guide activities, possibly strengthen them and publicise them where appropriate, in order to spread "best practice" and ensure it serves as an inspiration elsewhere. In this respect, one of the Council of Europe's tasks is to provide a system of communication between states in terms of information, relevant activities and appropriate strategies;

- combining the two areas above by extending monitoring mechanisms such as those that already exist for the Framework Convention and the European Charter for Regional or Minority Languages, or as used by ECRI and the Commissioner for Human Rights. States are responsible for the situation within their own boundaries, and the texts that they have signed and ratified must result in implementation, which has to be monitored. In Resolution 1740 (2010), the Parliamentary Assembly dwelt on this responsibility of states as well as the need for evaluation and therefore the introduction of the necessary instruments. It urged member states to:

   collect reliable statistical data – including ethnic and gender-disaggregated data – with the necessary strict safeguards to avoid any abuse, in line with ECRI's recommendations and the opinion of the Advisory Committee on the Framework Convention for the Protection of National Minorities, and to analyse these data carefully in order to assess the results and to enhance the effectiveness of the existing plans and programmes.

- guidelines, derived from this general position to structure a clear overall political strategy in which local, regional and national strategies can be incorporated. The current multiplicity of activities and programmes requires a framework to make them part of a coherent whole. States can call on Council of Europe expertise when developing their strategies. The MG-S-ROM has for example contributed, sometimes through direct assistance, to the development of national programmes in over 20 member states. There are also tried and tested logistical resources for helping to define local and regional policies: reference has already been made to the development of a network of cities, within the Congress, concerned with provision for Roma in local authority areas;

- in-house cross-cutting activities to build Council of Europe capacity in terms of management and expertise, in the shape of interdepartmental co-operation and projects covering a number of sectors. We have seen that various sectors of the Council of Europe have been invited as permanent observers to MG-S-ROM meetings, encouraging the appointment of contacts who can follow Roma issues in the long term;

- synergies not only between activities but also between approaches that can enrich each other. Mention may be made, for example, of the difference in approach and content, and therefore in impact, of the European Convention on Human Rights and the European Social Charter, as Pierre-Henri Imbert noted at the seminar on Exclusion, Equality before the Law and Non-discrimination:

   I would say that social rights are now really excluded from human rights. On the one hand there are noble rights, civil rights and the rest, which – even though we use the term "rights" – are not human rights. ... Now, allow me to play devil's advocate for a moment and ask how is it that the odd instance of tapping of a drug trafficker's phone can end up as a violation of the European Convention on Human Rights, but not the eviction of a family living in the Fourth World or the disconnection of water or electricity supplies for non-payment of bills?

...

The second problem ... is that these days, there is no longer any cause. Exclusion does not have a cause, there are no clearly identified culprits ... An excluded person is a victim of fate, of bad luck, or some real crisis or illness, and once that has happened, the remedy is simple compassion, not politics ... There are victims, but no culprits, nobody accepts responsibility ... [We must] reflect ... on ways of making the law a more effective instrument for combating discrimination and exclusion.

We can thus appreciate the importance of reference to texts such as the European Social Charter and understand the increasingly frequent use of this text (see earlier chapter on this subject) to protect Roma rights.

The period starting in 2010 must build on the achievements of the previous periods to make practical progress on two fronts: tackling discrimination and exclusion, and promoting the historical, cultural and linguistic presence of a minority of 10 to 12 million people in Europe.

Instruments have been created to tackle discrimination and exclusion; they are beginning to be used, and their use and impact ought to be increased. Michael Banton notes that:

If there is to be further research, it should be directed towards the discovery of why existing agreements are not better implemented and of how obstacles have been overcome.[65]

There is a huge amount of work to be done. These issues recur on virtually every page of this publication, in all the texts adopted, and in each activity programme launched. Let us take a recent European survey as just one example, "the first EU-wide survey to ask immigrant and ethnic minority groups about their experiences of discrimination and criminal victimisation in everyday life".[66] This first report of a series on different population groups concerned the Roma:

Experiencing Discrimination as a Roma

– On average – every second Roma respondent was discriminated against at least once in the previous 12 months.

– Roma who were discriminated against experienced on average 11 incidents of discrimination over a 12-month period.

Reporting of Discrimination

– Between 66% and 92% of Roma, depending on the country surveyed, did not report their most recent experience of discrimination in the last 12 months to any competent organisation or at the place where the discrimination occurred.

---

65. Banton M. (1995), "Exclusion, equality before the law and non-discrimination: the point of view of the international lawyer", *Exclusion, equality before the law and non-discrimination*, seminar proceedings, Council of Europe Publishing, Strasbourg, p. 39.
66. FRA (2009), *European Union Minorities and Discrimination Survey, Data in Focus Report: The Roma*, European Union Agency for Fundamental Rights, Budapest.

- The main reason given by Roma for not reporting discrimination was that "nothing would happen or change" by reporting their experience of discrimination.
- 23% of Roma respondents avoided places because of potential discriminatory treatment, which suggests that levels of discrimination would be higher if avoidance measures were not adopted

...

Being Victims of Crime, and Racially-Motivated Crime

- On average – 1 in 4 Roma respondents were victims of personal crime – including assaults, threats and serious harassment – at least once in the previous 12 months.
- On average – 1 in 5 Roma respondents were victims of racially-motivated personal crime – including assaults, threats and serious harassment – at least once in the previous 12 months.
- Roma who were victims of assault, threat or serious harassment experienced on average 4 incidents over a 12-month period.
- 81% of Roma who indicated they were victims of assault, threat or serious harassment in the previous 12 months considered that their victimisation was racially motivated.

...

- On average – 1 in 3 Roma respondents were stopped by the police in the previous 12 months, with every second person indicating that they thought they were stopped specifically because they were Roma.
- Roma who were stopped by the police experienced on average 4 stops over a 12-month period.

The survey "shows the extent to which discrimination against Roma is grossly underreported. Officially recorded incidents of discrimination only reveal the 'tip of the iceberg' when it comes to the real extent of discrimination against the Roma".

We have seen that this discrimination derives from and is sanctioned by prejudice and stereotyping and that its social and political consequences are widespread and serious across Europe. Such omnipresence obviously has adverse effects on Roma themselves in terms of loss of confidence and a wish to remain invisible. As far as this loss of confidence is concerned, we have stressed the danger that, because of stigmatisation and disparagement from their environment, the victims of these processes will end up belittling themselves. Roma, who are prisoners of the collective perceptions developed with regard to them, do not dare declare themselves Roma and adopt the strategy of invisibility that has for centuries been a condition of their survival. The consequences are not just psychological but also cultural and political: a permanent denial of their culture, which eventually becomes destructive.

We can see here the importance of a campaign such as *Dosta!* and also why priority should be given to education projects, which give Roma communities the tools to adjust and the instruments to define their cultural position. Education is also necessary for all the Roma's neighbouring communities: it is through education that change can be consolidated and domestic laws and international conventions can be applied, for it is impossible to legislate against ignorance and lack of knowledge; educating and informing people is the only way to lessen the latter.

We thus come to the second front: promoting the historical, cultural and linguistic presence of a minority. Together with schooling and training programmes, the establishment of a Roma cultural route is pivotal in this respect, enabling actual progress to be made rather than recycling old problems. Cultural dynamics is of vital importance in collective thinking. Over the centuries, the Roma's environment has been constantly constructing their "otherness", on the basis of stereotypes manipulated for policy ends: we have seen that Roma have been defined not as they actually are but as they should be for policy reasons. Their identity has been reduced to that of "the Other".

Roma want to avoid the danger of the same environment now unilaterally constructing or inferring a short-term identity from the outside for its own purposes and political requirements. Personal and collective identities are constantly being shaped and reshaped. In this continual work of construction, all programmes must promote a process that is chosen rather than endured.

Thanks to one of the Council of Europe's European cultural routes, it has been possible to use knowledge and recognition of history, culture and language to develop action that is constructive rather than defensive and proactive rather than reactive.

This is to the advantage not only of the Roma but of European society as a whole, as Imbert stresses:

> The Council of Europe looks upon exclusion as a challenge that must be met if all human beings are to find a recognised and enhancing place in society. The very credibility of all its action is at stake, for a society is defined just as much by the values it seeks to promote as by those it rejects.[67]

It has been said (following the example of Václav Havel, Günter Grass, etc.) that the treatment of Roma is a good indication of the level of democracy in the country where they live, since their situation typifies everything that is most negative about Europe in terms of heightened discrimination, rejection, racism and inability to accept and manage diversity. But, with their presence in every country and their transnational ties, they are pioneers of the future Europe. It is a supreme paradox that these supposedly anachronistic outcasts are living tomorrow's values.

Roma are the promoters of a Europe that they have been building for centuries and analysers of the policies stopping it from being implemented in practice. They have anticipated a trend that is gradually taking shape and have thrown down a challenge to the management of these new social, legal and migratory issues. They are helping to define new concepts and open up new avenues for reflection.

---

67. Imbert P-H (1995), "Opening speech", *Exclusion, equality before the law and non-discrimination*, seminar proceedings, Council of Europe Publishing, Strasbourg, p. 15.

Appendix I

The Council of Europe and Roma: references to the principal texts and key dates

1949   Creation of the Council of Europe, including the Parliamentary Assembly (Consultative Assembly).

1957   Creation of the Conference of Local Authorities of Europe.

1967   The World Gypsy Community becomes the International Gypsy Committee.

1969   Adoption of Recommendation 563 (1969) of the Consultative Assembly on the situation of Gypsies and other travellers in Europe (rapporteur: Daniel Wiklund, Sweden).

1971   The International Gypsy Committee becomes the International Rom Committee and adopts a flag, an anthem and 8 April as International Roma Day.

1975   Adoption of Committee of Ministers Resolution (75) 13 containing recommendations on the social situation of nomads in Europe.

1978   Creation of the International Romani Union (IRU) at the World Romani Congress in Geneva.

1981   Adoption of Resolution 125 (1981) of the Conference of Local and Regional Authorities of Europe on the role and responsibility of local and regional authorities in regard to the cultural and social problems of populations of nomadic origin.

1983   Adoption of Committee of Ministers Recommendation No. R (83) 1 on stateless nomads and nomads of undetermined nationality.

1985   Publication by Council of Europe Publishing of *Gypsies and Travellers*, a first European survey by Jean-Pierre Liégeois (with a network of experts). It covers the situation in the 21 member states at the time (the book was to be reissued in new expanded editions in 1994 and 2007).

1993   Adoption of Resolution 249 (1993) of the Standing Conference of Local and Regional Authorities of Europe on Gypsies in Europe: the role and responsibility of local and regional authorities.

Adoption of Parliamentary Assembly Recommendation 1203 (1993) on Gypsies in Europe (rapporteur: Josephine Verspaget, Netherlands).

1994 The Congress of Local and Regional Authorities of Europe (CLRAE) replaces the Standing Conference of Local and Regional Authorities of Europe.

1995 Adoption of Recommendation 11 (1995) and Resolution 16 (1995) of the Congress of Local and Regional Authorities of Europe, towards a tolerant Europe: the contribution of Roma (Gypsies).

First hearing of the Network of Cities in Košice, Slovakia (part of CLRAE work) to address issues of Roma education, culture and employment.

Creation of the Group of Specialists on Roma/Gypsies.

1996 Second hearing of the Network of Cities in Ploiesti, Romania (part of CLRAE work) to address the legal and institutional framework for Roma/Gypsies in local authority areas.

1997 Third hearing of the Network of Cities in Pardubice, Czech Republic (part of CLRAE work) on provision for Roma in local authority areas (housing, encampment, health, social issues).

Creation of a European Network of Cities on Provision for Roma/Gypsies in the Municipalities covering Ankara, Berlin, Budapest, Cordoba, Pardubice, Strasbourg and Thebes.

Adoption of Resolution 44 (1997) of the Congress of Local and Regional Authorities of the Council of Europe, towards a tolerant Europe: the contribution of Roma.

1998 Entry into force of the Framework Convention for the Protection of National Minorities and of the European Charter for Regional or Minority Languages.

Creation of the Migration and Roma/Gypsies Division.

Adoption of ECRI General Policy Recommendation No. 3 on combating racism and intolerance against Roma/Gypsies.

2000 Adoption of Committee of Ministers Recommendation No. R (2000) 4 on the education of Roma/Gypsy children in Europe.

2001 Adoption of Committee of Ministers Recommendation Rec(2001)17 on improving the economic and employment situation of Roma/Gypsies and Travellers in Europe.

The Migration and Roma/Gypsies Division becomes a department with two divisions: the Migration Division, and the Roma and Travellers Division.

Appendix I – References to the principal texts and key dates

The President of Finland, Ms Tarja Halonen, launches the idea of creating a consultative assembly for Roma at European level (which will become the European Roma and Travellers Forum).

2002 Adoption of Parliamentary Assembly Recommendation 1557 (2002) on the legal situation of Roma in Europe (rapporteur: Csaba Tabajdi, Hungary).

The Group of Specialists on Roma/Gypsies becomes the Group of Specialists on Roma, Gypsies and Travellers (MG-S-ROM).

Implementation of the Education of Roma/Gypsy Children project begins.

2003 Adoption of Parliamentary Assembly Recommendation 1633 (2003) on forced returns of Roma from the former Federal Republic of Yugoslavia, including Kosovo, to Serbia and Montenegro from Council of Europe member states (rapporteur: Mats Einarsson, Sweden).

The CLRAE is renamed Congress of Local and Regional Authorities of the Council of Europe (no abbreviation).

2004 Adoption of Committee of Ministers Recommendation Rec(2004)14 on the movement and encampment of Travellers in Europe.

Signing of partnership agreement between the Council of Europe and the European Roma and Travellers Forum (ERTF).

2005 Adoption of Committee of Ministers Recommendation Rec(2005)4 on improving the housing conditions of Roma and Travellers in Europe.

First judgment of the European Court of Human Rights recognising a violation of Article 14 (discrimination) in conjunction with the violation of another article in a case involving Roma victims.

2006 Adoption of Committee of Ministers Recommendation Rec(2006)10 on better access to health care for Roma and Travellers in Europe.

The Group of Specialists on Roma, Gypsies and Travellers becomes the Committee of Experts on Roma and Travellers (MG-S-ROM).

Launch of *Dosta!* campaign in five countries of South-Eastern Europe as part of a joint programme between the Council of Europe and the European Commission.

First judgment against a member state for violation of a right enshrined in the European Social Charter (revised) of which Roma were the victims.

2008 Adoption of Committee of Ministers Recommendation CM/Rec(2008)5 on policies for Roma and/or Travellers in Europe.

Gradual extension of the *Dosta!* campaign to other member states with a Roma population.

First annual conference of Roma women in Stockholm, Sweden.

2009 Adoption of Committee of Ministers Recommendation CM/Rec(2009)4 on the education of Roma and Travellers in Europe.

Route of Roma Culture and Heritage launched.

The IRU declares 5 November the International Day of the Romani Language.

2010 Adoption of Parliamentary Assembly Recommendation 1924 (2010) and Resolution 1740 (2010) on the situation of Roma in Europe and relevant activities of the Council of Europe (rapporteur: József Berényi, Slovakia).

Second annual conference of Roma women in Athens, Greece.

Appendix II

Testimonials from former and current MG-S-ROM members

(extracts from testimonials received from members of the MG-S-ROM, listed in alphabetical order)

Mr Serkan Bozkurt,
MG-S-ROM member for Turkey

Thanks to its activities and achievements in the area of Roma and Travellers, this committee fulfils a crucial task concerning the Council of Europe's main principles, such as the protection of minorities, the fight against racism and intolerance and the fight against social exclusion.

The Council of Europe should encourage governments to include or implement serious campaigns or initiatives for ensuring equal rights and equal treatment for Roma and Travellers in Europe and for combating anti-Gypsyism.

Mr Samo Drobež,
former MG-S-ROM member for Slovenia

I believe that the MG-S-ROM has the basis for adequate written standards, in the form of recommendations, to ensure that Roma, Sinti, Kalé, Gypsies, Travellers and related groups in Europe have the same conditions for life and work as other groups in the member states of the Council of Europe. From this perspective, I believe that the group of experts of the MG-S-ROM has fulfilled its objective.

However, we have reached the point where the work accomplished by the MG-S-ROM has to produce results and benefit the targeted groups. This means that the adopted recommendations must be implemented, otherwise all our efforts will have been in vain. And this is not always or only dependent on the MG-S-ROM.

What role can the MG-S-ROM play?

It is my opinion that, through the work accomplished so far, the MG-S-ROM has justified its role within the Council of Europe. Moreover, I do not see any reason why it cannot continue its work, on a broader foundation, in the future. In this follow-up work, the committee should observe the developments in the life and work of Roma, Sinti, Kalé, Gypsies, Travellers and related groups in Europe, as well as propose changes to, and amendments of, the existing recommendations or propose new recommendations in the fields that have not been regulated so far. Reports prepared by the MG-S-ROM based on such observations could serve as a useful indication of further work that needs to be done by all member states.

**Mr Henry Hedman,
MG-S-ROM for Finland**

In my opinion, the Council of Europe has elevated the status of Roma and challenged the member states to invest and improve it on both educational and socio-economic levels, as well as in terms of human rights. It has also raised general awareness of the Roma situation in Europe. Moreover, The Council of Europe has been able to unite European decision makers concerning the Roma issue.

My objective for the future work of the MG-S-ROM is to improve and enhance the level of education and the socio-economic situation of Roma even further, as they will otherwise become more and more marginalised and driven to inferior positions compared to the majority populations in member states. A better level of education and quality of housing will ensure improved living conditions for Roma. It is vital to incorporate local and regional actors to commit themselves to improving the situation of Roma. There is also a need to add emphasis in many member states on sanctions against violence, discrimination and racism directed towards Roma, which threaten their future.

Appendix II – Testimonials from former and current MG-S-ROM members

**Mr Peter Jorna,
MG-S-ROM member for the Netherlands**

Of course I remain constructively critical about the proceedings of this committee. The efficiency of its work will always depend on the new terms of reference that are adopted each year. But on the other hand I have confidence in the dedicated presidency of the committee (sometimes "triumvirate", sometimes strong chairwomen, from the west and east, "gadje" and "non-gadje"). In the long run, a lot remains to be done, such as maintaining the human rights and democratisation function of the Council of Europe, while working on the profile of the MG-S-ROM/Council of Europe in relation to the European Commission/European Union, and keeping a constructive, as well as critical, relationship with the European Roma and Travellers Forum (ERTF), the European Roma Information Office (ERIO) and other Roma "umbrella organisations". My specific topics of interest include the legalisation of situations faced by Roma (housing, ID documents, etc.), unregistered Roma residents who are still without personal documents, the pros and cons of early marriages, the process of "civilisation" in general (that is how to balance civil rights and duties of citizenship), together with a "Romani-culture respectful" approach towards housing (and halting sites), work, education and law. I hope this anniversary publication will contribute to that as well.

Some additional remarks: what struck me while participating in the sessions of the MG-S-ROM was a certain lack of *esprit de corps* between the members of the committee of experts. Of course, it is complex to generate such an *esprit* in a forum consisting of very diverse characters and functions, and which represents so many different countries, "local" contexts and divergences in interests and scope. However, bringing those differences together in order to work for the same cause is also one of our challenges.

**Ms Louiza Kyriakaki,
MG-S-ROM member for Greece,
Vice-Chair of the committee in 2009
and Chair since March 2010**

The combating of racism and discrimination vis à vis Roma, and in particular, the fight against anti-Gypsyism, could be reasonably identified as the main and eminent component of the Roma issue, though not the only one. Poverty and all forms of exclusion in public and social life are, unfortunately, still intense in most European states, even if to varying degrees. Roma, as one of the most vulnerable population groups, remain largely handicapped by bureaucratic procedures at best, and lack of attention at national and local levels at the worst. Not least, ineffective representation of Roma in decision-making mechanisms requires our attention while establishing channels for dialogue to the benefit of Roma but also of our societies at large. Undoubtedly, the progress made is not the one desired or expected considering the variety of recommendations and of internationally binding conventions adopted. This in turn causes, in principle, even greater difficulties in reversing aggravated conditions of discrimination, zero tolerance and above all, violations of fundamental rights.

Among the international organisations operating in the field and the wide range of international texts on human rights, the MG-S-ROM and the Council of Europe offer a valuable framework for possible fruitful co-operation among member states, free of the "domination syndrome" in the human rights domain. The Council of Europe and the MG-S-ROM have proved that international organisations may successfully provide positive synergies and not simply repeat actions or initiatives. It is in that sense that, within its mandate, the committee provides the possibility for each and every person concerned to participate in its sessions, regardless of full membership or observer status. It is in this way that the committee has assured a high level of representation and participation from member states, regional and local authorities, grass-roots Roma organisations and international governmental bodies. After all, the most valuable asset of democracy based on human rights is to provide all citizens, whether Roma or not, the possibility for full and active access to participatory procedures.

Among the lessons learned through the years, it appears that although Roma problems may vary among different states, they require a common understanding and a case-by-case approach, depending on the social context within which a solution should be envisaged. Inevitably, pertinent solutions may not be prescribed or come as a result of an exhaustive list. Wise use of existing resources, in human and financial terms, is conditional on the ability to explore efficiently, and sometimes in advance, the needs, demands and resources. A persistent challenge for the whole international community is the ability to achieve a common understanding of different and even unequal situations, to acknowledge problems or gaps and assess possible failures to address them effectively and to work further towards their resolution.

Appendix II – Testimonials from former and current MG-S-ROM members

Mr Claudio Marta, former Vice-Chair and former MG-S-ROM member for Italy

We should do more and better for the implementation of national policies and practices of member states concerning Roma and Travellers. We have to keep in mind that "we can and must play an important role in improving the general situation of the Roma and their living conditions" as stated by the Committee of Ministers (CM/AS (2003) Rec 1557 final).

We should start to monitor the situation of Roma and Travellers in member states at regional and local levels seeing that, as underlined by the Commissioner for Human Rights of the Council of Europe, "concrete improvements at local level remain largely insufficient, irrespective of existing recommendations and commitments undertaken" (CommDH(2006)1, page 5 of the final report on the human rights situation of the Roma, Sinti and Travellers in Europe). For this aim it is important to build a new, strong co-operation with the Congress of Local and Regional Authorities of the Council of Europe.

Concerning future perspectives, we have to be aware that new problems may turn up for Roma and Travellers in Europe. Unfortunately, discrimination and racism are growing throughout the continent and Roma and Travellers are still one of the most vulnerable groups. Good co-operation with the established bodies of the Council of Europe and with the European Roma and Travellers Forum (ERTF), can help us to understand these problems and draw up better plans for the future.

Mr Ian Naysmith, MG-S-ROM member for the United Kingdom, former Chair and Vice-Chair of the committee

MG-S-ROM has provided a focus for Roma and Traveller issues at the heart of the Council of Europe, for example by providing expert advice and opinions to the Committee of Ministers. Its recommendations have assisted governments and public bodies to develop legislation, policies and strategies to address Roma and Traveller issues – often for the first time. And its fact-finding missions, such as those to Bosnia and Herzegovina and to Kosovo, have helped to highlight the interests of Roma minorities in these areas and ensure that they are not ignored.

**Mr Nicolae Radiţa,
MG-S-ROM member for Moldova**

It is clear that being a member of MG-S-ROM implies responsibility but also an expectation that the different problems that the Roma face today can be discussed. On the basis of that analysis, recommendations and the different forms of racism are addressed, legal frameworks are adopted and services are adapted to the needs of the Roma and made available to them. Thus the discrimination they face can be potentially reduced if not only governments and local authorities but also other international actors, such as international organisations, are involved. The experience of non-governmental organisations also plays a very important role.

**Mrs Anne-Ly Reimaa,
MG-S-ROM member for Estonia**

MG-S-ROM has provided a focus for Roma and Traveller issues, expert advice and recommendations which have assisted the Estonian Government and public bodies in developing legislation, policies and strategies addressed to Roma issues, and in getting closer to incorporating a European focus on Roma issues into the work of relevant bodies dealing with integration issues in Estonia. Council of Europe action, such as research and practical initiatives, is a valuable resource which offers concrete and useful support for the Estonian Integration Strategy 2008-13.

The MG-S-ROM has provided the necessary grounds based on adequate written standards. By participating in the MG-S-ROM committee, we are able to partake of the joint efforts and Council of Europe policies, get a better understanding of the relevant regulations and participate in networking on an international level. It is a great opportunity to be directly informed of the relevant problems, to have a comprehensive overview of the policies towards the Roma, including matters regarding non-discrimination, statelessness and lack of citizenship faced by so many Roma everywhere in Europe, and also to witness the confidence and belief in people and a better tomorrow.

Appendix II – Testimonials from former and current MG-S-ROM members

**Mrs Małgorzata Różycka,
MG-S-ROM member for Poland**

The MG-S-ROM's work and its very existence force the member states to deal with Roma problems in an active way and simultaneously provide diagnosis of these problems.

This forum is all the more unusual because each of its members is an expert who deals with Roma problems on an everyday basis. Therefore our meetings provide an opportunity to share experiences, promote best practices, establish contacts and co-operation, which – as in the case of Poland – is also transferred to the local level.

One of the most important qualities of our meetings is the fact that they are attended by Roma – sometimes as representatives of the member states, sometimes as leaders of the Roma community. The Roma participants provide a view from the inside that helps us maintain the right perspective and purpose of our meetings.

**Mrs Tove Skotvedt,
MG-S-ROM member for Norway**

For me, and for Norway, with little previous knowledge and a small population of Romani/Travellers and Roma, the MG-S-ROM has been a valuable source of information and competence building. Through the help of the secretariat and the network in the MG-S-ROM, Norway has been able to carry out Roma projects in various countries such as Romania and Moldova and to contribute and co-operate with Roma organisations including the Forum of European Roma Young People (FERYP).

In addition to networks, competence building and exchange of experience, the strength of the MG-S-ROM lies in its development of methods and guidelines for countries to help them improve the living conditions and the participation of the Roma in a democratic society, thus helping to ensure human rights for the Roma. These efforts usually result in recommendations adopted by the Committee of Ministers. The MG-S-ROM thus contributes to distinguishing the role of the Council of Europe from those of the European Union or the Organization for Security and Co-operation in Europe, but not at the expense of the close and constructive co-operation with these institutions.

Mr Sergey Tolkalin, MG-S-ROM member for the Russian Federation

It is easy to underestimate the significance of the efforts made by international organisations, first of all by the Council of Europe, to overcome the deplorable situation of Roma and Travellers and to change states' attitude to the solution of the problems they face. It is a difficult and complex task. The activities of the MG-S-ROM are very important and practical in nature for the protection of the rights of Roma and Travellers.

As a member of the MG-S-ROM for the Russian Federation since 2000, I have had an opportunity to forward to Russian state structures and civil society institutions the information received by the committee on positive experiences, achievements and problems encountered in this area.

We realise the relevance of improving the approaches on how to ensure and protect the rights of national minorities, including Roma. I am convinced that our participation in international co-operation programmes on Roma and Traveller issues, including within the MG-S-ROM, is one of the most effective tools to achieve progress in our work.

Mrs Josephine Verspaget, former MG-S-ROM member for the Netherlands, former Chair of the committee and former member of the Parliamentary Assembly of the Council of Europe

With remarkably good co-operation among experts, Roma and non-Roma, delegates from governments and international organisations, representatives from NGOs, parliamentarians and bodies of the Council of Europe, we developed a strategy and guidelines regarding the most important issues for the Roma. We involved many international organisations such as the United Nations High Commissioner for Refugees, the World Bank, the Organization for Security and Co-operation in Europe, the European Union and the European Parliament in our work. We were successful in putting the Roma cause high on the pan-European and global agendas.

The creation of European standards for policies on Roma, in the field of human rights and anti-racism, education, employment, health and housing, is still a big achievement.

However, standards still have to be implemented in many member states.

Missions to Bosnia and Herzegovina and Kosovo underlined the necessity of a special approach to the problems of Roma in conflict areas.

When I left, I had a very good feeling about what we had achieved at international level, but I felt worried about the ongoing violations of human rights of Roma in our member states. The dream that Roma rights could be realised in practice within one generation seemed to be far away.

In recent years the MG-S-ROM has been working hard on many important issues, and since the creation of the European Roma and Travellers Forum (ERTF), the European voice of Roma is even more present in the Council of Europe.

But despite all this, discrimination and lack of human rights for Roma are still an overwhelming issue: even the High Commissioner of the United Nations mentioned their plight before all other kinds of violations in the 12th session of the Human Rights Council last September.

It is clear that Europe itself has the obligation, and has to show the will and the means, to speed up the implementation of the rights of Roma.

The first priority is the full participation of Roma children in the mainstream educational system. This should be implemented in one or two years through a common effort of all member states.

Without a good monitoring system, developed by the mechanisms of the Council of Europe, this will not happen. If necessary, sanctions have to be applied, together with the European Union.

The refusal to give Roma children a normal education, or simply inaction, robs Roma and society of welfare, jobs and peaceful coexistence.

A second priority is still full citizenship of all European Roma, especially for refugees and internally displaced persons from former conflict areas. A special taskforce should be set up for this purpose.

In general, a more powerful monitoring mechanism regarding the implementation of the Council of Europe guidelines (and recommendations) on Roma is needed: from a soft to a tough approach.

The Roma people's flag, which was adopted by the International Gypsy Committee in 1971 at the same time as it adopted the hymn Gjelem, Gjelem *and 8 April as the date for International Roma Day.*

On 24 January 2001 at a Parliamentary Assembly meeting Tarja Halonen, President of Finland at the time, proposed to create a pan-European consultative committee for Roma (which was to become the European Roma and Travellers Forum).

On 15 December 2004 the Secretary General of the Council of Europe at the time, Terry Davis, and the President ad interim of the European Roma and Travellers Forum, Rudko Kawczynski (later elected as its president), signed a partnership agreement.

The 2nd plenary meeting of the European Roma and Travellers Forum at the Council of Europe (Strasbourg, 6-8 November 2006).

Dosta! Enough!
Go beyond prejudice, discover the Roma!

Toolkit

Toolkit for the campaign Dosta! *("Enough!" in Romani), designed to raise awareness of and fight against anti-Gypsyism, prejudice and stereotyping with regard to Roma, and open to all Council of Europe member states.*

Poster for the 2nd International Conference of Roma Women (Athens, 11-12 January 2010), which discussed subjects such as early marriage.

Maud de Boer Buquicchio, Deputy Secretary General of the Council of Europe, and Fanny Ardant, ambassador for the Dosta! *campaign, at the press conference marking the adoption of the Parliamentary Assembly's Berényi report on the situation of Roma in Europe (Strasbourg, 22 June 2010).*

Sales agents for publications of the Council of Europe
Agents de vente des publications du Conseil de l'Europe

BELGIUM/BELGIQUE
La Librairie Européenne -
The European Bookshop
Rue de l'Orme, 1
BE-1040 BRUXELLES
Tel.: +32 (0)2 231 04 35
Fax: +32 (0)2 735 08 60
E-mail: info@libeurop.eu
http://www.libeurop.be

Jean De Lannoy/DL Services
Avenue du Roi 202 Koningslaan
BE-1190 BRUXELLES
Tel.: +32 (0)2 538 43 08
Fax: +32 (0)2 538 08 41
E-mail: jean.de.lannoy@dl-servi.com
http://www.jean-de-lannoy.be

BOSNIA AND HERZEGOVINA/
BOSNIE-HERZÉGOVINE
Robert's Plus d.o.o.
Marka Maruliça 2/V
BA-71000, SARAJEVO
Tel.: + 387 33 640 818
Fax: + 387 33 640 818
E-mail: robertsplus@bih.net.ba

CANADA
Renouf Publishing Co. Ltd.
22-1010 Polytek Street
CDN-OTTAWA, ONT K1J 9J1
Tel.: +1 613 745 2665
Fax: +1 613 745 7660
Toll-Free Tel.: (866) 767-6766
E-mail: order.dept@renoufbooks.com
http://www.renoufbooks.com

CROATIA/CROATIE
Robert's Plus d.o.o.
Marasoviçeva 67
HR-21000, SPLIT
Tel.: + 385 21 315 800, 801, 802, 803
Fax: + 385 21 315 804
E-mail: robertsplus@robertsplus.hr

CZECH REPUBLIC/
RÉPUBLIQUE TCHÈQUE
Suweco CZ, s.r.o.
Klecakova 347
CZ-180 21 PRAHA 9
Tel.: +420 2 424 59 204
Fax: +420 2 848 21 646
E-mail: import@suweco.cz
http://www.suweco.cz

DENMARK/DANEMARK
GAD
Vimmelskaftet 32
DK-1161 KØBENHAVN K
Tel.: +45 77 66 60 00
Fax: +45 77 66 60 01
E-mail: gad@gad.dk
http://www.gad.dk

FINLAND/FINLANDE
Akateeminen Kirjakauppa
PO Box 128
Keskuskatu 1
FI-00100 HELSINKI
Tel.: +358 (0)9 121 4430
Fax: +358 (0)9 121 4242
E-mail: akatilaus@akateeminen.com
http://www.akateeminen.com

FRANCE
La Documentation française
(diffusion/distribution France entière)
124, rue Henri Barbusse
FR-93308 AUBERVILLIERS CEDEX
Tél.: +33 (0)1 40 15 70 00
Fax: +33 (0)1 40 15 68 00
E-mail: commande@ladocumentationfrancaise.fr
http://www.ladocumentationfrancaise.fr

Librairie Kléber
1 rue des Francs Bourgeois
FR-67000 STRASBOURG
Tel.: +33 (0)3 88 15 78 88
Fax: +33 (0)3 88 15 78 80
E-mail: librairie-kleber@coe.int
http://www.librairie-kleber.com

GERMANY/ALLEMAGNE
AUSTRIA/AUTRICHE
UNO Verlag GmbH
August-Bebel-Allee 6
DE-53175 BONN
Tel.: +49 (0)228 94 90 20
Fax: +49 (0)228 94 90 222
E-mail: bestellung@uno-verlag.de
http://www.uno-verlag.de

GREECE/GRÈCE
Librairie Kauffmann s.a.
Stadiou 28
GR-105 64 ATHINAI
Tel.: +30 210 32 55 321
Fax.: +30 210 32 30 320
E-mail: ord@otenet.gr
http://www.kauffmann.gr

HUNGARY/HONGRIE
Euro Info Service
Pannónia u. 58.
PF. 1039
HU-1136 BUDAPEST
Tel.: +36 1 329 2170
Fax: +36 1 349 2053
E-mail: euroinfo@euroinfo.hu
http://www.euroinfo.hu

ITALY/ITALIE
Licosa SpA
Via Duca di Calabria, 1/1
IT-50125 FIRENZE
Tel.: +39 0556 483215
Fax: +39 0556 41257
E-mail: licosa@licosa.com
http://www.licosa.com

NORWAY/NORVÈGE
Akademika
Postboks 84 Blindern
NO-0314 OSLO
Tel.: +47 2 218 8100
Fax: +47 2 218 8103
E-mail: support@akademika.no
http://www.akademika.no

POLAND/POLOGNE
Ars Polona JSC
25 Obroncow Street
PL-03-933 WARSZAWA
Tel.: +48 (0)22 509 86 00
Fax: +48 (0)22 509 86 10
E-mail: arspolona@arspolona.com.pl
http://www.arspolona.com.pl

PORTUGAL
Livraria Portugal
(Dias & Andrade, Lda.)
Rua do Carmo, 70
PT-1200-094 LISBOA
Tel.: +351 21 347 42 82 / 85
Fax: +351 21 347 02 64
E-mail: info@livrariaportugal.pt
http://www.livrariaportugal.pt

RUSSIAN FEDERATION/
FÉDÉRATION DE RUSSIE
Ves Mir
17b, Butlerova ul.
RU-101000 MOSCOW
Tel.: +7 495 739 0971
Fax: +7 495 739 0971
E-mail: orders@vesmirbooks.ru
http://www.vesmirbooks.ru

SPAIN/ESPAGNE
Díaz de Santos Barcelona
C/ Balmes, 417-419
ES-08022 BARCELONA
Tel.: +34 93 212 86 47
Fax: +34 93 211 49 91
E-mail: david@diazdesantos.es
http://www.diazdesantos.es

Díaz de Santos Madrid
C/Albasanz, 2
ES-28037 MADRID
Tel.: +34 91 743 48 90
Fax: +34 91 743 40 23
E-mail: jpinilla@diazdesantos.es
http://www.diazdesantos.es

SWITZERLAND/SUISSE
Planetis Sàrl
16 chemin des Pins
CH-1273 ARZIER
Tel.: +41 22 366 51 77
Fax: +41 22 366 51 78
E-mail: info@planetis.ch

UNITED KINGDOM/ROYAUME-UNI
The Stationery Office Ltd
PO Box 29
GB-NORWICH NR3 1GN
Tel.: +44 (0)870 600 5522
Fax: +44 (0)870 600 5533
E-mail: book.enquiries@tso.co.uk
http://www.tsoshop.co.uk

UNITED STATES and CANADA/
ÉTATS-UNIS et CANADA
Manhattan Publishing Co
670 White Plains Road
USA-10583 SCARSDALE, NY
Tel.: +1 914 271 5194
Fax: +1 914 472 4316
E-mail: coe@manhattanpublishing.com
http://www.manhattanpublishing.com

Council of Europe Publishing/Editions du Conseil de l'Europe
FR-67075 STRASBOURG Cedex
Tel.: +33 (0)3 88 41 25 81 – Fax: +33 (0)3 88 41 39 10 – E-mail: publishing@coe.int – Website: http://book.coe.int